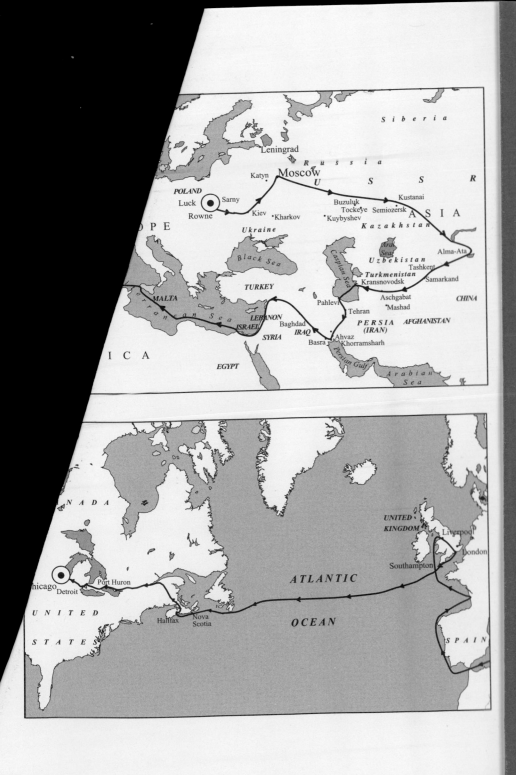

WESLEY ADAMCZYK

When

God

Looked

The

Other

Way

AN ODYSSEY OF WAR, EXILE, AND
REDEMPTION

FOREWORD BY NORMAN DAVIES

THE UNIVERSITY OF CHICAGO PRESS
CHICAGO AND LONDON

Wesley Adamczyk is a retired chemist and tax consultant who lives in Illinois.

The University of Chicago Press, Chicago 60637

The University of Chicago Press, Ltd., London

© 2004 by The University of Chicago

All rights reserved. Published 2004

Printed in the United States of America

13 12 11 10 09 08 07 06 05 04   1 2 3 4 5

ISBN: 0-226-00443-0 (cloth)

Library of Congress Cataloging-in-Publication Data

Adamczyk, Wesley, 1933–

  When God looked the other way : an odyssey of war, exile, and redemption / Wesley Adamczyk.

    p. cm.

    ISBN 0-226-00443-0 (alk. paper)

    1. Adamczyk, Wesley, 1933–   2. World War, 1939–1945—Personal narratives, Polish. 3. World War, 1939–1945—Prisoners and prisoners, Soviet. 4. World War, 1939–1945—Children—Poland. 5. Prisoners of war—Poland—Biography. 6. Prisoners of war—Kazakhstan—Biography. I. Title.

D805.S65A33 2004

940.53'175845—dc22

                                                                2003022321

This book is printed on acid-free paper.

FOR MOTHER AND FATHER,

who died so their children could live.

And for all the proud Polish people

who endured the Inhuman Land

with the hope that their children

might one day live in freedom.

CONTENTS

Generally speaking, most Britons and Americans are vaguely aware
that the Second World War molded the world in which we live. It is a
world where the United States is, for the present, the strongest state on
earth, where freedom and democracy thrive, and where the totalitarian
monsters who threatened us fifty and sixty years ago no longer exist. The
Cold War, which may be seen as the unfinished business of 1945, succeeded in dominating the second half of the twentieth century. And it is
only very recently, after September 11, 2001, that we have been forced to
recognize new terrors and new challenges on the international scene.

Yet despite the passage of time, our memories of World War Two remain curiously stunted and selective. We remember the battlefields in
which our own soldiers were involved; we watch films ranging from *The
Dam Busters* and *The Bridge on the River Kwai* to *Battle of the Bulge* and
Saving Private Ryan; and we continue to be left in no doubt concerning
the undiluted evil of the enemies against whom we fought. Above all, we
are constantly and rightly reminded of the Jewish Holocaust—the most
extreme example of the crimes of our enemies.

Unfortunately, this conventional scenario does not present the full
picture. It contains many blank spots, and it does not address the central
moral dilemma that was created when, in order to defeat Nazi Germany,
the Western powers joined forces with the Soviet Union. At the time,
many people were led to believe that Joseph Stalin was a benevolent
Uncle Joe. Blinded by the feelings of relief and admiration generated by
the heroic sacrifices of the Red Army, they easily imagined that the Soviets shared our own goals, that Soviet Communism was fostering "a
different sort of democracy," or that the Red Army was liberating the nations it had overrun. We know that these wartime beliefs were fundamentally false. In reality, Stalin's regime was responsible for mass murder on an unparalleled scale. Soviet-style Communism proved to be a
dire disaster for all who embraced it. And in 1945, the same number
of European nations were left enslaved as had been liberated. In other
words, the Allied Victory for Freedom and Justice was strictly limited.

Wieslaw (Wesley) Adamczyk redresses this imbalance in the most
convincing way. He recounts the story of his own wartime childhood with
exemplary precision and immense emotional sensitivity, presenting the

ordeal of one family with the clarity and insight of a skilled novelist. The ordeal begins in eastern Poland at a time when, in the western half of the country, the Nazis were building Auschwitz and creating the Warsaw Ghetto. It begins with the author's tearful farewell with his father, who would soon be murdered by Stalin's police, and by the family's terrifying expulsion from their home. It proceeds through a three-week journey in crowded cattle cars, through the starvation and snowy deprivations of distant Siberia, through constant interrogations and humiliations to "the darkest hour" of all, when his mother dies from maltreatment on the threshold of liberty. The author ends the war as one of the 50,000 Polish orphans who had survived Siberian exile but who still faced years of bewilderment and loss before reaching a safe refuge, and a promising future, in America.

It is remarkable that Mr. Adamczyk kept his colorful memories to himself for more than fifty years. The floodgates of his suppressed recollections were not released until the 1990s, when President Mikhail Gorbachev's admission of Soviet guilt for the Katyn massacre solved for the author the mystery of his father's fate and when survivors like himself were able to visit "the inhuman land" in person to pay their respects to their long lost relatives and compatriots. In the meantime, he has obviously conducted a great deal of historical research to ensure the accuracy of his narrative, and he has somewhere learned to order his thoughts, and to wield the pen, with great skill. In so doing, he has rendered a valuable service to all who wish to read about the triumph of the human spirit or to gain a deeper understanding of World War Two.

I have read many descriptions of the Siberian odyssey and other forgotten wartime episodes. But none of them is more informative, more moving, or more beautifully written than *When God Looked the Other Way*.

Norman Davies

When President Mikhail Gorbachev of the Soviet Union met in the Kremlin with President Wojciech Jaruzelski of Poland on April 13, 1990, it turned out to be a historic day. Millions of people in Poland and throughout the world had been awaiting such a day for decades. During this meeting, Gorbachev admitted that the Soviet NKVD (forerunner of the KGB) was responsible for the massacre at Katyn of fifteen thousand Polish POWs, more than half of whom were army officers—including my father—who were taken prisoner by the Soviets shortly after the outbreak of World War II. Had Stalin made such an admission nearly fifty years earlier, when the Germans first discovered mass graves in the Katyn Forest, the course of European and world history might have been changed dramatically.

The belated admission of guilt revealed the secrets of the graves only gradually. Gorbachev, still determined to protect the fast-fading image of the Communist Party and the Soviet government, did not take responsibility for the murders of many thousands of other Polish citizens buried in mass graves in the Soviet Union. Nevertheless, his revelation stunned the Soviet citizenry. It also further tarnished the reputation of many well-known government and military leaders in the West, most of whom were no longer alive.

A fifty-year chain of lies, deceit, and cover-ups had been broken. For all those years the Soviets had maintained a façade of innocence regarding the Katyn massacre, blaming the Germans for the one crime the Germans did not commit. At the same time, the American and British governments, knowing that the Soviets were guilty of the crime, officially remained silent about the truth of Katyn and prolonged the cover-up by going along with the Soviet version of the story. The Polish people, who had lost about half of their homeland's intellectual and military leadership, were forced to live not only with the gruesome tragedy but also with anger and frustration regarding the continuing deception surrounding it.

The Katyn massacre is only one chapter of the forgotten holocaust that Polish people endured at the hands of the Soviet Communists. The other chapter is the forced deportations of hundreds of thousands of Poles to the Soviet Union for the purpose of their gradual elimination by means of murder, slave labor, starvation, and disease. My family and I endured this ordeal as well. (The number of deportees is a matter of controversy, discussed on pages 257–59 in a note to chapter 4.)

While Gorbachev's admission of Soviet guilt in the Katyn massacre sent shock waves throughout the world, for me it was like the bursting of a dam. I was flooded with painful memories of events in my life that occurred half a century ago, beginning when I was a young child—events that had been frozen in time but never completely lost to me. Nightmarish visions of my father's murder flashed before my eyes, and I could not help but relive many tormenting details of my family's deportation and enslavement. I agonized again about the early death of my mother, who sacrificed her life to save her children from Soviet captivity, and I was unable to push out of my mind the memories of a lonely and confused decade of wandering the world as an orphan, yearning for home.

The reader may wonder why I waited so long to begin writing about my childhood odyssey. The reason is that for most of that time the truth about my father's murder was buried with him. I had searched a lifetime to discover the location of his grave, and I had long dreamed of visiting his burial site and paying him homage at least once before I die. Had I written of my odyssey sooner, it would have been a story without an ending. And I was not willing to write such a story.

After Gorbachev's admission, I felt compelled to tell the world about my family's tragedy, and that of the Polish people, at the hands of the Soviets. What remained for me to do was to find the way—and the courage—to bring back the events of the past as accurately as I could. I began by spending hundreds of hours in interviews with my much older brother and sister, aunts and uncles in Poland and in the United States, dozens of Polish deportees who followed the same route that we did, and natives of the countries in which we traveled. Then I contacted Polish museums in Chicago, London, and Warsaw, the Military Archives in Warsaw, the Railroad Museum in Cracow, and the Hoover Institution in Stanford, California. I reviewed hundreds of photographs, documents, and letters from family archives in America and in Poland, as well as poems and memoirs written by my sister during our journey. When all the pieces were put together, the mosaic of my early life lay before me, some of it in vivid color and some in shades of gray and black, and my innermost feelings, long buried, began to come to the surface. Nothing stood out more clearly than my childhood memories of the Inhuman Land, as the Soviet Union is commonly known by Polish people throughout the world. The appellation refers not to the harsh Siberian winters or to the heat of the Russian steppes in summer but to the extreme cruelty and brutality of the Soviet Communist regime.

In June 1998, at the invitation of the Polish government, I boarded a plane at O'Hare International Airport in Chicago and began my pilgrimage to Kharkov, Ukraine (formerly USSR), where I would attend a memorial service for the murdered Polish officers. Even before the plane left the tarmac my heart pounded with anticipation and my emotions were in turmoil. The last time I had seen my father had been fifty-nine years earlier in Poland, when I was a little boy. He had held me close and kissed me before leaving for the war. Soon I would stand for the first time over the mass gravesite where he is buried along with thousands of other officers.

After our arrival in Cracow, the others destined for the memorial service and I boarded a train to Kharkov sponsored by the Polish government. As we crossed the border into Ukraine, until recently the Soviet border with Poland, I realized that it had been exactly fifty-eight years earlier on these very same tracks that I and thousands of other Polish deportees had been forcibly loaded by Soviet soldiers into cattle cars to be shipped to Siberia, many never to return. The tragic events of my ten-year childhood journey began to replay themselves in front of my eyes as if I were watching a film. I clearly saw myself on that cattle train, frightened and shaking from fear while clinging to my mother for comfort. Once again I saw and heard Soviet soldiers shooting innocent and defenseless people trying to escape. As time passed and the train continued to bore deeper into the former USSR, a door I had firmly shut for half a century opened, and out tumbled the memories of that little boy, who to my amazement never forgot what happened.

Two months after I returned to the United States, a documentary about the pilgrimage and the memorial service in Kharkov was aired on BBC radio and television. One of the voices heard by millions of people throughout the world was that of a husky, gray-bearded man from Chicago who, choking on his tears, spoke with passion for his silent father. But another spoke through that voice as well: a young boy from Poland for whom time had stopped, who for more than half a century had remained silent about all he had witnessed. This book is his story.

ACKNOWLEDGMENTS

I am grateful to many people of various nationalities (too many to mention here) who helped me survive my childhood odyssey, to those who encouraged me to write this book, to those who brought past to present, and to all others who if only in a small way made this book what it is: an exercise in the best of the human spirit. In particular, I thank Czeslawa Adamczyk (my sister-in-law), Sohail Bahu, Massoud Banan, Barbara Basinski, Mary Jean Coulson, Kenneth and Ellie Dubrau, Maryla Dudziak, Alicja Edwards, Lee and Kay Esworthy, Richard Greb, Iwona Gronkowska-Rzeczkowski, Diane Inglot, Teresa Kaczorowska, Yvonne Kaminski (my niece), Jan Kawecki, Boris Liechten, Steven Luckew, Stanislaw Machnik, Zofia Machnik-Hamarneh, Roberta Marsh, Casimir Moneta, Aneta Naszynska, Veneta Popova, Barbara Procop (my niece), Janice Ryder, Joseph Sturgis, Adam Szymel, Father Zygmunt Waz, Leopold Witkowski, Jagna Wright, Adolf Wrobel, Krystyna Ziemlo, and Miles Zimmerman.

I thank as well the following institutions and persons for allowing access to their archives and for providing other information: Irena Czernichowska, Archives, the Hoover Institution, Stanford, California; Zdzislaw Kowalski, Central Military Archives, Warsaw; Liverpool University; Wladyslaw Dusiewicz, Katyn Families Foundation, Warsaw; Jan Lorys, Polish Museum of America, Chicago; Franciszek Kostrzewa and Roman Sikora, Polish Railroad Museum, Cracow; George Kaminski, Turn Key Communications Services, Chicago; Kresy-Siberia Group, Stefan Wisniowski, founder and moderator, Sydney, Austrialia; and Professors Wojciech Materski and Andrzej Korzon, Polish Academy of Sciences, Warsaw.

I would also like to express my deep appreciation to those who read my manuscript at various stages and offered valuable criticism and advice: Olenka Frenkiel, for teaching me what not to do in writing a book; Anne Brashler, for reviewing the first draft of the manuscript; Leslie Keros, my consultant extraordinaire and reviewing editor, for her professionalism, unique insight, and keen sense of perspective; David Bemelmans, editor of an early draft of the manuscript, for his encouragement, patience, and sensitivity; Jane Zanichkowsky, copyeditor of the final draft, for her conscientiousness and dedication; and Professors M. K. Dziewanowski and Christopher Flizak, Edward Kaminski, and two anonymous readers for the Press for their informed and fruitful suggestions. I am also deeply grateful to Doctor Ewa Gruner-Zanoch and Waclaw Godziemba-Maliszewski for their firsthand accounts of some of the historical events described herein.

In addition, I would like to express my very special thanks John Tryneski, editorial director of social sciences and paperback publishing at the Press, for accepting my manuscript for publication and thereby giving my story a life of its own; Erin Hogan, publicity director of the Press, for her zeal in promoting the book; and Mike Brehm and Vin Dang, book designers at the Press, for their creativity. I also thank Robert Gutierrez for drawing the map of Poland that appears on page 21 and Jennifer Kohnke for drawing the map of my odyssey that appears on page ii.

And finally, I offer my profound gratitude to members of my family. To my brother Jurek and my sister Zosia I owe eternal thanks for maintaining our family's pride and honor in Siberia and all the other foreign lands we traveled as nomads, and for keeping alive all the precious memories of home. To Zosia, who became my adoptive mother while a teenager herself, I still owe much of who I am today. I thank my son George, whose offer to accompany me to my father's gravesite was the greatest Father's Day gift of all. I am grateful to my aunt Maria Adamczyk-Siepak, the lady who lived in three centuries and the matriarch of our family, who brought me to America and gave me a start, and to Geraldine Siepak-Luckew, her daughter, who graciously revived for me some of the most precious memories of my childhood in Poland. I thank Maria and Geraldine for maintaining our family's archives on American soil for nearly a century.

To the love of my life, my wife, Barbara, the one who through the many years of writing this book ever so gently cuddled my soul, wiped my tears, and soothed my aching heart—I offer everything.

For ease of reading and to avoid ambiguity, Polish names and terms appear without diacritical marks. The surname of the famous Polish general Casimir Pulaski, for example, is spelled without the slashed *l*, reflecting the common American practice. In a more complicated example, the same English spelling legally applies to a person of the same name born in this country and to a naturalized American of Polish descent, but a relative of either person by the same name who is a Polish national would have to use diacritical marks. Doing so would surely create the false impression that the two names are not the same or that one of them is spelled incorrectly.

In a few cases, diminutive expressions of Polish first names are used, showing varying degrees of endearment frequently used between parents and children (or other intimates). My first name in Polish is Wieslaw, but I am often called Wiesiu. Similarly, my brother Jerzy is often referred to as Jurek, and my sister Zofia is often called Zosia. In addition, depending on the context, the endings of these names sometimes change as well.

Finally, a number of notes appear in the back of the book; these are keyed to the text by page number rather than note number to avoid impeding the flow of the narrative.

PART I

Poland

Family members and neighbors sitting on the porch of our home in Sarny, Poland, 1935. In the top row, second from left, I am on my nanny's lap, and my mother is on my left. My brother, Jurek, is in the row below, at far right, and my sister, Zosia, is in the bottom row, fourth from left.

CHAPTER I

SARNY

Like most wintry days in Warsaw, January 14, 1933, was cold and miserable. When I arrived in this world on that day, my mother and my nanny were convinced that a great Polish poet had been born. I did not learn of this until well after I was able to utter my first words, and why my elder brother or sister was not chosen for this lofty profession instead of me remains a mystery to this day. Whenever I asked Mother, she only smiled.

We lived on the outskirts of Sarny in eastern Poland, in a large wooden house surrounded by birch, pine, and oak trees. A wooden fence circled the property, mostly to keep deer away from the garden and the orchard in back. An old gate in front opened freely to welcome visitors. I liked to swing the door back and forth to hear it creak.

Behind our house was a large yard with a stable, a garden, and a small pond. The yard was our playground, the site of summer cookouts, a gathering spot for hunting expeditions and trips to pick berries and mushrooms, and the place where gypsies came to entertain and tell fortunes. Mother always had her fortune told when the gypsies came. No matter how much I pestered, she would never tell me what they said.

My sister Zofia played hide-and-seek with me in the stable, which housed horses and wagons, a sleigh, and a carriage, as well as chickens, ducks, and geese. Some mornings Mother would send us there to pick up fresh eggs for breakfast—one of the few chores I never refused—and if we were lucky we would see the hens lay the eggs. When the day came for the young to hatch, we would spend hours waiting for the chicks to peck their way through the shells.

On one side of the stable was the garden, where many herbs and vegetables grew, including my favorites, corn and cucumbers. On the other side of the stable was the pond, where ducks and geese splashed around. I loved to feed bread to the flock and watch as chicks, ducklings, and goslings followed their mothers, carefree and happy, learning how to grow up. I often wondered how they were able to learn so much faster than human babies.

Sunflowers grew along the fence in back, stretching their smiling faces toward the sky. We waited all summer long for them to ripen so that we could pick their seeds. Deer often came to the fence, sticking their heads between the sunflowers and imploring me with their beautiful eyes to give them cabbage and lettuce. Though skittish, they were never afraid of me, but would bolt when adults came near.

Beyond the fence was the forest, where our family and friends went to pick mushrooms. The sun rarely broke through the heavy canopy of leaves, and moss carpeted the ground. Even on the hottest days, the air was fresh and cool with a profound intermingling of scents of wild berries, flowers, moss, and decaying wood. Mushrooms were hidden under the moss cover or under moist leaves, and finding them required a keen eye. What a delight to carefully brush away the leaves and uncover a bulging cluster of mushrooms! Their gold, brown, green, and red hues blended cleverly with the ground cover. The most colorful and beautiful mushrooms were often the poisonous ones. My brother, Jerzy, was a connoisseur of mushrooms, and he checked the ones I found to be sure they were not poisonous.

At the front entrance of our house stood a heavy wooden door, which opened onto a small reception room with a cloakroom. From there, a long hall ran the length of the house, joining all the rooms. The one I spent the most time in was my bedroom. It was my playroom, with lots of toys and books, and it was the place where my mother, my nanny, and my sister told me stories and taught me to read and write. My favorite story was about the Lilliputian kingdom, its people so small that I could hold them in the palm of my hand. Their kingdom was hidden someplace deep in the forest, and once in a great while, according to the story, it was possible to find a Lilliputian sleeping under a mushroom. How I wished that I could find one. Just once! But they worked only at night and slept hidden away during the day.

The most interesting room in the house was Father's study. Oak paneling covered the walls from floor to ceiling, making the room seem dark and mysterious. The heavy aroma of cigar smoke hung in the air. The old parquet floor showed much wear, as did the old rug lying under a huge oak desk inlaid with green leather, which was embossed with gold trim. Maps and survey drawings were piled high on one side of it and stacks of papers that never seemed to get smaller on the other. A large blotter with brown leather corners and leather underside spotted with ink covered the area of the desk where Father worked.

Directly behind the desk hung a large portrait of Josef Pilsudski, the first marshal of Poland. Father served under him in the defense of Poland against the Bolsheviks in the War of 1920. On either side of this painting hung the portraits of two other great Polish generals, Casimir Pulaski and Taddeus Kosciusko, both of whom fought in the American Revolution. Paintings of their most famous battles hung nearby, as did portraits of the most renowned Polish kings. Opposite the desk was a large brick fireplace, with wood piled high on each side. Above it, Father's army rifles, handguns, and shining officer's saber were displayed. Above them in a glass enclosure were his hat, insignia, and decorations. In the remaining space by the fireplace hung colorful paintings depicting Polish battles of long ago.

Father's study was his sanctuary. No one was allowed to enter it without knocking first and asking, "May I come in?" But unless Father was extremely busy with some pressing business, no one was ever denied entry. Once inside, I would sit on his lap and he would tell me a short story or answer many questions about the adventures we had talked about earlier. Even when he had little time, just being in his study for a few minutes made me feel a part of the past of my ancestors, a world so different, yet so much my own.

Father's army fatigues and dress uniforms hung on a coatrack next to the doorway. They were neatly pressed with sharp creases and always at the ready. Tall leather officer's boots, shining like a mirror and reflecting the flickering flames of the fireplace, stood under the coatrack. On the other side of the entrance was a glassed-in cabinet containing single- and double-barreled shotguns, rifles for big game, and hunting paraphernalia of all sorts.

Father would sometimes tell me about the wild hordes of Mongols that once swept in from the east, led fearlessly by Genghis Khan, to conquer vast lands and form an empire larger than that of the Romans, the Greeks, or even the Persians. I would also hear how, years later, the Tartars, descended from the Mongols, would also attack Europe from the east, on one occasion invading as far west as Cracow. They would overrun villages and brutally slaughter the men, then take the women and children hostage and return with stolen goods to Asia. Listening to these tales, I could not help but wonder whether invaders from the east could descend on us again. Father always assured me that there was nothing to fear.

Of all the stories Father told me, the one I liked best was the story of the Battle of Grunwald. It took place more than five hundred years ago between the German-Christian Order of Teutonic Knights and the Polish-Lithuanian armies. Father said it was the biggest and bloodiest single-day battle in the recorded history of Europe up to that time.

One cold and blustery evening, Father let me into his study. Once inside, I talked him into telling me one more time the story of Grunwald, though I had heard it many times. Father lifted me onto his lap and covered me with my favorite wool blanket. I waited for the action to begin, my eyes glued to the painting of the battle that hung on the opposite wall.

The story began, and at once the battlefield came to life. Thousands upon thousands of men on both sides were facing their enemies in silence. Knights in heavy armor with lances and swords and foot soldiers armed with spears, chains, knives, iron nets, and ropes were standing still as if nothing were going to happen. Only the colors held by standard bearers were swirling in the wind. The knights bowed their heads. The foot soldiers dropped to their knees, all in humble prayer.

"Papa, why do the soldiers pray before the battle?" I asked. Father answered solemnly, "They ask God for forgiveness for their sins, knowing it could be the day when they meet their maker."

Bugles broke the silence on the Polish-Lithuanian side. The lines began to move, slowly at first and then faster and faster. I could hear the thunder of the horses' hooves at full gallop and the running footsteps of thousands of men screaming the battle cry. I could see the knights dressed from head to toe in shining armor, their visors down, their heavy lances lowered at the enemy. Then, suddenly, the thunder stopped and turned into a screeching and horrifying crash of steel against steel, knight against knight. The tumult became a furious whirlwind of men and beasts. Knights fell to the ground, unable to move, only to have their throats cut by the foot soldiers. Heads of foot soldiers toppled to the ground after a single swing of a sword from a powerful knight. The wounded were trampled. Horses with fear in their eyes and steam pouring from their nostrils reared high in the air, their riders holding on with one hand while fighting their enemy with the other. Before me was a bloody entanglement of humans and horses lying in pools of blood, limbs sticking out here and there. How horrible!

For many hours the battle was nearly even. Then out of the tumult appeared a knight wearing no armor or helmet but only a white silk tunic with a black cross in front and back, a symbol of the Teutonic Order. He was Grand Master Ulrich von Jungingen, riding a magnificent white stallion. His sword, drawn high, was ready to strike. But before he could draw a drop of blood from his enemy, two long-haired, heavily bearded Polish foot soldiers charged him with a spear and an axe. His horse reared. At that moment, the spear of one of his attackers went through his heart while the axe of the other split his head. It was the turning point of the battle; hours later the clamor was over. Only the cries and the moans of the dying men could be heard on the battlefield. The crows and the vultures, having hovered for hours, descended on the dead. Women from neighboring villages came carrying buckets of water to quench the thirst of the wounded. Others came to pray for the souls of the departed. So it went for hours until darkness fell.

For a long time Father and I sat in his leather chair, watching the dwindling flames in the fireplace and saying nothing. With the crackling of the fire, tiny flames seemed to jump from log to log and then disappear, only to come back again like the ghosts on the battlefield, teasing and scaring me. Surely some of them had to be in the room, though I could not see them. I closed my eyes and curled closer to my father's chest. A barely audible knock on the partially opened door broke the silence. I opened my eyes and could see the door moving ever so slightly. I trembled. Could it be the ghost of one of the fallen men?

Before Father could answer, a soft-spoken voice came from behind the door. "Wiesiulku," Mother said, "it is way past your bedtime." Hearing this, Father scooped me up and carried me into the kitchen, where warm milk and cookies awaited me.

In contrast to the stories of fierce battles Father liked to tell me, the ones Mother told me were usually about God and the guardian angels. Mother taught me about the Almighty, who sits high up in heaven, knows everything, sees everything, and hears everything. For this reason, she said, I should always be a good boy and obey my parents. Mother also explained that every person has a guardian angel to protect him and that there are other angels who also help.

Every night with Mother beside me I prayed to God and my guardian angel. With eyes closed and hands folded, I would ask them to look after my father, mother, brother, and sister, my nanny, and the servants all through the night. Then I would ask them to look after me as well. The following morning, when I saw them all healthy and smiling, I knew my prayers had been answered. Gradually I began to believe in the existence of God and the power of prayer. Sure enough, nothing bad ever happened to my family or me.

Later I began to appreciate the importance of religion in our history and tradition. Religion was not a separate area of our lives; it was part of our heritage. Religious holidays defined the order of the year. Easter and Christmas in particular, with their deeply rooted traditions, were beautiful and memorable, and I awaited their arrival with eager anticipation.

Life in our house was carefully structured, with an appropriate time for everything. There were times to eat, to play, to learn, to relax, to say prayers, and to go to sleep. Growing up in this atmosphere, I knew what was expected of me and what the consequences were for not toeing the line.

When Father was home, everything went most smoothly for me because it was pointless to break rules. On a few occasions, when Mother told him I had misbehaved, Father would tell me to go to his study. "Mother says you are not listening to her. I want to know why not," I remember him saying on one such occasion.

"I listen, Daddy," I answered timidly. What I meant was that I listened, but did not always do as she said.

"Wiesiu," he said, "listen to me, and listen carefully. In this house, we do not believe in physical punishment unless someone repeatedly steps out of line regarding something important. And the worst thing you can do is to fail to listen to your own mother. Do you understand?"

"Yes, Daddy."

"Good, and do not let there be a next time or you will be punished by your mother and when I find out, you will be punished by me again."

Then Father took me by the hand and led me to his bedroom. Pointing to a hook on the wall, he asked, "Do you see what is hanging there?"

Did I see it? How could I not? But I surely did not want to look at this big, thick, wide belt.

"This time," said Father, "I will let you go, but not the next time. Remember that. Now go and apologize to your mother."

I ran as quickly as I could to apologize to her. Never did I experience that belt on my seat, but I imagined how it would feel. It remained a symbol reminding me that there was a line that was not to be crossed. Even so, when Father was away, I sometimes took liberties just to see what I could get away with. Much to my surprise, Mother, as loving as she was, did not bend, either.

One day, to test Mother's resolve while Father was away, I refused to join the family for lunch. I told Mother that I wasn't hungry. She explained to me that I did not have to eat but that it would be very rude not to join the others. I refused and told her I was going to leave home. She nonchalantly replied, "If you want to, go ahead." She even handed me a suitcase. Her words and actions stunned me. I could not understand why my doting mother was now so mean to me.

It suddenly dawned on me that if I left home I would have to care for myself. There would be no food to eat, no place to sleep, and no family to be with. This scared me. I wanted desperately to run up to her and apologize, but I could not. I had my pride, too. When my father said something, he always kept his promise, and I wanted to be just like him. There was no backing out. I hoped that Mother would break down at the last minute and beg me not to go. But she didn't.

I put some clothing into the suitcase and said, "Good-bye."

She replied calmly, "Good-bye." She didn't even kiss me or ask me where I was going or whether I would be coming back. This lack of concern, so unlike my mother, hurt me deeply. I walked slowly from the house toward the old wooden gate. With each step, I hoped I would hear her calling me back. As I turned into the road, I glanced at the windows, but there was no one standing there. Suddenly, for the first time in my life, I experienced fear. I began to feel what it would mean to lose my family and my home. I started crying, turned back, and ran into the house, straight to Mother's outstretched arms. Without speaking a word, she taught me the most cherished lesson of my life: the importance of having a home and a family.

My mother was born in Warsaw in 1897 as Anna Schinagel. Unlike my father's parents, hers were well educated. Her mother was a teacher and her father a successful attorney. By all accounts Mother was a beautiful woman. Her raven hair flowed onto her shoulders, contrasting sharply with her light complexion and smooth, soft skin. She lived near Cracow until she married.

My father, Jan Franciszek Adamczyk, was of humble beginnings. Born in 1893 in the small village of Ciezkowice, he was the second eldest of eight children and the only one to obtain a higher education. He financed his schooling largely by tutoring other students. In this way he met my mother, to whom he taught French and German. It wasn't long before they fell in love. Their romance blossomed despite Father's intermittent absence during six years of military service, and they were married in 1921. My brother, Jerzy, was born in 1922, and my sister, Zofia, four years later.

When World War I erupted in 1914, my father was inducted into the military. At the time, Poland did not exist in name; it had been partitioned and occupied by Germany, Russia, and Austria for more than 120 years. Each of the three governments inducted into their own armies Polish men in the territories they occupied. Because Father lived under the Austrian occupation, he had to join the Austrian Army. He moved up in rank quickly and was invited to attend the officers' school. By the time the war ended in 1918, he had attained the rank of first lieutenant. At that time Poland regained its independence, and Father joined the newly forming Polish Army. He organized his own infantry company in the Cracow region and rose to the rank of captain.

Between 1919 and 1920, Poland found itself in another war, sometimes referred to as the War of 1920. The Russian Communists, the Bolsheviks, who were determined to spread Communism around the globe, attacked Poland. Their intention was to conquer the country and make her a stepping-stone to the conquest of the rest of Europe. Though the newly formed Polish government was still in partial disarray, officers such as my father staunchly supported it. The last and decisive battle, which the Poles refer to as "the miracle on the Vistula," took place near Warsaw, where the Bolsheviks were defeated and driven back. Not only Poland but also all of Europe was saved.

As a result of this victory, Poland regained some of its prepartition lands in the east, whose inhabitants included Ukrainians and Belorussians. The Polish government offered the soldiers and peasants plots of land and financial assistance to resettle; those who did were subsequently referred to as settlers. The government commissioned my father, who was still a regular army officer, to supervise the parceling and distribution of Polish lands in the Sarny region. He was given a small estate on the outskirts of Sarny (which in Polish means "deer"), and he was assigned two adjutants, who resided in separate quarters on the property, to assist him in his work. Sarny was our home until 1938.

Father's duties required much traveling within the recovered lands, which were considered the most productive in all of Europe. There he supervised and worked with engineers and architects to divide the land. He also helped peasants, many of them illiterate, complete the paperwork transferring the parcels to them. After the required number of years as a regular army officer, Father became a reservist but continued his assignment in land distribution.

Over time Father's primary responsibilities shifted dramatically from land surveying and distribution to finance and banking. In the fall of 1938 the family moved from Sarny to Luck, a larger and more urban town, and Father rented an apartment close to the government-owned agricultural bank in which he worked.

Our apartment was on the first floor of a two-story brick building located on one of the main streets. It included four bedrooms, a large dining room, a sitting room, a kitchen, and living quarters in a sort of basement for our cook, Marysia. Being very attached to our family, she insisted on coming along with us from Sarny and even expressed her strong desire to go with us to America, where some of Father's brothers and sisters lived, if we ever decided to move there.

Although many of our belongings were still in boxes, we began the Christmas season just as we always did. From early December onward, joy was in the air, heightened by expectations of special delights to come. Father rented a huge sledge drawn by two horses, and all of us piled in to go out of town for our usual Christmas tree–cutting ceremony.

Two hours later we were back, eager to start decorating the tall fir. Its fragrance filled the room and seemed to remind us all that the long-awaited Christmas season had officially arrived. Decorating it was a family affair. All of us looked forward with excitement to this annual event— even Mother, who was always extremely busy at this time of year. This was one activity of the season that we never had to talk her into doing with us. And when Mother finished arranging the Nativity scene in the corner of the room, Father grandly asked the question we had eagerly awaited.

"Children, is everybody ready for the angel?"

I had earlier taken the angel in my hand before anybody else could and now quickly ran up to Father. He lifted me high in the air and I placed it on the top of the tree. Beaming with delight, I slid down his shoulder, scratching my face on his whiskers. After supper, Father lit the candles that we could not reach and then Jurek, Zosia, and I lit the rest of them.

As we hoped, it snowed heavily the next day. We arose early to start building a snowman. We packed and packed the snow, piling it up higher and higher until I could not reach anymore. When the snowman was five feet tall, Mother came out with two pieces of coal for his eyes. Then she stuck a carrot below the eyes for his nose. Zosia took her scarf off and wrapped it around his thick neck.

My excitement increased with so many things to do and so much to share. On the day of Christmas Eve, we scurried to prepare for the traditional supper. In the late afternoon, Jurek, Zosia, and I helped set the table. First we placed straw under a white linen tablecloth, a custom relating to the Nativity that was meant to remind us of the humble surroundings of Christ's birthplace. Then we placed the dishes, silverware, hand-embroidered napkins, and tall candles on the table and put a small fir branch next to each plate.

With the Christmas tree, the table, and the Christmas Eve supper ready, my anticipation mounted. Every few minutes, I ran out the front door with my sister and brother looking for the first star. Soon tired of waiting, I pointed my finger toward the sky and shouted, "There it is. I saw it!"

"I do not see a single star," responded Jurek and Zosia almost simultaneously.

"That's because you two do not look hard enough," I told them with assurance.

"Show me, then," said Zosia.

I stretched my hand as far as I could with my index finger pointing in the general direction where the first star was expected to appear. Zosia and Jurek looked intently, yet they saw nothing. "You're getting silly again, little brother," said Jurek, "just like last year."

"Fine, I will go and get Father. Then you will see who is right."

I rushed into the house proclaiming that I had sighted the first star. Father came out and looked for a long time. With great disappointment he said, "Wiesiu, you must have better eyes than I do, for I just cannot find it."

"Papa," Zosia said, "this is only his imagination playing tricks again. Last year he did the same thing."

"Maybe not," Father answered. "Let's all look a little harder."

A few minutes later they spotted the star, sparkling like a tiny diamond in the velvety black sky. Then we all went inside and lit dozens of candles on the tree. We sat down at the dinner table, and Father gave thanks for our blessings. Then we shared the Holy Wafer, a large, white, very thin piece of unleavened bread, sometimes blessed by a priest, that is used to exchange good wishes at Christmastime. The custom of sharing the wafer represents family unity, like the solidarity symbolized in breaking bread with guests. That night, each person broke off a piece from the wafer. We then hugged and kissed each other while exchanging wishes for health, happiness, and all other good things. When my turn came to exchange wishes with my father, I was well prepared. I wished him more time for hunting in the coming year. When he asked me what I wished for, I told him that I wished we all would go to visit our family in America and take a side trip to see the cowboys and Indians. Father smiled and told me that he would like that, too. Perhaps, he said, we could even go to the World's Fair in New York City.

After supper, we sat down in a circle around the Christmas tree to sing carols and tell stories. Each member of the family told at least one. Mother's story was the best. She told us about the Nativity and explained the meaning of Christmas. After the stories, all of us went singing outside neighbors' houses. When we returned home, Mother tucked me into bed and my parents, Jurek, and Zosia attended midnight Mass.

Christmas morning, after a late breakfast, Father surprised the whole family with an unexpected treat. He told us to open the front door. A beautiful bay mare and a sleigh were waiting for us. The driver was invited inside for refreshments that Marysia served him while all of us went for a ride. Father took the reins while we covered ourselves up with sheepskins. In a short while, we were out of town.

The air was crisp, the sun shone brightly, and the trees were laden with snow. The mare started slowly, then picked up the pace on her own as if she, too, were eager to go for a spin. The ground slipped away quickly behind us. The wind whistled by in tune with our joyous caroling. The mare whinnied now and again, and the bells jingling on her mane seemed to be singing with us. The faster we went, the louder we sang until we were out of breath. After a while, Father pulled to the side of the road and announced that everyone would take turns driving the sleigh. Just like the year before, Mother declined, but we coaxed her into trying. When my turn came, Father handed me the reins. With Father beside me, my family caroling, reins in my hands, open road in front of us, and the powerful bay mare with her jingling bells pacing along, I felt as though I were in heaven. It was Christmas!

CHAPTER 2

THE HUNT

During the holidays, my father and brother went hunting whenever they could. From the time I was aware of the hunt, I had wanted to join a party. To my great disappointment, I was never permitted to go, even when the hunt was only for small game. Mother always insisted vehemently that I was too young to be around such a dangerous sport, and all my pleading fell on deaf ears. Once in a while, aggravated by my insistence, she would ask me if I understood the meaning of the word *no*. I did, but I also knew that once in a while Mother was known to give in.

Certainly, I was not about to give up, and I tried again to persuade her to let me go hunting with Father, "just to observe, that's all." I explained to her that when Father was away at work and my elder brother Jurek was living at school, I was the only male left in the house, and I wanted to see what men were doing when they went hunting. I reminded Mother that in only two weeks I would be six years old. She looked at me and said, "Wiesiulku, my little boy, don't you think I know how old you are? I am your mother."

Judging by the tone of her voice, I knew she was hesitating with her answer, so I quickly asked her before she could continue, "Does this mean, Mama, that I can ask Papa if he would take me hunting?"

"No, it does not mean that at all, but . . ." She paused, took a deep breath, and said, "Yes, you are welcome to ask him."

At that moment, I knew I had a good chance of going. When Father returned home, I was the first to greet him at the door. Before he could take his coat off, I made my request. "Papa, can we please go hunting tomorrow?" Father picked me up as he always did to greet me. Surprised by the urgency of my request, he responded, "Tomorrow? Absolutely not! But, if you want to go so badly, this weekend would be fine, if you get permission from your mother."

Mother relented, on condition that I listen to everything Father told me to do or not to do and that I never leave his side, not even for a second.

I promised. Father, meanwhile, assured her that we would hunt only for jackrabbits and would be back within four hours. He added gently, "Dear mother, do not be so afraid. Wiesiu will be with me. Not only that, every boy must learn how to grow up and be a man. It is much better that he learn sooner rather than later."

"But he is still such a young boy," she said.

"Yes, dear, I know that well."

Father put his arms around her waist and kissed her on the lips. Mother did not say anything, yet I could see that she was happy.

On Friday, Father came home early to prepare for our hunting trip. I went to sleep that night eager for the morning to come.

It was still dark when we woke up. We ate a hearty breakfast and then dressed warmly, putting on extra layers of clothing to guard against the winter cold. No sooner were we ready than we heard a commotion in the street. We could hear men talking and a dog barking. My heart pounded with excitement. It was time to go hunting!

Mother wished us good luck and reminded me to listen to my father. Seeing how uneasy she was about my going, I promised that I would be careful. I gave her a big hug and kiss and I ran out the door.

One of Father's army friends, Mietek, and his son, Kaziu, who was sixteen, the same age as Jurek, waited for us on the street in front of our apartment. So did a large hired sledge with three benches piled with sheepskins. In front sat a husky old man with a long, heavy mustache twisted to a sharp point on each side. He owned the sledge and the two frisky young horses harnessed to it. Mietek's hunting dog pranced around, probably as eager to join the hunt as I was. The men loaded their gear onto the sledge: shotguns, shooting jackets, first-aid supplies, ammunition, game bags for the rabbits, sandwiches, and thermoses filled with hot tea with honey. We boarded, making ourselves as comfortable as possible.

"Wojtek!" Mietek called out to his dog, which jumped into the sledge. The driver cracked his whip in the bitterly cold morning air, mumbling something under his breath that only the horses understood. Off we went! I was going on my very first hunting trip, sitting between my father and brother. Cold wind bit my face, but I could not have been happier.

While we were riding, Father instructed me in some of the safety rules every hunter should follow. Always keep the shotgun's safety catch on until you are ready to shoot. Never point a gun at anyone at any time.

Never, ever shoot until you know exactly what you are shooting at. After explaining the basic rules to me, he said, "Today, son, you will learn by watching us."

After half an hour, we stopped by a snow-covered meadow with waist-high hedges on both sides and a forest adjoining it. The driver pulled in by a clump of trees and we all got off. Wojtek, who jumped off at the first chance, eagerly sniffed the ground around the sledge. Father, Jurek, Mietek, and Kaziu put their hunting gear on and loaded their shotguns, making sure to click the safeties on and pointing their double barrels away from everyone. The old sledge owner tied the horses' reins to a small tree and placed a feeding sack filled with oats over each one's head. He climbed into the back of the sledge, took a sip of something from a small bottle, covered himself with sheepskins, and said, "Good hunting, gentlemen."

"Thank you, Stanislaw," Father replied. "We will be back in about two and a half hours."

We split up, walking on either side of a hedge toward the forest. Mietek, Kaziu, and their hunting dog were on one side, and we were on the other, walking in an even line next to one another. Here and there, clumps of black dirt and piles of fallen leaves showed themselves through the freshly fallen snow. Some time passed before we found jackrabbit tracks leading in and out of the hedge. Father cautioned me to be on the lookout and told Jurek to take the first shot. We continued walking. Nothing happened for a good while. There was not even a sound, but through the leafless hedge I could see Wojtek becoming more active, circling and sniffing the underbrush.

My feet dragged over the uneven surface. Inadvertently, I stepped on a pile of dried twigs. They cracked loudly and at that very moment I heard a rustling sound in front of me. A moment later, something darted into the open from the hedge. A gray jackrabbit jumped high into the air, left and right, getting away from us. Almost simultaneously, Father and Jurek raised their shotguns in the direction of the zigzagging animal but, for what seemed to be the longest time, neither of them pulled the trigger. Finally, Jurek took a shot. The rabbit seemed to take one more hop into the air before coming down on the white snow and lying there, still. Within a second or two, we heard two more shots from the other side of the hedge. "They shot at least one. The other one probably got away," Father said. My heart pounded with excitement, while my curiosity boiled over. Why did Father and Jurek almost let the jackrabbit get away instead of shooting immediately? I turned to my brother for an answer. He asked me if I remembered Father's rules of hunting.

"I thought I did," I answered.

"What if it had been the hunting dog that darted out of the hedge and I shot him to death instead of a jackrabbit?" Jurek reminded me that a safe hunter never shoots too soon, not before he can see exactly what he is shooting at. I was impressed by my brother and hoped that when I grew up I would be as good as he.

Jurek and I went to pick up the jackrabbit, which he put into the game bag slung over his shoulder. We went back to the hedge and continued walking. Our party bagged four more jackrabbits over the next hour and a half. Then Father announced the end of the hunt. This seemed a good time to ask him whether I could fire a shotgun. He granted permission but said that I could do it only one time. Because Mother was waiting for us to get back, he wanted to surprise her by returning sooner than promised.

Father chose a clearing adjacent to the forest with a snow-topped tree stump some distance away. He explained to me how we were going to get set up for my first shot. He knelt down on his right knee, while resting his left elbow, shotgun in that hand, on his bent left knee. He showed me how to align my line of vision from the sight at the end of the barrel to the object at which I was shooting.

"With your index finger on the trigger, safety off, you aim, take a slow, deep breath, and squeeze the trigger slowly. For your first shot, pretend that the wooden stump is a wild boar charging directly at us. If you miss, we could be in trouble. Make your shot count and do not get impatient by shooting too early." Father paused and told me to listen carefully.

"When you see the whites of his eyes, squeeze the trigger gently."

I came up closer to Father's left side, took my gloves off, put my head next to the shotgun, and placed my right hand over it with my index finger on the trigger. It felt as cold as ice.

"Ready, Wiesiu?"

"Yes, Papa," I answered nervously.

Father's voice reverberated in the cold winter air. "The boar is charging straight at you. Aim . . . deep breath . . . and . . . *baaang!*"

The shotgun fired. My eyelids closed reflexively. Momentarily, everything went dark. My ears were ringing, and my nostrils were filled with gun smoke. To my surprise, when I opened my eyes, everything in front of me was snow white except for the wooden stump. There was no wild boar charging at us. Yet I was very glad that Father was still kneeling beside me.

"Bravo!" shouted the men standing behind us.

"Son, you did very well for the first time," Father said, and then he gave me a firm pat on my back. I was so proud of myself that I could not wait to get home and tell Mother all about our hunting trip, and especially about how I had learned to shoot a wild boar.

Heading back to the sledge turned out to be the most exhausting experience I had ever had. My clothes seemed to weigh a ton. My boots, covered with sticky snow, were twice as heavy as usual and dragged over the ground. If Father or Jurek would only carry me for a while, I would feel so much better, I thought, but neither offered to do so, and I knew better than to complain because if Mother found out about this, that would be the end of my hunting for a long time to come.

With every step, I fell further behind. Now and then, Father looked back, but he offered only encouragement.

"Won't be long, son. You're doing well," he said but did not pick me up. How I wished he would have! What seemed like hours later, we arrived at the sledge. The old man was getting the horses ready for our return trip. "Thank goodness," I said to myself, and somehow managed not to cry.

"Greetings, gentlemen," Stanislaw said with sincerity, bowing ever so slightly.

"Greetings to you, too, sir," we answered, also bowing slightly.

When the jackrabbits, the shotguns, and the rest of the hunting equipment were loaded onto the sledge, we quietly took our positions on the benches. The driver helped cover us with the sheepskins. Even the dog was more subdued by now, only wagging his tail as he jumped on and made himself comfortable at the feet of his master.

Exhausted from feverish excitement and fatigued by strenuous walking, I leaned on my father's chest, and my eyelids closed. The last sound I remember in the meadow was the piercing crack of the whip as it again cut through the bitterly cold air.

What seemed like only seconds later, Father whispered in my ear, "Wake up, Wiesiu, we are home." I opened my eyes to see nothing but sheepskins covering my head.

"Home?" I asked.

"Yes, son. Run along and be the first to greet your mother. That should make her happy."

Then he turned to our companions, saying, "Gentlemen, everybody is cordially invited for dinner."

I did not have to knock on the front door. Mother was already standing in the open frame, wearing only an apron over her light dress. In my excitement, I forgot to greet her.

"Mama," I shouted as I ran up to her, "didn't I tell you that nothing was going to happen to me? I was right!"

"You certainly were, and you have no idea how happy that makes me, my little boy," she answered with a radiant smile. Why did Mother have to call me a little boy when I was almost six and already hunting with grown men? But I thought it would be best to ask her some other time.

As soon as we were inside, Mother helped me take off my heavy boots and peel off all the winter clothes. Then, unceremoniously, she placed her hand on my forehead and told me to sit down by the kitchen table. She put a tall glass of hot milk with honey and freshly baked cookies in front of me. Strange. Milk with honey and cookies before our main meal?

Mother went to assist Marysia with finalizing dinner preparations. Totally exhausted and without appetite, I only toyed with my treat. The heat from the stove and the hot milk made me very sleepy, and I could not keep my eyes open. I put my head on the hard wooden table. It was to be just for a little while, but instead I fell asleep instantly.

Some time later I awoke in my own bed, resting comfortably on a goose down pillow. Mother was standing next to me. As soon as my eyes opened, I told her about a very scary dream I had.

"About a wild boar?" she asked.

"Yes, Mama. How did you know?" I answered in disbelief. "And I shot him dead right between his eyes."

She smiled. "Come, Wiesiu, you can finish telling me about it later. You slept all afternoon. I do not want you to miss your supper since you already missed your dinner."

PART II

We Are Enslaved

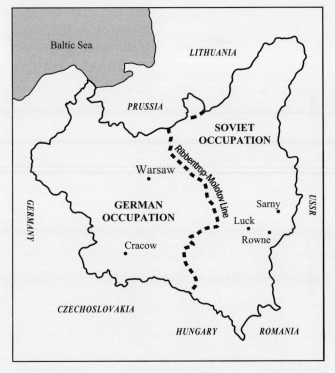

Map of Poland, August 1939. The Ribbentrop-Molotov Line shows the partition of Poland secretly agreed to by the Germans and the Soviets.

CHAPTER 3

A KNOCK ON THE DOOR

The exhilaration of hunting and Christmastime lingered for weeks into the new year, long after the glitter of holiday decorations and the scent of the fir tree had faded. My imagination turned to the stories I heard about pilgrims, cowboys, and Indians and to the wonders of the distant land we called *Ameryka*. Father's offer to take us on this exotic adventure only added to my anticipation.

Yet as the months passed, my excitement about the trip began to lessen as I struggled to adjust to life in a new town. I missed our home in Sarny, and I longed to play with my old friends, feed the wild deer, pick mushrooms and berries in the forest, and watch the gypsies dance and tell fortunes.

Making matters worse, the atmosphere in and around our home began to change, becoming more gloomy and secretive. Army officers came to our apartment to speak with Father privately, and young people came to our door to collect empty cans and other metallic objects we no longer needed. My parents and nanny took to speaking in whispers when I was around and refused to explain why. Even Zosia began acting toward me the way Mother did, telling me not to be concerned and abruptly changing the subject.

Now and then I overheard my parents talking about imminent war with Germany. The uncertainty of what life would be like frightened me. Would the war last only one day, like the battles of old my father told me about? I wanted to know, but nobody would give me an answer.

On the first day of September 1939, the Germans attacked Poland across its western border. I did not understand what being at war meant, so I asked Mother. She only held me close and said she would explain some other time. Later that day, I overheard Father say to her, "Do not tell the children yet. Do not tell them what might happen."

That evening I overheard Father expressing his fear that the German attack might spread into a wider war. He explained that the Soviets could easily take advantage of this situation to also attack Poland in an attempt to get back the land Poland had recovered after the victory over the Bolsheviks in 1920. If that happened, Poles could be in grave danger from local Belorussians and Ukrainians, whose relationship with the Poles was uneasy at best. For the first time in my life, I had the scary feeling that all the good things I took for granted—my family, my home—could be lost.

Several days after the German invasion, this feeling intensified as our nanny left our home in Luck, advised by Father to stay with her relatives in Warsaw. Then Mother told us that our father, a captain in the Polish Army, would be leaving us to join the troops. That evening, a short time after my parents told me to go to bed, papa came to my room.

"Dear Wiesiu, I must say good-bye to you." He picked me up and kissed me. "Take care of your mother," he said. Overcome with fear, I felt that our life would never be the same again. Somehow I knew that I would never forget the moment when my papa kissed me, and I hoped it would not be for the last time. Even today, when I recall that moment, I am filled with a boyish wish that I could have stopped the clock and given Father another chance at life.

After he left, our life began to unravel. The Germans attacked with warplanes. Sirens blared, bombs fell, and we ran and hid in previously dug trenches by the river Styr. During the bombing I could taste the dirt that fell on us while Mother held my head close to her body to protect me. For the first time, I feared for my life and the lives of my family. Although the German Army did not advance as far as Luck, the bombing raids continued, and Mother decided we should return to our country home in Sarny, which was smaller and less likely to be a target.

On September 17, however, a second horror began. The Soviets, despite having signed a treaty of nonaggression with Poland and without declaring war, entered from the east on the pretext of helping the Poles fight the Germans. With the Germans winning and occupying the country in the west, chaos had ensued, and the Soviet double-cross worked. Small Polish Army units, composed mainly of reservists, that were scattered along the eastern border were surrounded by massive Red Army forces and were forced to lay down their arms or die. In the confusion some furious fighting broke out, but it was too little too late. Within a very short time, the Soviets took about two hundred thousand Polish soldiers prisoner.

Officers, including my father, were separated from the others. For months we knew nothing of what happened to him. Some time later we started receiving letters from him and learned of his capture. He had been taken to the Starobelsk prison in the Soviet Union along with other officers.

Just as the Gestapo followed in the wake of the advancing German Army, the Soviet secret police followed the Soviet troops and began to plunder villages and arrest, torture, and murder civilians. Soon after entering Poland the Soviet story changed from "We are protecting you from the Germans" to "We have come to liberate the workers from the Polish bourgeois oppressors." The Soviets also announced that the liberated lands would be annexed to the Soviet Union to satisfy "the will of the people." Suddenly the battle's theme changed from defending Polish territories from the Germans to class warfare. The intent now became clear: it was to take over Poland permanently and to spread the Communist revolution westward, something the Bolsheviks had failed to do twenty years earlier.

The Soviet secret police, or NKVD, was equivalent to the Gestapo. In the beginning the NKVD sought out professionals and army officers and then their families. Because our father was a banker and an army officer, we were prime targets for arrest. I sensed how my mother's fear for our safety intensified, which made me more afraid. I had the horrible feeling of being hunted. I could not, however, understand why I was anybody's quarry, nor could I understand why people would want to kill other people.

In February 1940, shortly after my seventh birthday, word began to spread that the Soviets were forcibly deporting Poles to the Soviet Union, particularly those whom they viewed as a threat to the Communist takeover. The time soon came when persons with any kind of material possessions, including peasants who owned small plots of land, were targeted as well. All were considered members of the bourgeoisie and thus "enemies of the people" who were prime subjects for deportation.

Our family's bank account was seized for the benefit of the Soviet treasury. Firearms, if found, were confiscated, too. Late one night, Jurek gathered all of Father's guns, oiled them, wrapped them in rubber sheets, and placed them and some jewelry in a steel box, which he buried among the fruit trees in our orchard. At that point I realized that we would soon be leaving our home behind and had to prepare for that day. Mother busied herself designing ways to hide our jewelry from the invaders. Since our return to Sarny, she had been making dried bread. "It is for emergencies," she would say. But I watched her insert into the dough many pieces of jewelry including her grandmother's gold earrings, a gold crucifix, and gold bracelets. After the bread had baked, I helped her and Zosia cut it into large pieces. Later the bread was dried in the oven and packed into large potato sacks. How Mother identified the pieces with jewelry hidden inside, I have never learned. Mother and Zosia sewed other small pieces of jewelry and gold coins inside hems of dresses.

We had heard that watches and clocks were of great value in the Soviet Union and had observed for ourselves that the Soviet soldiers walking the streets would ostentatiously wear many watches on each arm, some proudly displaying many alarm clocks attached to their belts. We gathered together all the family's watches, even those that didn't run, and I watched as Mother and my sister spent long hours sewing them into the hems of winter coats.

On the night of May 14, 1940, we went to sleep anticipating the next day's celebration of Zosia's name day. In the middle of the night, however, we were awakened by heavy pounding on the front and back doors. Jurek, Zosia, and I jumped out of our beds to see what the commotion was about. It was 2:00 A.M. We came out of our rooms to see Mother standing in the middle of our guestroom, trembling. Her face was ashen, her black hair tumbling in disarray over her white nightgown. Her feet were bare and her hands were clasped together as though in prayer. She stood frozen, looking toward us as we ran up to her. I had never seen Mother like this before. Her usual smile was gone, her eyes were distant and filled with fear, and her lips were open as if she were trying to tell us something.

"Who is it, Mother?" Jurek whispered.

"Dear Lord! The Russians have come to get us!"

In haste, she motioned us closer and embraced us.

"Listen carefully, children, to what I am going to tell you. No matter what happens, God will be with you. Whatever they do, do not talk back. Keep your composure because they can kill us all. Remember, no matter what they ask, you know nothing."

The pounding on the door became louder, and we heard male voices shouting something in a language I did not understand. As we started toward the door its latch shattered and it swung open; soldiers rushed in with rifles and fixed bayonets extended before them. The next thing I knew, Jurek was lying on the floor bleeding from his face, Mother bending over to help him. The first soldier who came in pushed her away toward the wall with his rifle, screaming at her not to touch Jurek. Zosia was crying. I was petrified, thinking that they would kill us. Nobody had ever treated my mother or my brother so terribly. When gentlemen guests had come to our house, they had always kissed her hand and bowed with respect. Now this brute had shoved her against the wall with a rifle. The soldiers charged into our home with all the manners of the wild boars that Father used to shoot in the forest. If only Jurek had not buried all the guns in the orchard, I thought, maybe I would shoot them all the same way.

A half-dozen soldiers rushed through the rooms, knocking down lamps, crystal vases and decanters, paintings, and furniture while two soldiers with fixed bayonets stood guard over us. They all looked alike— short and stocky with round faces, drab-looking green uniforms, and hats adorned with red stars. I looked into their blank eyes and expressionless faces. I had never seen such people before. It took the invaders fifteen minutes to ransack our house. Then they left through the front door, leaving us huddled together in the middle of the room. A minute later, two of them returned with an officer, a captain of the Soviet secret police. He was dressed in a bluish-gray uniform with red stripes running down his trouser legs and a round hat with a blue band around it and a red star in the middle. He looked directly at Mother and said something in Russian.

When Mother replied that she did not understand, he switched to broken Polish.

"Is your name Anna Adamczykova?" he asked.

"Yes," she answered.

"Your husband is Jan Adamczyk, captain in the Polish Army?"

"Yes."

"You have three children: Jerzy, age seventeen; Zofia, age thirteen; Wieslaw, age seven?"

"Yes."

"You are all under arrest."

"But this must be some mistake," Mother protested. "We have done nothing wrong."

"You are Polish elite," he said scornfully. "You are Polish lords and masters. You are enemies of the people."

"We have no enemies," Mother replied.

She was right. How could she, my brother, sister, and I be enemies of the people? I was getting angry. Everybody knew we had nothing but friends and I wanted to tell the man that, but I remembered what Mother had said about keeping quiet.

The NKVD captain ignored her, and we stood quietly as he issued orders. He allowed us one hour to pack our things. We could take anything with us except guns, jewelry, money, and books.

Mother asked where he was taking us.

"To our great country," he answered.

We had all heard the stories of how the Soviets were deporting innocent Polish people, killing many in the process, stealing money and jewelry, and confiscating their possessions. We had a surprise for this Russian, however, because there were no guns or jewels for them to find. But still we had only one hour to pack, to choose what we valued most and leave everything else behind. Mother told us to collect our things and not to waste any time in the process. We rushed to our bedrooms and began to gather underwear, summer and winter clothes, boots, heavy scarves and hats, mittens, and shoes, which Mother packed into suitcases and bundles made from bed sheets.

On the third or fourth trip to my bedroom, I began to gather my toys and fairy tale books, which I loved so much. Before I could take them to where Mother was packing, the NKVD captain with the red star on his hat blocked my way and barked, "Where are you going with all of this, little Polish prince?"

"These are my toys and books," I answered. "I am taking them with me."

"No!" He turned to Mother and ordered her to tell me not to pack such things. There was no need for them where we were going. "Russia is a great country," he explained. "In Russia, we have everything. He will read Russian books."

He paused for a second, his eyes bulging with anger. Then he roared, "Everything! Everything! Even matches, we have in our great country."

I replied that I wasn't interested in matches; I only wanted my toys and books.

"No!" the man bellowed.

Jurek ran up to me, clearly shaken, and grabbed me by the arm to drag me back to my bedroom. He pushed me toward my bed.

"Sit here, brother, and listen. Don't you remember what Mother said? You must be quiet or you will get us all in big trouble."

I sat down, frustrated and angry. All I wanted to take with me was my toys and books, but the man with the red star kept bellowing, *No! No! No!* Why was he so angry? Why would an adult talk about having matches in his "great country"? We had plenty of matches in our home. So what? I did not understand what was happening. The longer I sat, the more distraught I became. If I could not have my toys and books, then maybe all of us should escape. Maybe we could all sneak one by one through a back window of the house into the orchard and then into the forest. After a while, seeing that no one watching me, I went on a scouting mission from window to window in the back of the house. To my amazement, outside each of them I saw one or two soldiers with rifles with fixed bayonets looking straight at me. Each one wore a hat with a red star in the front, the same red star worn by the soldiers who had burst into the house. I looked at them, but they just stared back at me without moving. They stood there like the tree trunks in our orchard. Their round faces were all the same, no smile and no expression at all.

As I moved from window to window, even the blank faces of the soldiers seemed to disappear. I could no longer distinguish people but saw only red stars and bayonets reflecting the dim moonlight. There was no escaping. If only Father were here, I kept thinking, he would shoot them all just as he did when they attacked Poland earlier. If only Jurek hadn't buried the guns.

Someone put an arm around me. Startled, I turned. "Come, Wiesiu," Zosia whispered in my ear, "you cannot look out the windows any more. We have to leave in a few minutes."

"But I do not want to go. How is our father ever going to find us? Who is going to take care of our house and feed my deer, the chickens, the ducks, and the geese?"

"We will talk about it later," she said.

But we never did.

While we were packing, the soldiers made a list of our household possessions that included furniture, tools, and belongings we were not taking. Shortly before it was time to leave, the NKVD captain shoved it at Mother and demanded that she sign it. When Mother asked why, the officer replied that it was necessary to show that he and his soldiers did not steal anything. Mother looked perplexed. "I do not understand," she said. "You seized our money from the bank. Now you are taking our house and our furnishings, and you want me to sign papers that nothing was stolen? I do not understand what is happening. It is you who should be signing the inventory list for me."

Whether Mother said this in earnest or whether she could no longer contain her indignation at what was happening to us, I will never know. It was in any case a very dangerous thing to say. Blood rushed to the captain's face, his eyes bulged, and foam appeared at the corners of his mouth. He looked like a possessed man just escaped from an asylum.

"Citizen Adamczykova!" he screamed. "I could send you to Siberia to do hard labor for disobeying a representative of the people of the Union of Soviet Socialist Republics!"

Mother paled and started sobbing. Two Soviet soldiers stood next to her armed with their rifles, motionless, their faces without feeling.

"You would never see your children again!" the tyrant carried on, pointing at my brother and sister and me.

In all my seven years of life, I had never heard anybody scream like this or act so boorishly, particularly in front of a woman and children. So this is a Soviet, I thought to myself; this is what they're like. Scared for Mother's life, the three of us surrounded her, pleading with her to sign. She looked at each of us with deep sadness and barely whispered, "Were it not for you children, I would never sign this paper." She took the pen and, with trembling hands, signed her name.

Still in a rage, the captain went into Father's study and brought out the framed picture of him in full military uniform, his saber at his side. He raised it above his head, smashed it on the floor in front of us, and stomped on it, raving in Russian as he did. Then he turned back to us and hissed, "This is what the Soviet liberators will do with all you Polish lords and masters." With that he began screaming incomprehensible commands to his soldiers. As if prodded by a hot iron, they rushed to carry the books from Father's study, my bedroom, and the rest of the house, searching all its corners. They grabbed all our family pictures and paintings of Polish generals and famous battles and carried them into the back yard. A short time later, I saw the glare of flames lighting the back windows of our house.

Despite Zosia's earlier gentle warning, I went closer to the windows to see what was happening. Our books and pictures had been piled high and were being engulfed by fire. All the books full of enchanting stories that my family used to read to me, all the history books that taught me the greatness of Poland—they were shriveling into ash. Why were the Soviets doing this to us? Why did they hate us so much? Anger and frustration overtook me. Recalling a phrase used by my parents, I whispered to Jurek, "These Soviet soldiers behave like uncouth boors." He grabbed me firmly by my hand and took me back to my room. There he said, "Wiesiu, I am telling you for the last time to be quiet. If you love your mother, you will not say another word this night."

"Your hour is up," announced the captain. "Take your belongings and put them on the truck outside."

Our suitcases, bundles, and three sacks of dried bread were lying in the middle of our front room. We put on extra sweaters, coats, and winter shoes so we would not have to carry them. Then we took as much as we could and walked out of our house for the last time. Jurek, visibly shaken, tried to maintain his composure, but Mother, Zosia, and I wept as we entered the yard, our tears running faster when we saw Soviet soldiers everywhere. They loaded us into an army truck with four soldiers to guard us.

Why so many? I wondered. But I could not ask Mother, because I had been told not to talk.

As the truck pulled away, I looked at our home for the last time. Though its outline faded into the darkness of the night, I could still plainly see the red stars and the bayonets reflecting the moonlight.

CHAPTER 4

TRAIN TO NOWHERE

The NKVD captain and his soldiers took us to an eighteenth-century prison in Rowne, about three hours away. There we joined hundreds of others who had been through a similar ordeal and were now jammed together, sleeping on floors and waiting for deportation to one of the Soviet republics. We were held at the prison for several weeks, during which time Mother tried desperately to convince the authorities not to send us to the Soviet Union. It was futile. When the day came for us to leave, she told the officer in charge that she was sick with some awful disease and could not travel. A Red Army doctor came to examine her but declared her fit. Even I knew that Mother was faking illness in one last effort to spare her children from deportation. But only a few hours later, our journey began. We were the third wave of Poles to be deported by the NKVD.

We were taken to a railroad station in army trucks. There, soldiers armed with the now-familiar rifles with fixed bayonets herded us into waiting cattle cars with kicks and shoves. Between forty and fifty people were crowded into each car. At each end of the car, the Soviets had built two wooden shelves to serve as bunk beds, leaving a little space at the bottom for storing personal belongings. Straw was spread over the bunks and on the floor of the car. Those who entered first immediately took the bunks, which could not fit everyone; later men gave up their places to women with small children. Those who did not have a space on one of the bunks had to lie on the floor.

Mother, Jurek, Zosia, and I found space on the bottom bunk at the front of the car, as far as possible from the opening in the middle of the floor that served as a latrine. Next to us we kept our few possessions and the dried bread that Mother had brought from home.

When the train was loaded, soldiers locked the sliding iron doors of the cars from the outside, just as is done with cattle. We heard the heavy bar drop into the lock to seal us in like animals, with no regard for our safety should the train overturn. The car was dark. Even during the day only a tiny amount of light could penetrate the two small, barred windows high up on either side of the car. In the daytime, it was also unbearably hot. And, in a short time, owing to lack of basic toilet facilities, the stench of unwashed human bodies hung heavily in the air and made us retch on almost empty stomachs.

Many Polish children died in such transports on the way to the Soviet Union, most of them in the winter of 1940. The youngsters, in particular the infants, who were stuffed into those cars during the winter had little chance of surviving the ordeal. Even in June, when we were deported, though the days were miserably hot, the night winds chilled one's bones and choked one's lungs.

As the train started rolling, the old cars began to vibrate and shake. After a while all I could hear was the clicking and clattering of the wheels. The train was going to Nowhere, which to the Poles meant an unknown, dreaded place somewhere in the Soviet Union.

Not long after the train left, people began to whisper that we were close to the Soviet border. We would soon be leaving Poland behind. Mothers began to hug their children. Other people caressed each other. We all cried. We cried for our country and our homes, for the land we loved so much. Then someone in our car said we had just passed the border. In a deep voice laden with emotion, he began singing the Polish national anthem: "Poland has not yet perished / As long as we live. . . ." In seconds, others picked up the words until everyone in our car was singing. We could hear singing from the cars in front of us and behind us as well. Our nation's anthem rang out on Soviet soil. A breath of hope, no matter how futile, was in the air.

The train braked to a sudden stop. We heard rifle shots, pounding on doors, and shouting by the soldiers to stop singing.

Silence fell.

More shots rang out. More pounding and shouting followed. "Those who disobey will be shot like dogs!"

The cattle train stood still, the silence broken only by the soldiers, who ran back and forth shouting commands in Russian. In due time, this too died down and the train started moving again. Minutes later, from the cars jammed with people—now without a country, homeless, and scared—voices again united in singing Polish national hymns. This time the wheels kept rolling.

After we had passed into Soviet territory but were still close to the Polish border, some people tried to escape. Such attempts were possible only when, under close guard, we were let out of the train for some reason or another. Most who tried to escape were shot immediately by the guards or the NKVD. The farther we traveled away from Poland, the fewer such attempts were. We had said good-bye to our country. With each passing meadow and each lonely tree, it receded into the distance. The birds were free to fly above us, crossing borders at will, but we were imprisoned on a cattle train. We cursed the Soviets for what they did to us. We prayed to God not to forget us in our misery.

To this day I remember what it was like on that train to Nowhere, though I have wished a million times to be able to forget. When the car's doors were slammed shut and locked for the first time, I felt as though a dagger had pierced my heart. I can still hear the heavy doors shut and lock, the wheels spinning and clicking as the train travels on and on.

I remember how the train was packed with hungry and thirsty people. I remember young children crying, people trying to escape and being shot. I remember the bodies of people who had died of illness, exposure, or hunger being thrown out of the cars at night like garbage. I imagine how my mother must have felt, and the others, too, trapped on this journey of humiliation and deprivation. Meanwhile the train kept going and going. To some place. To no place.

The train bore deeper into the Soviet Union. Attempts to learn its destination from our captors invariably failed. It was hard to understand why they were so reluctant to tell us because most of the passengers were either old men or women with young children and were unlikely to escape. Their plan, it turned out, was to disorient us. For the first two days, the train usually stopped a good distance away from the railroad station. Even when it did stop at a station, we noticed that the signs were all covered or missing, so that we had no idea where we were. But there were clues that some people in the car were able to read. At some point we saw a large city in the distance that the adults agreed had to be Moscow. We discovered that in the Soviet Union the trains, especially those carrying deportees, prisoners, or the condemned, usually went around the big cities. In due time we crossed the Volga River, the pride of the Russians. Later, when we were deeper into the Soviet Union, we occasionally stopped at stations where our captors opened the doors, which might have been locked for two or three days. But even then the guards would let only a few people off. At these times, people from different cars could trade belongings or beg for food from the locals at the stations.

During long stops, if we were allowed out, Mother and I would run to get boiled water, which the Russians called *kipyatok*. In the Soviet Union boiled water was available to all travelers free of charge and was used primarily for drinking. Often boiled water was not available because the stoves at the station were broken or there was no fuel; at these times Mother and I would get boiling water from the locomotive's boiler. Even if it had a foul odor and taste, at least it was hot and sterilized.

On some days, our captors fed us a thin cabbage or fish soup, really little more than hot water, with a piece of stale bread. On many days we received nothing. People ate what they were lucky or smart enough to have brought with them. Those without supplies had to depend on the kindness of others in the car. Their last resort was at the stations, where they would beg; sometimes, to their amazement, the local people would beg them for food and clothing.

In the Communist world, I quickly discovered, working toilets were considered a bourgeois indulgence. We were expected to use the small hole in the floor of our car. You had to take your pants down and relieve yourself in front of everyone, a great humiliation for the deportees who had lived all their lives with private flushing toilets. Worse still, you had to squat down on a moving train and maintain your balance with nothing to hold onto, and your aim had to be true so as not to miss the narrow opening.

The first time I tried to answer nature's call, Mother had to hold my hand because I could not keep my balance well. Embarrassed, I could not relieve myself in front of all the people, especially young girls and women. It was revolting. At home, Mother had admonished me at times for not fully closing the bathroom door behind me. Here there was no door, and any pretense of civility had to be abandoned for the sake of necessity. Many people cursed the Soviets for putting us in this predicament. I was not allowed to curse and did not even know how, but I wished I could. This impossible situation only made me more tense and frustrated. The more I thought about it, the worse it became. My stomach tightened up like a drum and for three days Mother had to massage my abdomen before I was able to return nature's due. So it went the rest of the journey, for I could not get used to using the hole in the floor.

I remember overhearing a man sitting next to us remarking sarcastically upon this Soviet innovation. Unlike most copycat inventions and patents stolen from the West by the Soviets, he said, this design was "truly Soviet," and the inventors should be given credit for their ingenuity. Someone who took him seriously interrupted, wondering why the hole in the floor would be considered ingenious. The first man answered that one had to be very smart to design a hole "small enough to prevent the escape of a child and yet large enough for anyone to take a piss squatting down on a moving train and hit the bull's eye at least some of the time."

The laughter that greeted his comment was the first I had seen or heard since we had been loaded into the car. The man then posed a question. "Can anybody here tell me why the Soviet engineers placed the hole off-center, near one wall, rather than in its very center?" No one volunteered an answer, so the man continued. "They figured out all on their own that if they placed the hole in the center, the floor of the car would be more likely to collapse and thus prisoners more likely to escape. This engineering feat was motivated by nothing more than their fear of being sent to Siberia or even being shot for sabotaging the Communist system."

I wondered whether the man was being serious or joking, and another person asked whether it was true. The first man answered, "Sad, but true. The Soviets send people to Siberia or kill them for much less than that."

Even when stops and layovers became more frequent as our train dragged toward its unknown destination, we were usually not allowed to leave the train. When we were permitted to stretch and walk along the tracks, we could see a seemingly continuous pile of feces between the rails, an indication of the thousands of Poles who had preceded us along the same route. The deprivation of personal hygiene and privacy was a powerful weapon designed to demoralize us. I was getting an education in human relations and politics faster than a young boy's mind could comprehend, but I learned that I did not have to understand something to know that it existed. Germans, the modern Teutonic Knights, started the war. The Soviets, the modern hordes from the east, deprived us of our freedom, our home, and our country. I knew these things but could not understand why they happened.

Through it all, our mother kept praying, and she urged us to do the same. But I did not want to pray. The only thing I wanted was to be back home in Sarny. I missed my father, my nanny, my toys, my books, and listening to fairy tales. I missed feeding my deer and going to the forest to pick mushrooms and look for the tiny Lilliputians. I would be willing to do anything to be back home. But the cattle train kept rolling along.

PART III

The Inhuman Land

Left: Jurek as a recruit in the newly forming Polish army on Soviet soil, Totskoye, USSR, November 1941. *Right:* Zosia, in recovery from a serious illness after our escape from the Soviet Union, Tehran, 1942–43.

CHAPTER 5

THE RUSSIAN STEPPES

After a three-week journey of about nineteen hundred miles into north-eastern Soviet Kazakhstan, east of the Ural Mountains and bordering Siberia, we were close to our destination. Unlike Siberia, Kazakhstan is composed mainly of what are often referred to as the Russian steppes. These are vast tracts of level grasslands, barren of trees. In the summer, the steppes, scorched by the sun, become desertlike. Temperatures vary from about 95 degrees Fahrenheit in the summer to minus 40 degrees or lower in the winter. Only tough people can survive in this harsh and desolate place. The Kazakhs, as did their brave ancestors, have done so for centuries.

The train stopped in the middle of nowhere. No habitable place could be seen in any direction. Mother, Jurek, Zosia, and I were taken off the train and, along with some others, loaded into army trucks. We were the only family, however, to be taken to a small, dirt-poor, government-operated Kazakh farm named Sharmamulzak. It was made up of fewer than a dozen flat-roofed huts, each with only one small window, arranged in a circle. They were situated that way to prevent the inhabitants from being isolated when snowstorms came. The huts were made of clay bricks, chinked with mud and straw. A tiny space in one of them was to be our new home.

The hut we were taken to was roughly forty-two feet long and nineteen feet wide. Two Kazakh families lived there. The NKVD officer in charge shoved us through the lone opening in its walls and led us to a space on the beaten earth floor that was roughly thirteen by thirteen feet. He pointed to the spot with his finger and said in barely understandable Polish, "This is where you will live." He then straightened himself out by sucking in his stomach and puffing out his chest, like someone about to make a grand pronouncement, and continued speaking in his broken Polish. "As a representative of the USSR, I want you people to know that you were fortunate to be brought to our great country out of the kindness of our great leader, Joseph Stalin, and the great Soviet government at no cost to you. I also want all of you to know that in our great socialist country everybody is equal. There are no masters, no slaves as in capitalist countries. There is no more 'mister,' 'missus,' 'sir,' or 'madam,' as in Poland. Everybody in our great country is called *grazhdanin,* a citizen." He paused and took another breath.

"Tomorrow," he said, "you all get a day off and after that you go to work. I also want you to know that in our great country of working people, we follow the rule that 'He who does not work does not eat.'" For emphasis, he repeated the rule in Russian: "Kto ne rabotayet tot ne kushayet." We stood dumbfounded, not knowing what to make of all this. I thought the man was talking gibberish or was just plain stupid. I did not understand most of his rhetoric except for something about working or not eating. He did say everybody had to work, didn't he? Exhausted from the three-week journey, smelly, hungry, scared for our lives, all we wanted to do was lie down and go to sleep.

The hut had no furniture, no carpets, no interior walls, no toilet, no kitchen, and no running water. The floor was a flattened area of earth. We sat down. In a matter of seconds, we were infested with fleas. It wasn't much longer before we also became infested with lice. I looked around the hut and at the Kazakhs, who eyed us curiously. I had never heard of Kazakhs, but one look seemed to tell me more than I wanted to know. I was reminded of how Father had described the Mongols and the Tartars who used to attack Europe. Our new companions were short and wiry, with narrow, slightly slanted eyes, dark hair, and dark complexions. The men looked rugged, with thin, scraggly beards and slightly bowed legs. All of them hissed through gaps in discolored, separated teeth when they talked. Fierce in appearance, they were loud and uncouth in their behavior, spitting constantly. They seemed terrifying to my boyish eyes. I remembered Father's description of the Mongols' and the Tartars' brutality and feared that the Kazakhs might be the same. Why did they stare at us so strangely? I spent that first night in the grip of terror that they would kill us all—that they would cut open our stomachs and chop off our heads. I quietly begged for the Lord to hear my prayer and spare our family. We would later discover them to be a simple people, very kind, friendly, and hospitable, and with a hatred of the Soviets who had conquered them that matched our own.

Less frightening yet still disturbing was the terrible stench in the hut. We later realized that the Kazakhs worked and slept in the same clothes and rarely had a chance to bathe. The stink of unwashed clothing repeatedly soaked by perspiration permeated the stagnant air and was so overpowering in the heat of summer that we choked on our breath at first. It didn't help matters that the Kazakhs let their goats, sheep, and dogs have the run of the hut, contributing not only to the stench but also to the infestation of fleas and lice. With no wood available, bricks cut from dried cow and horse dung were stacked next to the huts or stored inside for winter fuel.

On the day of our arrival in Sharmamulzak, after being taken to the mud hut that was to be our home, not only was I petrified with fear of the Kazakhs and hardly able to breathe because of the stench, I was also struck with disbelief that this was our final destination. My heart ached and I began to cry. Exhausted, we lay down—my mother, brother, sister, and I—on the bare clay floor and went to sleep hugging each other.

Our first full day in Sharmamulzak was equally memorable. When we arose, the head of the communal farm took us around to show us where we would work. Seeing the primitive surroundings and work methods, Mother and Zosia became very depressed, Jurek became withdrawn and gloomy, and I was in a state of shock. Was it just a bad dream? Mother told us that in these surroundings, we would be lucky to survive the winter, which in northeastern Kazakhstan is much the same as in Siberia, and sometimes worse because the open steppe provides no protection. She promised to make every effort to get us out of this place to a small village or town. When we returned to the hut, Mother began rearranging our clothes, which had been quickly shoved into suitcases and bundles during the night of our deportation. There was no need to totally unpack. The hut had no storage cabinets or shelves of any kind. Everything we brought with us was lying on the floor in our sleeping area.

While Mother occupied herself with this project, Jurek, Zosia, and I went out to take our first good look at the steppe. We were struck by the vast flatlands that never seemed to meet the horizon, like an unending illusion where nothingness met nothingness. The land was scarred, scorched, cracked, and blistered, giving the impression that everything on it had died. I wondered whether that would be our fate as well. Where would we get water, food, and the necessities to sustain life? I asked my brother and sister to give me an answer, but they did not have one. As if talking to herself, Zosia asked, "Has God abandoned us?" I looked at my elder brother, thinking that after years of Jesuit school he might have an answer of some kind. He kept gazing into the distance, saying nothing.

We walked to the other side of the compound to see if the view from there was different, only to find the same scorched earth stretching as far as the eye could see. But then we noticed something different in the landscape. Strange-looking objects in the shape of balls, some as big as I was, appeared like mysterious apparitions, rolling and swirling in every direction on the parched surface of the steppe. Their motion changed from back and forth to sideways as they bumped into each other, flying up into the air as if they had wings. Then they plunged down to earth and continued their dance.

Whichever way the wind blew, so went the balls. When the wind subsided, the balls slowed down. When the wind stopped, they stopped. The mysterious balls had no life of their own but danced with the wind as their partner. Our curiosity got the better of us. Jurek, Zosia, and I went to investigate this incredible sight two hundred or three hundred yards away. As we neared them, there was still no telling what this was all about, until a heavy gust of wind blew in our direction. Within seconds, the balls descended upon us as though they were possessed. There was no time to escape. As the first ball rolled toward me, I stretched my arms out, trying to push it away. It was a mistake. Dozens of sharp, needle-like prickles penetrated the skin all over my body. When the wind shifted again, the balls danced away from us.

"Devils on the steppe!" Zosia screamed, while pulling thorns from her skin and clothing.

"Welcome to Kazakhstan, sister. Just be thankful that they were not the Russian devils," said Jurek.

We rushed to our hut for help. The minute we walked in, Mother exclaimed, "Dear God, what happened to you, children?" As we were trying to explain, an old Kazakh woman who lived in the hut came over and, communicating in the only way possible, motioned us to sit down on the floor. She did not seem surprised by our condition; she merely squatted down next to us. In one hand she held a bottle of dark liquid in which roots of some kind were soaking, in the other, a bowl of cotton, half of which she gave to Mother. She soaked a piece of it in the liquid and began pulling the prickles from my body, cleaning the bleeding areas. She motioned to Mother to do likewise for Zosia and Jurek. The itching and the prickling pain disappeared in minutes. I thanked her very much, even though I knew she did not understand. Mother, taken with the woman's kindness, went to one of our suitcases and picked out an embroidered handkerchief to give to her. At first the woman refused to accept it and only took it because of Mother's insistence. When she did, her eyes brightened, and her wrinkled face glowed with a smile. For the rest of the day, she displayed her gift to her family and us as well, overjoyed.

Painful as the experience was, our encounter with the mysterious dancing balls was a lesson well worth learning, and from that day on we called them, appropriately, "devils on the steppe," as Zosia had named them. We were to learn shortly after this incident the truth about their devilish behavior. Under the summer's scorching heat, the many grasses and shrubs indigenous to the steppe become bone dry, break off, and are carried with the wind over the flatlands. In the process, the flying twigs, branches, and razor-sharp grasses with thousands of prickles and thorns intertwine, roll with the wind, and pick up more and more of their companions along the way. By the process of constant rolling, they form extremely light and buoyant balls that might look harmless yet pose a painful danger to those not familiar with life on the steppe.

Although the Kazakhs appeared at first to be fierce and frightening, they turned out to be kind and charitable. Despite their extreme poverty, these generous people shared with us their meager food supplies. The very first day, they gave us thin pancakes made of flour, water, and a little salt, which they baked on hot bricks. They also gave us cheese made from sheep's milk and goat cheese full of dead flies, which I refused to eat. After being scolded by Mother, I took a bite of this cheese and promptly threw up. The Kazakhs laughed. For the most part, this was to be our diet and I had to adjust to it quickly or starve. I dreaded feeling the dead flies being crushed between my teeth, but there was no way to pick them all out. The Kazakhs also treated us to crude tea made from crushed fruit stones and branches, occasionally some lamb, and koumiss—fermented mare's milk—which they kept in leather pouches buried in the ground to keep it cool. This milk smelled and tasted terrible, but over my bitter objections, Mother saw to it that each of us drank our portion. She would admonish me to eat and drink what the Kazakhs gave me and to thank God for their generosity.

There were no knives or forks. We ate with our fingers, and we followed Kazakh etiquette, sharply different from our own. Here the men ate first, then the women, and then the children. I was flabbergasted to observe that among Kazakhs, unlike Poles, women and children were not given preferential treatment. Mother explained to me that customs and etiquette often vary from country to country and sometimes for good reason.

I still had a hard time understanding why the Kazakhs sat on the floor while eating, ate with their dirty fingers, and did not treat their women with more respect. When I asked my brother if he ever saw a Kazakh kissing the hand of a woman in greeting, he surprised me by saying

I should not ask foolish questions. But why was my question foolish? Hadn't we been taught that this was how men were to greet women?

We learned immediately the truth of the Soviet rule that if you did not work, you did not eat. In practice, the small amount of produce raised at each farm that remained after the government took its share was distributed according to each worker's productivity. We also learned that few dared ask about what happened to the Marxist motto "From each, according to his ability, to each, according to his need"; to do so might invite a trip to the hard labor camps of Siberia.

All able-bodied people tended cattle and other livestock, made clay bricks, hauled water, picked up cow and horse dung from the fields to be dried for fuel and fertilizer, and did menial chores. At age seven, my first gainful employment came a few days after our arrival in the USSR. Indeed, if I did not work, I would not eat. That is, I would not get my daily ration of flat bread, mare's milk, and cheese studded with flies. For those who were unable to work, the alternative was to depend on the charity of those who worked, usually the family, or to steal.

My job did not require any previous education or training. I simply picked up *kizyak,* cow dung, with my bare hands, piled a few pieces together, and carried them closer to the huts where later the adults would add straw and stack them into large piles. After a few months of drying in the scorching sun, the piles would be cut into large, bricklike squares and stored both inside and outside the huts to be used in the winter. The job did require a certain amount of skill and technique. If one were to pick up dung too soon after the cow dropped it, it would fall apart in one's hands. Conversely, if one were to pick it up too late, when it had dried too much, it would fail to bond adequately with the straw.

After only a few days of this work under a cloudless sky, cow dung all over my hands and body, and flies torturing me, I felt so angry and frustrated that I was anxious to tell the first Soviet official who came along what I thought of his country. As it turned out, I didn't have to wait long. One day the NKVD officer who gave us the rhetorical speech on our arrival came toward me. He strutted over like a peacock in his bluish-gray trousers with red stripes running down both sides. He started parading in front of me. At first sight of him my fear overpowered me. Then my anger and frustration took over.

"How are you, Wieslaw?" he asked in broken Polish. I did not even look his way; I simply picked up soft cow dung while trying to decide whether I should trip accidentally and drop it on his boots. He started quizzing me and I did not move.

First he asked where my mother was, then where my brother and sister were, then whether my family "liked our great country." I recalled Mother's advice not to answer any questions posed by the Soviets, especially the NKVD, and not to do anything foolish. So each time he asked a question, I answered, "I do not know."

"Don't you know anything?" he retorted, getting red in the face and neck. I then realized that he was getting very angry with me.

"I know some things, sir," I replied with traditional politeness to an older person, while choking on the words as I remembered what he said the first day we met: that there are no "sirs" in the Soviet Union, only citizens.

The man jerked like a fish in a hot frying pan and screamed back at me, "I am not a 'sir.' My friends call me *tovarishch,* or 'comrade.' I am your family's and your friend, and I want you to remember that."

"I will remember, tovarishch," I answered uncertainly, not knowing how I should address him.

Only a short time earlier he had told us that everybody in the Soviet Union was equal and called a *grazhdanin,* or citizen. Now he was telling me a different story: that some people called him "comrade" rather than "citizen." It was confusing. This seemed a good time to ask him for an explanation.

"Tovarishch, does this mean you are not a grazhdanin?" I asked him.

"Yes, I am, but I am a member of the Communist Party, and for respect, we address one another as 'tovarishch' to remind all citizens that we are also their comrades and friends," he bellowed.

If this man insists on being my friend, I thought to myself, maybe I should test him. What are friends for if not to help one another? This is what my mother had taught me at home. Let's see if this friend will help an exhausted citizen like me. I already had two piles of cow dung stacked and ready to be moved. I told him how hard and how long I had worked in the sun, how tired I was, and how I was not used to doing this kind of work, all of which was true. Without the slightest hesitation, I picked up one pile, came up close to the officer, and pleaded as politely as I could in a tired voice.

"Tovarishch, please help me carry one pile of this cow dung closer to the huts so that I do not have to come back for the other pile."

That did it.

"You little Polish spoiled prince," he screamed. "I am an NKVD officer and a representative of the Union of Soviet Socialist Republics. I do not have to pick up cow shit like you do and the rest of you Polish capitalists.

You keep on doing this and one day we will make a good Communist citizen out of you and you will learn to appreciate our great country. I will forgive you this time. At least you remembered to call me tovarishch." He spat on the ground and angrily walked away, mumbling something under his breath in Russian. After I calmed down a little, I realized what I had done and hoped that this man would not take revenge on my family.

When Jurek came back to the hut, Mother and Zosia were still away. I told him what had happened, repeating the conversation almost word for word. His face turned pale. The first thing he told me was not to say anything about the incident to our mother or sister. Then he explained how the NKVD and its informers interrogated young children in the hope of uncovering information that could be used against their families. From now on, he instructed, no matter who talks to you, tell them that you have not seen anything or heard anything, that you don't know anything, or, better yet, that you don't remember anything. "You never know which of them may be an NKVD informer," he said.

When I pointed out that this seemed to amount to lying, Jurek replied that there was a difference between lying and refusing to tell the truth. "If you tell them what we really think about Communism and the Soviet Union, we may end up in Siberia, which would be much worse than being here." Then he told me that what I had done was very foolish and dangerous. He gave me a stern warning never to do anything like it again. I promised, but I knew that it would be a very hard promise to keep.

Jurek, then eighteen, had been put to work at the commune's clay pit, where water from a well was poured over clay and stirred by a mechanism driven by oxen. The resulting mixture was poured into molds and dried in the sun to make bricks that were shipped to other parts of the Soviet Union. Jurek also hauled water. Higher production earned him larger rations, which he shared with us. Without his extra efforts, we would have had little to eat. Mother and Zosia were put to work tending animals, hauling water, and doing other miscellaneous chores.

When not working, we spent much of our time killing fleas and lice. The Kazakhs spent hours each day on this pursuit, crushing the vermin in their teeth and throwing them into the fire. We crushed them between our fingernails before tossing them on their funeral pyre.

Because I was only seven and a half, I was not expected to do as much work as the others. While they were out, I often stayed behind, spending the time looking out across the steppe and meditating on our misfortune. The steppe nurtured feelings of hopelessness and emptiness. You could look and look and look, only to see barren land stretching to meet an empty sky. Underfoot was flat, scorched, fissured earth filled with dry twigs and dried-up grass. There was no green vegetation of any kind. I spent hours looking in every direction and wished every minute that I was back home in Sarny, where I belonged. Mother continually reminded us to have faith and to pray that soon we would return home. She taught us that without hope there is no survival. That, in the end, was the lesson I remembered most.

After our first day's experience with the devils on the steppe, we learned that the Kazakhs used them as fuel for cooking during the summer. Highly flammable and plentiful, this source of fuel was much more expedient for cooking than cow dung. Within a week of my confrontation with the NKVD agent, my sister and I received an additional work assignment: collecting the dried-up balls. The problem was finding a way to gather a sufficient supply safely, without getting all cut up. To do so in lightweight summer clothes would be impossible. The only clothes we had that offered some protection were our winter clothes, hats, and gloves. We well remembered our painful first encounter with the "devils" and chose the lesser of the two evils. Donning our winter clothes in the scorching summer heat won out easily.

Another incident occurred when my brother took me on a wagon ride to fetch water for the farm from a well some distance away. I sat on the side of the wagon, dangling my feet and daydreaming while Jurek walked, leading the team of oxen. Suddenly I fell off the wagon, flat on my stomach, straight in the path of the approaching wheel. Hearing me scream, Jurek, who fortunately was on the same side of the wagon, jumped toward me. Just as the heavy wheel was about to crush my legs, he grabbed me and pulled me away. Though I was saved on that occasion, the experience had the effect of impressing upon me that there was not always going to be a family member to pull me out of danger.

A month and a half after we arrived at the Kazakh farm, news spread of impending disaster. The dried grasses and low-lying bushes of the steppe were burning, and we could see the approaching flames and black smoke on the horizon. Ironically, the balls of dried twigs and grass that the Kazakhs used for fuel now were fireballs blown about by the wind, exploding like firecrackers. We thought we would burn to death, which was frightening enough, but having to watch the wall of flame come nearer and not being able to get out of its path is a feeling difficult to explain. My body tensed, my blood flowed faster, my senses of sight, smell, and hearing became more acute as the fire crept closer and closer. I could hear the crackling of burning grass in the distance.

My first impulse was to run in the opposite direction, where I thought it would be safe, but the Kazakhs, who were often in this predicament, knew it was better to take a stand. Using all available teams of oxen, they plowed circles around the buildings. Every person, including children, helped dig ditches in the freshly turned ground. By this time I was filled with the urgent desire to do all I could to save my family and the others. With the ditches dug, we all picked up dung, which otherwise would feed the fire, on both sides of the ditches. As the fire came closer to us, it seemed to rage like an inferno. At that point, other than carrying buckets and buckets of water, there was nothing we could do but pray for salvation. Pray we did, until the devils on the steppe and any loose twigs burned themselves out. To my amazement, the fire stopped at the ditches. Again I was impressed with the Kazakhs' knowledge of what it took to survive in such a harsh environment.

We lived with the Kazakhs on that government farm for about three months. Just as I can still hear the clicking and clattering of the cattle train's wheels, I still see the steppe stretching without end before me. Envisioning that barren land evokes feelings that I cannot escape—that I am in no place, that I am going to no place, that I am inexorably trapped in nowhere.

CHAPTER 6

SEMIOZERSK

Almost from the time we arrived in Sharmamulzak, Mother had been imploring the NKVD officers who regularly checked up on us to transfer us to Semiozersk, a town some distance away that she had learned about from the Kazakhs. Her persistence was prompted by an earlier incident with an interviewing officer. She had asked him when we could return to Poland. "You will no sooner see Poland," he snapped, "than you can see your own ears."

Mother was convinced from the beginning that the poor living conditions on the steppe did not bode well for our survival. She knew our prospects would improve in a town, where we might also have a better chance of getting information about Father and the war.

After listening to her pleading for weeks, the NKVD allowed our family to move. We traveled to our new home in a cart drawn by a team of oxen. Measuring time while traveling across the steppe, especially by oxcart, is difficult. With no identifying reference point, one develops a feeling of timelessness because of the sameness all around. Travelers on the Sahara Desert experience the same sensation.

Though also situated on the steppe, Semiozersk was a much different place. It had buildings made of logs as well as of clay bricks and mud. The surrounding area offered us at least a semblance of life, with a small lake, scattered green trees, and a forest reachable by horse in a half-day's journey. The town was populated by Russians, Ukrainians, Belorussians, Poles, and Jews, most of whom had been deported by the czars after speaking out against oppression. It was also home to a small number of Kazakhs and about fifty newly deported Poles. Some had been sent there by the Bolsheviks after the Russian Revolution of 1917; others, as punishment for refusing to accept the regime's dogma, had been sent to be reeducated in the Communist way of thinking.

When we arrived, the local NKVD took us to an empty mud hut. Unlike Sharmamulzak, here we had boards for beds. Mother would later find the materials she needed—burlap and straw—to make mattresses for us. We would use them for the rest of the time we were in Semioz-ersk. The straw mattresses were very uncomfortable, but they were bet-ter than sleeping on bare wood or clay.

This hut too was infested with fleas and lice, apparently an accepted part of life in the Soviet Union. Nevertheless, especially where the lice were concerned, it was a major and time-consuming preoccupation of Soviet citizens to kill these slimy, opaque creatures that invaded one's privacy day and night. With no running water or medicines and only an occasional cake of soap, there was not much anyone could do to get rid of them. Mother and Zosia spent hours each day combing the lice and nits out of our hair. Washing them out, even when we could get soap, did little good. The lice survived. The only remedy that really worked was kerosene, if and when we could get any. We soon found that the use of kerosene only created new health hazards from prolonged skin contact with it and from breathing its fumes. The situation was hopeless no mat-ter what we did, because we would always pick up more lice from those around us.

Bedbugs presented a different nightmare. They interrupted our sleep by crawling over our bodies and sucking our blood. We spent countless hours killing them and devising methods to prevent their attack. Squish-ing them only compounded the problem because their blood had a ter-ribly foul odor. Fighting the bedbugs was futile, but we did so anyway.

The Communist regime in Moscow knew about the infestation of the citizenry with fleas, lice, bedbugs, and other indigenous pests. Rather than try to eradicate the problem by improving basic living conditions, they resorted to superficial, stop-gap measures such as building steam baths to be used free of charge by anyone. Most of these baths, which the Russians called *banya,* were crude imitations of saunas. Water was poured over heated stones, creating dense steam. The user would scour himself with birch twigs, or have someone do it for him, to open the pores to enhance cleansing. In small villages, men and women often used such places together. In larger towns, the baths were more sophis-ticated, with tile floors and showers, as well as hot water and steam pro-duced by coal-fired boilers.

The Soviets clearly intended the steam baths to serve as delousing stations but for obvious reasons never called them by that name. When people entered, they would give their clothes to an attendant who was supposed to process them according to prescribed methods for disinfes-tation. At the same time the bathers would receive a smelly and gummy substance to apply to themselves as a delousing agent. The major problem with these baths was that they very often lacked soap, had no fuel for the heaters, or were broken. As a result they were themselves a good place to pick up lice. Bathers, after putting on their clothes on the way out, would often leave more heavily infested than when they entered.

Our steam bath in Semiozersk was extremely small and used by both sexes. We very seldom went there because Mother did not want us exposed to such an environment and it was inoperative most of the time anyway. So we fought the lice and dirt as best we could, sponging ourselves with wet cloths during the winter and bathing in the lake when it was warm enough. Even the lake proved to be a problem because the locals bathed naked at the beach nearby and some of the younger ones made love openly on the sand. This was something my sister did not want me to see, and she did her best to drag me away from such exhibitions.

A few weeks after we were settled in our new hut, I told my mother that my eyelids were itching and sore. At first she didn't know what the problem was, but a day later, when they became very red and were swollen so I could barely keep them open, she realized that nits between my eyelashes were hatching, leaving my lids severely infested. We had no tweezers, medicine, or ointments to get the nits out or to soothe my raw eyelids. Mother had no choice but to try to dig them out with a needle. When I first heard this, I panicked. But I soon realized that I had no other choice. I felt scared because of the pain but also because I could see that Mother agonized more than I did at the prospect of what she had to do. When the time came, I sat there for what seemed an eternity, with my hands in her lap, grinding my teeth. I kept quiet. I did not want to cry out. I knew I should be brave because my father would have expected it of me, and I knew that Mother needed me to be brave. When she was finished, Mother kissed and cuddled me. I felt much better, though my eyelids were red and almost swollen closed, not to mention extremely sore and itchy. It took about two weeks for my eyelids to heal, during which time Mother maintained constant vigilance against new infestations.

That was not my only mishap during the autumn of 1940. I walked barefoot to save on shoes and one day drove a rusty nail all the way through my foot. There was no doctor to go to and no medicine, but again, Mother came to the rescue. The nail had to come out and the wound had to be thoroughly cleaned, no matter how much it would hurt. She instructed Zosia to boil water and to get some cotton and tincture of iodine, which we had brought with us from Poland. When the water was ready, I was told to sit on a chair and hold on to it with both hands, and I was given a towel to bite on. Jurek held my foot firmly enough so that I could not move it. I closed my eyes. Shortly afterward, I fainted. Whether it was from fear alone or from the pain of the procedure, I did not know. Mother pulled the nail out, washed the wound, and applied a homemade medicine made of herbs, hoping my foot would not become infected. Later we visited a nurse in town, but owing to the lack of medical supplies she could do no more for me than Mother had already done.

Not long after our arrival in Semiozersk, Mother got permission for us to move to another one-room hut, which we shared with another Polish family of four, making a total of eight people. Except for the overcrowding, it was a marked improvement over the two previous places we had lived since our deportation. The new hut had a tiny adjoining room that served as a kitchen and storage area. It had a wooden floor and a brick stove. Zosia and I befriended the daughters of the other family, who were the same ages as we were. For the first time since leaving Poland, I had a playmate. Then, during the winter, we moved again, this time to a small hut in town that we had to ourselves. It had one room with two windows and a storage area.

Moving from a small town to a city was very difficult, if not impossible. Restrictions were imposed not only on deportees but also on all citizens of the USSR. Moscow, Leningrad, and Kiev were off-limits to everyone except those asked to move there by the government. Permission to move within the same town was more easily obtained but still required much paperwork.

Mother was always on the lookout for a better place to live and repeatedly pleaded with the NKVD for permission to relocate. She was always interrogated about why we wanted to move and was asked to return for subsequent interviews and to wait for final approval, a decision that depended on the whim of the local NKVD official.

From the time we arrived in Semiozersk, the NKVD forced Mother, Jurek, and Zosia to go to work. Jurek was sent with two other young Polish deportees to a forest to cut and haul timber. There he lived in a work barrack for almost three months before moving back with us as winter approached. The work was exhausting and dangerous, and he and his coworkers were beset by mosquitoes. This required them to cover their heads with specially made paper hoods with gauze-like screening in front in order to protect their faces and necks. Despite the heat, they also had to wear gloves and heavy clothing. Zosia, then fourteen, was also sent to the forest, grouped with other young Polish women to load and haul timber.

Mother, because of her pleading, was given a job in a factory making felt boots—a blessing because many of the jobs given to deportees were beyond their physical capabilities and served mostly to weaken and eventually kill them. As for me, unlike in Sharmamulzak, I had nothing to do and spent most of my time thinking about our home and fantasizing about how to escape to Poland. Even in my imagination, nothing I tried ever worked because the NKVD was always watching us.

Meanwhile, Mother wasted no time in learning all she could about the Soviet system. She learned that there was a law that all children under sixteen had the right to attend school for at least ten years. To save my brother and sister from hard labor, she again went to the local NKVD, asking that Jurek and Zosia be allowed to go to school. After her requests were shunted aside for two months, she threatened to write to NKVD headquarters. I will never know how she found the courage to threaten the local officials. She was granted permission not only for Zosia but also for my brother, who by then was eighteen years old. They began attending the Soviet *desyatiletka*, a ten-year school. We were fortunate that Semiozersk was large enough to have such a school. In smaller places, the Soviets either put the children to work or took them away from their parents to send them to school elsewhere. In many cases the parents and children never saw one another again.

Mother handled the question of my schooling differently. Under no condition would she send me to a Soviet school; she did not want to expose me to Communist ideas that she feared would poison my young mind. Mother talked to me in whispers about the Communists, their godless behavior, constant lies and deceit, restrictions on personal freedom, and attempts to control the thoughts of the population.

The Soviets began brainwashing children in preschool, Mother told me. They told the children how lucky they were to live in a workers' paradise. They told them that in all other countries there was persecution, disease, poverty, and suffering, but not in the Soviet Union. From the beginning, Soviets taught the children all to think exactly the same way, to talk exactly the same, "like robots," Mother explained. Children could not develop their own opinions, let alone express them. Older children who asked questions and voiced criticisms were punished or expelled. In some cases, parents lost their jobs because of what their children said.

"There have been cases of parents being sent to Siberia," she said, "because they were accused of bringing up their children in what the government called a 'subversive atmosphere.'"

Although I had wanted to be with other children, I understood Mother's reasons and went along without argument, though unhappily. She then announced in her customary self-assured manner that I was going to study what every Polish boy ought to be studying.

Mother asked Zosia to teach me whenever she found some free time from her own studies and chores. My sister taught me Polish, Polish history, geography, and math. We had no books written in the Polish language, so Zosia had to teach me from memory. History was my favorite subject. Hearing about my forefathers, just as I had heard about them from my own father, was a great source of strength because it gave me a feeling of identity and belonging, even though I was thousands of miles from my true home.

Being tutored at home instead of going to a Soviet school initially gave me a sense of adventure, but the excitement did not last long. During the day, when everybody went to work or school, I still sat there with nothing to do and no one to play with. With no books, the days dragged on, and I would long for my cozy room and toys in Sarny. As the times worsened and we struggled harder to survive, the tutoring I did receive became more sporadic. Sometimes I wished I could attend classes simply to be with children of my own age, even if they were being brainwashed. But for the two years I was in Kazakhstan, I never went to school.

The experience of my brother and sister soon vindicated Mother's stand against my attending a Soviet school. Jurek and Zosia often talked between themselves and with Mother about what went on in their classes. According to them, Soviet children did not go to school only for reading and arithmetic. Every day they were taught about the greatness of the Soviet Union and its people: the farmers, the factory workers, the mechanics, the fishermen, the engineers, the doctors, the musicians, the pilots, the sailors, and the brave Soviet soldiers who never lost a battle or a war. Then the children would be asked who of all the Soviet citizens were the greatest and the noblest and cared the most for the downtrodden workers. The students knew the answer expected of them, and all hands were immediately raised. The greatest were the Soviet leaders, who loved their people, especially the young children. Once in a while Jurek and Zosia would bring me a piece of candy from school, a rare treat because sugar and candy were not available in stores. At school, children were taught that the candy they received came from the benevolent father Stalin, all the way from Moscow, because he cared so much about all the children in the workers' paradise. The children were so impressed that with little encouragement from their teachers they were eager to join the young Communist groups to prepare them for their work for Rodina, the Motherland; their mission was to fight capitalist oppression and liberate those enslaved by it, so that eventually the whole world would be a workers' paradise like the Soviet Union.

The brainwashing of the public as to the glories of Soviet Communism was not confined to the schools, however. Propaganda posters were on every wall, in every room and corridor of government buildings, in railroad stations, hospitals, eating places, meeting halls, and all buildings frequented by the public. Such placards figured prominently in Semiozersk's Palace of Culture. The room was typical of those all over the country. They were decorated with posters, red fabric, and pictures of government officials. The "palaces," depending on their size, usually had a radio, a couple of newspapers, books about Communism, and a table and chairs in which citizens could sit and absorb the latest government propaganda. Keeping me home from school did not prevent me from seeing and hearing the proclamations of Communism.

My lack of formal schooling was the least of my concerns, though I wished to be with other children. The culture shock we experienced on our first day in Sharmamulzak was not lessened at all in Semiozersk, unless measured by Soviet standards. We went from horrible circumstances to merely terrible ones. At this point, the aspect of our life I found most difficult to deal with was the constant spying to which we were subjected by the secret police. Their visits to us greatly increased after our move to Semiozersk, though their purpose was not to inquire about our health and general welfare. The interrogations, whether subtle or blatant, became a fearful part of my life, particularly when I was at home alone. My family had warned me about the NKVD's tactics, and I was soon wise to them. But the threat they posed to me by their questioning—even when it seemed entirely innocent—was emotionally exhausting.

At first I thought the NKVD was concerned that we might escape and make our way back to Poland. Then I realized how unlikely that would be. We were thousands of miles from Poland on Soviet soil, a mother with children, helpless and unarmed. How could we possibly escape? The NKVD and their informants were in every town and every village in the Soviet Union. We surely could not walk back the way we had come, nor could we take a train without permits, passports, and money. Cross the Russian steppes? The heat would suffocate us in the summer and the blizzards and wolves would kill us in the winter. So why did they persist in spying on us?

Mother and Zosia most often replied the same way. "Do not ask such questions. Someone may hear you, and then all of us could be in trouble." Sometimes they would add, "When you grow up, we will talk about it. Right now, you're too young to understand."

Jurek, however, was more outspoken than they and agreed that the NKVD was not really worried about our trying to escape. They knew we could not do so successfully, he said, but they also realized the trouble it would cause were we to attempt it. Nor were they afraid of us as individuals. The NKVD could kill us or send us to Siberia any time they wished, and nobody would challenge their actions. What they were afraid of, Jurek explained, was what we represented—our way of life and our beliefs as Poles. They especially feared our telling the truth to Soviet citizens about life outside the USSR.

Whenever my brother talked this way it made me proud to be who I was. Despite my fear of the NKVD, it gave me a sense of hidden pleasure that the dreaded Soviet secret police were afraid of what my family and a little boy like me stood for and believed in.

The spying was only one of many culture shocks that initially traumatized us but that eventually we learned to live with. Equally trying was the lack of the barest provisions for public and private sanitation, coupled with the shocking habits of personal hygiene among the populace, which resulted in dangerous and sometimes deadly health problems. These problems were compounded by their being explained away or excused by Soviet propaganda. Having and using a handkerchief to blow one's nose, for example, was considered a capitalist luxury and might place one under suspicion of being bourgeois and perhaps even an enemy of the people. Instead, on streets and in other public places people put their fingers on their noses, blew out, and shook the mucous off their fingers, wiping the remnants on their clothing.

Another common method people used to clear their noses was to suck the mucous up into their throats and then spit it out with a powerful burst of air from the lungs. Bystanders and passers-by had to be always on guard, especially a youngster like me who tended to dart around here and there. It was not unusual to find someone's spit on your clothing when you arrived home.

Lack of public and private sanitation further added to the degradation in which we had to live. Although there were some public latrines in the town, these were almost always unusable, especially in the summertime. The stench was horrifying. Human excrement lay all over the floors and wooden seats, and the walls were covered with dried and fresh feces, the result of using fingers to wipe oneself, because toilet paper was unavailable. The reason for not providing it was that, like the handkerchief, toilet paper was a capitalist luxury.

There were, however, alternatives to using the latrines and one's fingers. In the summertime, many Soviet citizens would stop by the side of the road and gather fresh leaves with which to wipe themselves. If there were no fresh leaves, then round stones sufficed. If there were no stones, there was another option. Young children in particular would look for a clump of green grass down which they would gently slide on their bare behinds. This could prove dangerous, as it often did, if there were twigs or thistles concealed in the grass, but at least it kept the fingers clean. In winter, because the leaves, grass, and stones were all covered with deep snow, the only other way to wipe oneself was with a hardened snowball.

My sister's friend Iwona Gronkowska, the daughter of a Polish businessman, described the dilemma she and other deportees faced when assigned to work on a government farm tending eight thousand sheep with sheepdogs. Iwona was fourteen at the time. During the winter the dogs were kept outside with practically no food. The unsuspecting deportees who went outside to answer nature's call soon found themselves being attacked from behind by starving dogs competing for the feces before they even dropped to the ground. After such an experience, many began to carry sticks with them to fend off the dogs, but it soon became obvious that having to repel them from behind was too dangerous. Next came an invention born of necessity. A person would build a small igloo, large enough to stick one's behind into, and fend off the dogs from the front. Whatever the dangers of this method, at least one would not be bitten on one's bare behind.

Desensitized, the locals made no effort to conceal themselves in public. It was not unusual to see both men and women pull down their clothing and defecate by the roadside. One day shortly after our arrival in Semiozersk the four of us were walking out of town to look for a watermelon farm. It was not long before we noticed a couple we were familiar with squatting down by the same side of the road that we were on. Zosia became very flustered and asked Mother if we should cross to the other side. Mother replied that it would be more awkward to do so and that we should just keep walking as we were, without looking at the couple. As we went by they waved and greeted us. Mother answered in Russian and I waved back, thinking all along that the entire scene was comical. After we were out of earshot, Zosia derided what she had just seen but was promptly reminded by Mother that we were not in Warsaw or Paris and that we should adjust our expectations accordingly.

I once asked Mother why the people in this country were so crude. Her answer surprised me. "Do not pay any attention to these people, but remember that one cannot always blame them for the way they live," she said. "The Communist system has imposed much of their way of life on them. What I want you to always remember is how you were brought up and who you are."

Public eating places in Semiozersk and elsewhere that we had occasion to visit presented a microcosm of much of Soviet life and cultural practice. I went to such places with my family a number of times, but always under duress.

Soviet eateries usually were open for only a few hours a day, if at all. The two items almost always available, compliments of the state, were hot water and table salt. Fish soup and watered-down cabbage soup, if and when available, were the standard offerings. On special days patrons could buy a slice of heavy black bread. Everyone sat on benches at old, thick wooden tables riddled with cracks in which were embedded food particles from years of use. People sat wherever space was available because in the Soviet Union there were no strangers. Everybody was a citizen, a friend, or a comrade. At least this is what the citizens were told.

Minor problems did exist, however. For one, there were never enough utensils to go around. The best way to get a spoon was to sit down next to someone who was almost finished eating. After licking the spoon to be sure no food was wasted, the citizen, friend, or comrade would hand it over to the newcomer. Should the recipient be too sensitive to begin eating immediately with this unwashed spoon, his only option was to wipe it on his clothing, because there were no napkins. When diners wanted to use some of the salt freely available in the tin containers on every table, they would usually dip right in with their fingers or a spoon, with the result that the containers of chunky salt crystals also held particles of fish, cabbage, and barley as well as everybody else's saliva.

The slurping of the diners could be heard across the room. When finished, each would usually wipe his mouth with his hand or the sleeve of his shirt or jacket. Not to do so was considered *ne kulturno*, not cultured. He would then indulge in belching, never covering his mouth, which was an accepted way to show approval of the meal. Further words of approval—"Khorosho, Khorosho!" ("Good, Good!")—would follow.

I don't think we ever learned to ignore the nose blowing, another common feature of Soviet dining out. Most patrons of an eatery knew better than to let it diminish their enjoyment of the meal. After all, none of this could possibly constitute a health problem, they were assured, because there were no communicable diseases left in the Soviet Union. According to the government in Moscow, Soviet doctors had wiped them out after the revolution. And, anyway, the very same doctors had also discovered the best medicines to treat any illness. In fact, nothing could have been further from the truth, and among those not deluded by the government's claims it was often said that for the lucky ones there were two types of medicine: for any illnesses from the waist up there was aspirin; for any from the waist down there was castor oil.

CHAPTER 7

WINTER AND WOLVES

The winter of 1940–41 stormed in with all its fury—an awful Siberian winter with its heavy snows and deadly blizzards. Snow that fell in late fall did not melt until late spring. The roads in town were so thoroughly covered with compacted snow that travelers walked as much as four feet above the ground. Mother frequently braved these roads not only to get to work but also to stand in lines for food, barter with the Kazakhs, and visit NKVD headquarters to inquire about Father. We hadn't received a letter from him since April, before we were deported.

We called the blizzards "white foam." If caught in one while outside, you would be completely engulfed by it. We dared not even go to the outhouse for fear of losing our direction and freezing to death, so we used the buckets in the hut.

During a blizzard, life came to a standstill. Temperatures fell as low as minus 40 degrees, and snow driven by high winds produced impassable drifts. When such cold weather came, hungry wolves would venture into the town, and their howling outside our hut at night would make it nearly impossible to sleep. I kept imagining how horrible it would feel to be eaten alive by having my flesh torn by the white fangs of wild animals. The locals had told us that this happened now and then during the blizzards when the wolves were starving.

Travelers caught in a blizzard seldom survived, and their frozen bodies would either be eaten by wolves or found in the spring when the snow melted. The local people would comfort themselves by saying that freezing to death was the most pleasant way to die because in a blizzard's extreme cold, you could feel no pain or sensation of freezing. I appreciated the importance of this observation, but to me it had exactly the opposite effect. It put fear in my heart, because I was not ready to die in a blizzard or any other way. Still, every time a blizzard came I wondered how a person who froze to death could tell others how it feels to die this way.

In such extreme conditions, burying the dead was almost impossible.

Instead, the bodies were placed in wooden caskets bound with wire to keep the wolves from devouring them, and the caskets were left on top of snow mounds until springtime. Snows would later cover the coffins, but they would reappear with the thaw and then the dead could receive a proper burial.

During such times, those who had been provident enough to save some of their meager rations had something to place in the hollows of their stomachs, and they survived. Others did not.

We were often entombed in our hut during a blizzard by the mounting piles of snow that covered the windows and reached the top of the chimney, making the hut a dark and scary place. For days we had no place to empty our waste buckets, and the stench would be unbearable. We opened the door only to get snow, which we melted for water. Unable to communicate with anyone outside, we often felt that nothing else existed except the starving wolves. In the darkness, the only light came from the wood burning in the stove. This light kept us going.

After a blizzard, the first chore was to dig a way out of the hut. The second was to dig a tunnel to our neighbor's hut to maintain communication and give assistance if needed. The third was to dig a tunnel to the outhouse. The locals used a simple but occasionally lifesaving idea: running ropes between huts and from huts to outhouses. Early in the winter, before the snow piled up too much, these ropes allowed us to move around without getting lost even in a blinding blizzard. Once the snow was piled high, the ropes were useless.

During breaks between blizzards, it was not unusual to see some brave soul travel with a horse and sledge. And such a soul was indeed brave, because if the horse and the driver ventured even a short distance from the beaten path, they could sink deep into the snow and perish, unable to dig themselves out. Many did. Once, when the snow was deep, Jurek and I borrowed a horse and sledge to run an errand. Before we came to the road, the horse had disappeared in the deep snow. After hours of digging, we managed to lead it back to the barn, but we gave up on our trip.

Keeping warm required a tremendous amount of wood, and at one point we ran out. By then, Jurek had gotten to know a few friendly locals working on a government farm. One of them was willing to barter the use of a horse, a sledge, a couple of axes, and a shotgun for one of the men's watches Mother had stashed away when we were forced to leave Poland. In those days, bartering was the best way to acquire something or get anything done. Money was almost useless because there was prac-tically nothing to buy in the government stores and few people were will-ing to accept it.

It was common knowledge that for anyone to go to the forest in the middle of winter without a shotgun was tantamount to suicide because the hungry wolves would be likely to attack and devour humans. At the same time, for a Pole to be caught by the NKVD with a gun could be equally deadly. Jurek decided to risk it and, despite great objections from Mother, asked me to go with him to gather and load the wood. Mother told him that he should take one of his Polish friends instead. She was terribly afraid to let me go, but we reassured her as best we could. Though in truth I was scared to go, I didn't want to show it. Besides, I knew I would have the protection of my elder brother, as well as the axes and shotgun. Also, I reasoned to myself, I had hunting experience that could be useful if the wolves attacked us. Mother should have remembered my hunting with Father. I still remembered Father's instructions on how to hunt dangerous animals: "Do not shoot the boar until you see the whites of its eyes."

Before dawn on the day we were to go, a heavily bearded Russian pulled up on a horse-drawn sledge as arranged by Jurek and knocked on our door. As we came out, he greeted us warmly and we returned his greetings. It was so cold outside that spit seemed to freeze before hitting the ground. We were dressed in layers of clothing lined with newspapers and *fufaiki,* quilted cloth jackets filled with wool. We wore wool hats with earflaps, heavy gloves, scarves, and felt boots. We covered our faces with wool stockings. To complete our protection, Mother smeared ani-mal grease on our faces and gave Jurek and me some parting advice. She and Zosia hugged us, kissed us, and said a prayer for our safe return.

On our way, we dropped off the old Russian at his hut. Jurek thanked him politely.

"Go with God," he said. He waved and disappeared into the unlit hut.

"A good old Russian," Jurek said to me as we pulled away. "You see, brother, the old ones still believe in God."

The shotgun was hidden under straw on the bottom of the sledge, in case we should have a chance meeting with the NKVD. Two axes were clearly visible. We sat next to each other saying nothing until the snow-covered huts began to disappear in the grayish gloom of the Siberian dawn. Snow stretched to the darkened horizon, which gradually light-ened as the golden sun began to peek at the earth. The horse was pacing along on a lightly beaten path without much urging, as if he knew where to go. My brother loosened the reins and turned to me, saying that the only reason he had brought me on this trip was to give me a chance to be better prepared to care for our mother and sister in case something happened to him.

Going on this trip was scary enough for me, though, as I say, I hadn't admitted as much to anyone. But hearing my brother tell me that something could happen to him frightened me even more. What could I do? Up to now, everybody had been taking care of me. My still childlike innocence led me to ask my brother what could possibly happen to him. He told me that in the Soviet Union, you never know if you are going to live or die. And if you do live, you might spend most of your life in prison or, worse yet, in Siberia at hard labor.

"But what if you haven't done anything wrong?" I asked him.

"That doesn't matter," he said. "People are imprisoned for just speaking the truth and wanting to be free."

When I asked why, Jurek explained that the Soviets simply imprison people who disagree with them. Even Soviet citizens would say, in all seriousness, that in their country there are three kinds of people: those who are in jail, those who have gotten out of jail, and those who are waiting to go to jail. "All someone has to do who does not like you is to report you to the NKVD for saying or doing something you did not even say or do, and off you go to prison or Siberia."

We rode for a bit in silence. Then Jurek began to give me specific instructions about our mission. He was all business and sounded just like Father did when we went hunting in Poland.

"Listen carefully, little brother. What we are about to do will keep the family from freezing to death. There must be no mistakes. I am going to tell you exactly what to do and what not to do. This is one time I want you to behave like a grown man even though you're only eight. Do you think you can do it?"

I was scared, but then I remembered I was also a little scared when I went hunting for the first time. I remembered how Father assured me that there was nothing to be afraid of if I did exactly as I was told. I had also been scared of dying when the steppe was burning, yet I did not panic, nor did I hide under Mother's skirt then. I carried dirt and water and did whatever else the Kazakhs told us to do to stay alive. I thought to myself that in the past year I had seen and gone through a lot. I had already faced dying, so why could I not act like a grown man now? Besides, Mother and Zosia depended on us for help.

I assured him that I would do my best to act like a grown-up and that

I would do anything he told me to do. Jurek said that he would drive and handle the horse. Once we were out of town, my job was to take the shotgun and sit in the sledge with my back toward him. Above all, I was to remain calm and not to panic. If I saw wolves following us, I was *not* to shoot. If they were to charge us—which Jurek said was unlikely—I was to pick out the lead wolf, steady my hand, take a dead aim, and shoot only when I saw the whites of his eyes. If I missed, we would have to fend off the wolves with axes. "No matter what happens, you stay close to me. Do you understand?"

I told him I did, and then observed that he sounded just like Father did when he described wild boar hunting in Poland.

"I am glad you remember that," Jurek said, "because today you may have to use his advice."

Hours later, we arrived at the forest's edge without incident. As we entered its domain, it grew darker. The deeper into the forest we traveled, the darker and more eerie it became. A shroud of pure white snow blanketed the forest floor, except for dead branches sticking out here and there like skeletons. Tall, barren trees, half-frozen, soared high into the sky, their seemingly lifeless branches intertwined with each other like a massive spider web. No birds, no animals. Stark silence. I knew that ghosts had to be cleverly hiding behind the heavy tree trunks, just as in a cemetery, where you can't see them or hear them but still know they're there. The silence was so complete that we could clearly hear the sound of the horse's hooves and our own breathing. Surely, I thought, the wolves could hear us, too. Fear overpowered me, and my heart began pounding. Jurek pulled up to a spot laden with fallen branches. He maneuvered the horse and the sledge around in the direction from which we came.

"Just in case we have to make a fast getaway," he explained. Thank heaven we were not going any further into this forbidden place, I said to myself, and silently prayed that we would not be here too long, either.

Jurek tied the horse's reins firmly around the trunk of a medium-sized tree, telling me to lean the shotgun and the two axes against it. We walked back to the sledge and laid two long ropes over it crosswise, then wove them through iron loops on either side of the sledge. Jurek told me that later we would use the long loose ends to bundle the load. Wasting no time, we began to stack the fallen branches into the sledge, hardly ever using an axe to trim them. Heavy pieces were loaded first, medium-sized next, and the small ones on top. The work went slowly because breathing was so difficult. I grew tired quickly, and my lungs began to hurt. Remembering my first hunting trip two years earlier, when I became so exhausted, I convinced myself to stick it out until the job was finished. I had made it then, so I should be able to make it now.

When the sledge was nearly loaded, the silence was broken by a thunderous explosion nearby. Jurek dropped the bundle of light branches he was carrying and ran for the horse. So did I. The frightened animal tried to rear while jerking its head up and down on the tied reins. Then it shuffled its hooves in place, still pulling and jerking. Jurek grabbed the reins close to the horse's mouth and began petting the neck of the frightened animal and talking to it in Russian in a desperate effort to calm it down. The last thing we wanted was to have a spooked horse break loose, break up the sledge against the trees, and take off. It would be a long and dangerous trek home through the night. We might even freeze to death, and then the wolves would get us for sure.

After a while the horse grew calmer, but I was still scared out of my wits.

"What happened, Jurek?" I asked.

"Nothing that you should be afraid of," he answered. "It was only a frozen tree trunk that split open."

While petting the horse and with an obvious effort to calm me, he explained further. According to the people who worked in the forest, when the temperature was colder than minus 40 degrees for a long time, as it often was in these parts and in Siberia, many trees froze solid inside. The pressure from the expansion of the freezing moisture inside the tree eventually caused a violent split, sounding just like an explosion. Also, with the temperature so low, the air was extremely thin, which amplified the sound and carried it over long distances. This was the reason that the explosion had sounded so close to us.

"Feel better now?" Jurek asked.

"Yes," I answered. But no sooner had I done so then we heard the sound of a howling in the distance.

"Wolves!" I screamed.

"Quickly!" Jurek commanded. "Get the shotgun and one axe while I tie up the load." He was done in a flash. Then he helped me climb on top of the sledge, handed me the shotgun, set both axes in front close to where he would be sitting, untied the skittish horse, and with two quick moves was sitting in front next to me, snapping the reins over the horse's back. Ever so slowly at first, we started moving. Thank God we were on the way back. If we could only get out of the forest before the wolves caught up with us! I hoped and prayed.

Jurek turned back to me with a different set of instructions. He told me to sit with my back touching his and to spread my legs firmly against solid branches for support. Above all, I was not to do anything until I was told to. He then instructed me to hold the shotgun with both hands across my lap and to put one axe on my lap "just in case," and to keep my eyes and ears peeled. If I saw or heard anything moving, I was to hand over the gun immediately. Under no circumstances was I to shoot at anything. Once again, I was instructed not to panic.

If only our father had been with us, it would have been much safer and easier to bear. Nevertheless, I did what I was told. Sitting back to back with the shotgun and an axe on my lap and my legs riveted between branches, I continually scanned our surroundings as we made our way through the forest. There was still no sign of life, but we could hear the howling of the wolves getting closer.

Frightening images flickered in my imagination. Wild, hungry wolves with gleaming yellow eyes, mouths wide open with white fangs, ready to attack us. Then a wild boar charging straight at us with all his might. My first hunting trip with Father flashed before me, as well as my first shot at the pretend wild boar. My father had said, "If you miss, we will be in trouble." Then it was all make believe, yet seemed real somehow. Today, it was for real: the first shot *had* to be good. Jurek turned back to me and with a reassuring voice said, "Once we are in the open, we will be safer. Remember that there are two of us."

With each passing moment, the forest became thinner. But the horse began to labor pulling the sledge, and the time seemed to drag. As I turned my head toward the front to see how close we were to the clearing, my scarf came off my mouth and nose. The freezing air pricked my lungs. When I complained that my lungs hurt, Jurek replied that his did, too. "It always happens when you're out in this type of weather for a long time." He told me to cover my nose and mouth with a scarf and not to talk. "If you get tired and sleepy, do not close your eyes even for a second," he warned. "If you do, we may be in deep trouble."

I took his advice and leaned more heavily on his back for comfort. As time went on, my lungs began to hurt even more. I was in pain and feeling tired, dreamy, and dazed. Oh, how I wished to take a short nap! Just for a brief moment, only to rest my aching eyes. I would have except for those annoying tiny black dots dancing behind us in the distance, back and forth and sideways. I rubbed my eyes to get rid of them, but the black dots were still dancing around and moving faster. Minutes later, they grew bigger. The horse whinnied several times and quickened his pace without any urging. Suddenly I realized we were being stalked. I nudged Jurek with my elbow. As he turned, I barely whispered.

"Wolves!"

"I saw them a long time ago, brother," he replied. "Stay calm. The odds are that unless they are disturbed, they will follow us a little longer and then drop off."

How I wished my brother would be proved right. In the meantime I said a prayer, just in case. It was getting dark. The dancing dots in front of my eyes disappeared. Total exhaustion from the long day's events overpowered me and lulled me into a pleasant state of oblivion. I leaned more heavily against my brother's back and, despite his warning, allowed my eyes to close. The very last words I heard Jurek utter to me barely registered.

"Wiesiu," he said, "do not tell Mother anything about the explosion and the wolves."

The last thing I remember of that day's events was Mother and Zosia undressing me and rubbing me all over.

CHAPTER 8

THE PETROVICHES

With the spring of 1941 fully upon us, we moved again. Six months after our arrival in Semiozersk, Mother found an old Russian couple willing to share their one-room hut with us. The reason for yet another move was not entirely clear to me at the time, other than that we would be close to a small lake with easy access to fishing and had the use of a boat courtesy of our host. Another benefit, I was to learn, was that the place was much closer to the center of town where the stores were located. On the rare occasion when something became available, lines formed the night before the store would open. Mother, Jurek, and Zosia would take turns standing in line all night waiting and hoping that the goods would not run out before it was their turn to buy. If only for this reason, living closer to the stores was a big advantage.

Mother had to apply again to the NKVD for permission to move. She submitted her application at one of the regular visits to their headquarters. As with each previous request since we had come from Sharmamulzak, permission came with bureaucratic slowness but without objection. Shortly afterward, we moved into Ivan and Natalia Petrovich's straw-roofed, clay-brick hut. They were an old Russian couple whose stooped posture, wrinkled faces, and worn hands showed not only their age but also years of hardship. We greeted them, but the old man was the only one to answer. It made us all very uncomfortable. We could not decide whether they resented us or were afraid to talk to strangers. The hut had neither a kitchen nor a bathroom and only one door, but at least it looked and felt like a house. Our beds were elevated boards placed along the walls. We slept on the straw mattresses and pillows we brought with us. Close to the stove stood an old wooden table with numerous cracks that had become embedded with dried food particles over the years. Two wooden benches stood on either side of the table.

The hut was about 160 yards from the lake. Facing its door was a barn, largely in disrepair, in which Mr. Petrovich stored a small, leaky boat that he used for fishing several times a week, weather permitting. He later told me that many years earlier, before the Communists took everything away from the people, it had been a cattle barn.

He also tended a garden adjoining the hut, using human waste taken from the outhouse for fertilizer, as most of the locals did. He asked us all to defecate in his garden during the spring and summer to feed his crops, but we declined.

Spring dragged into summer, the time passing slowly. Mother continued to inquire of the NKVD about Father. When asked whether he was still in the Starobelsk camp, they said no. When asked what camp he was in, they said they didn't know. When asked whether he was still alive, they said they didn't know. When asked how it is possible not to know the location of a prisoner of war on their soil, their answer was always the same. They replied that he probably escaped.

Our suspicions and fear grew when the wives of other Polish officers inquired about their husbands and the NKVD's responses were identical to the ones Mother received. Mother cried after every visit to the NKVD office. Jurek became morose but did not want to speculate about what might have happened to our father. Zosia took comfort in writing poems about Father that today are treasured parts of our family archives. I fervently believed that he was alive, because I could not fathom the alternative. I loved him and missed him. He had to come back. He would find us and we all would go back home and live just as we did before, except for remembering the nightmare I wished never had happened.

Waiting for Father to find us became increasingly hard for me to endure. My hatred for our captors grew. It was no longer the Soviet Army and the NKVD but all Communists as well who became the object of this hatred. All of them now were my enemies, and I was forced to live among them, which made each day a chore that seemed to have no ending. Back home in Poland, I had said my prayers each night with eager anticipation of the next day. In Kazakhstan, I also prayed each night, but went to sleep dreading the next day.

Mother worked while Jurek and Zosia attended school. During that time, day after day, week after week, there was nothing for me to do. There were no Polish children close by to play with or to talk to.

"Do not talk to the Russians and do not trust any of them because you never know which one could be spying on us, and even on the children," Mother would constantly remind me. Neither could I forget what Father always said about listening to Mother, but it would be so much easier, I felt, if I had somebody to play with or to talk to, even if that person were

Russian. Later I found out that most Russians, like most people in the other Soviet republics, did not belong to the Communist Party. Most of them suffered under the Soviet regime just as we did and were sympathetic to the Polish deportees.

The Petroviches, although they proved to be pleasant, charitable people who helped us in every way they could, for the most part kept to themselves. Natalia almost never talked to us or her neighbors and did not talk much to her own husband. After busying herself with daily chores, she would sit and stare into space for hours at a time as though she were mad. Or could it be that she was afraid to trust anyone, including her own husband?

Ivan spent most of his time working in his garden or on his old boat. Now and then, he would say something to me in Russian. After a while, and to my great surprise, he began to talk to me a little in broken Polish. It became obvious that he wanted to be friends with me. Despite Mother's admonition, I started hanging around the old man more and more.

He was a kind man who seemed to like me, and I could not help liking him. Jurek was too busy to give me much of his time, and this gentle old soul offered me the warm, fatherly attention I needed. My Russian vocabulary increased daily, and I learned enough in a short time for us to talk about everyday things. I never told my mother that I was beginning to understand and speak the language. In turn, I taught the old man Polish, a smattering of which he knew already from Polish deportees brought to Russia by the czars.

One sunny morning when Mr. Petrovich was getting his boat ready to go fishing, he asked if I would like to join him. I told him I would like it a lot but that Mother forbade it because I could not swim. That, of course, was only part of the reason, but I could not bring myself to tell him the rest—that I was not to speak to or trust any Russian.

He assured me that there was nothing to fear, that he had been in the boat hundreds of times. "Come, Veslav," he said, "every boy has to learn how to fish. We will stay close to the shore. Do not be afraid. I will not tell your mother."

I hesitated. What if Mother asked me what I had been doing all day? I very much wanted to go fishing, simply to do something interesting for the first time since we had left Poland. But I did not want to defy Mother's instructions or hurt her feelings. She suffered enough without having to worry about me drowning. I could not lie to her, either. Maybe she wouldn't ask about what I was doing. Maybe I could just tell her part of it; that way I wouldn't have to lie.

"Thank you, Mr. Petrovich," I said at last. "I will go if you promise not to tell."

"I will promise if you will promise not to call me 'Mr. Petrovich' anymore. Why do you always call me 'mister'? Here we do not have any 'misters,' only 'citizens.'"

Surprised, I responded that in Poland, children always addressed older people as "mister" or "missus" as a sign of respect. He reminded me that I was no longer in Poland, but I told him that it didn't matter— he was still older than I was.

He looked at me for a long time. Then he put his big, heavy hand on my shoulder and bent over, coming close to my face, as though he didn't want anybody to hear what he was about to say, though there was no one else nearby.

"Veslav," he began. "I am a sixty-seven-year-old Russian peasant, and nobody ever called me 'mister' except you and your family. Thank you for being nice, but please do not call me 'mister' when other Russians are around because my wife and I could get in trouble."

"But you haven't done anything wrong. How could you be in trouble?"

"It doesn't matter, Veslav," he replied, looking around nervously. "Let's go fishing now, it's getting late."

We dragged the wooden boat to the lake, waded barefoot into the water up to our knees, and pushed off with an old, cracked paddle while staying close to the shore. I was given a fishing pole, a long, wooden stick with a string that had a hook at the end. Carp were biting well that day. In two hours, using worms from the garden for bait, we caught about half a dozen. In the excitement, I forgot about being afraid of the water. My only fear was of being discovered by Mother.

When it was time to go back, we went ashore, turned the boat over to dump water from its bottom, then dragged it back to the barn. We cleaned the fish and went home, and Mrs. Petrovich began frying them without saying a word.

Not long afterward, when Mother, Jurek, and Zosia returned home and we had exchanged greetings, we sat down by the wooden table to a fish dinner. Our Russian host and hostess never joined us at the table to eat but always sat on chairs in their corner of the hut, eating from plates held in their hands. Mother asked Jurek and Zosia about school. Sure enough, she then turned to me and asked me how I was.

"Fine, thank you, Mama," I answered, hoping that this would be the end of her inquiry.

"And what did you do today, Wiesiu?"

"Nothing."

"You did nothing? You have to have done something because you smell terrible, just like fish."

Maybe I made a mistake by sitting so close to her. Then again, she always managed to figure out when I was up to something. I told her I had helped Mr. Petrovich clean carp in the barn.

Jurek and Zosia looked at me, then at each other, but said nothing.

Mother looked at me as well, then said that in the future, whenever I clean fish I should scrub myself with sand and dirt and then wash with water, because we have no soap. "Maybe then you won't smell so bad," she said.

Mother looked in Mr. Petrovich's direction, but his back was turned. Either he didn't hear our conversation or he pretended not to.

Thank you, Mr. Petrovich, I said to myself, carefully not looking at Mother. My feelings of friendship toward the old man deepened. Somehow, I knew I could trust him.

As spring turned to summer, our hopes for an easier life than we had had in Sharmamulzak rose, but fate turned cruel.

On June 22, 1941, the Germans attacked the Soviet Union across its western border. The marriage of the Nazis and the Soviets, consummated with "eternal friendship" only two years earlier, was shattered. The German blitzkrieg advanced south toward Kiev and north toward Leningrad, in a move as treacherous as the Soviets' invasion of Poland in 1939. Unprepared for war with their bosom allies, the humiliated Red Army gave way in a short time. As we learned later, they took a tremendous beating in the first two months after the invasion.

The Communist government in Moscow engineered a full-scale propaganda offensive to rally the citizens. Communal meetings, newspapers, and the radio fed the public a litany of catchphrases intended to evoke nationalistic fervor: "The fascist pigs will pay for this!" "Citizens, rise against the oppressors and defend your Motherland!" "The workers will prevail!" At the same time, the citizens were assured that in a few days the fascist murderers would be defeated and that already the victorious Red Army was winning one major battle after another.

We saw the news of the German attack as a mixed and highly uncertain blessing. The Germans as well as the Russians were our bitter enemies. Mother and Jurek believed that had they remained allies, Poland would have been doomed and our home lost forever. It was foolhardy but impossible not to speculate about the effects of victory of one of our enemies over the other. At least we took comfort in knowing that our bitter enemies were at war with each other, giving us hope of returning home and seeing Poland free again. Mother reminded us that whatever the eventual outcome, the most important factor in our struggle was daily survival. And the conditions worsened. The Soviet government began to confiscate most of the food supplies from government farms to feed the Red Army and the war-zone population, leaving next to nothing for the people they robbed. Except for tempting displays of ham, sausages, fish, cheese, and bread all made out of wood and painted to simulate the real items, the stores were empty almost all the time except for minuscule portions of rationed bread and flour. Our only good fortune was that the lake nearby provided us with fish.

As time went on, Mr. Petrovich and I became better friends and went fishing at least once a week. Still, as much as my command of the Russian language improved, we seldom talked about anything except fishing. Occasionally, he spoke about how the war would end soon because the brave Red Army was beating the Germans. Jurek had told me earlier that he heard the same thing from other people but didn't believe them.

Soon it will be over, Mr. Petrovich would say confidently—maybe even before next winter. "Maybe then," he said, "your mother won't have to stand in line like a beggar all night to get a piece of bread."

By then, I hated the Germans and the Soviets equally, the Germans for starting the war and the Soviets for what they were doing to my family. I was convinced that both groups were terrible people. Maybe, I thought, it would be best if they killed one another to the very last man. Then there would be peace. I wanted to tell the old man how I felt, but something held me back. Though he was a Russian, I did not want to hurt his feelings. By getting to know him and his wife I was beginning to realize that there were good people in this country and that they were suffering in the same ways we were.

Adding to our tribulations, Mr. Petrovich became very ill. He lay in bed for many days. There was no more fishing. When nobody was around, he would ask me to come close and sit next to him. He complained about the miserable life that he had to live. There were always shortages of food, empty stores, and long lines, and there was no medical care.

He talked of the hard work he'd had to do all his life for nothing. He lamented that nobody cared about him, not even his wife. He told me that even some dogs had a better life than he had.

"Maybe," he said one afternoon, "it would be easier to just lie here and die."

Who knows? I thought. Maybe that is just what he wants to do.

The very idea of someone dying before my eyes scared me. I pitied the old man. But what could I do? Was he really so miserable? Tears welled in my eyes. I wondered what you tell a man who wants to die. If I were older, surely I would know the answer. Perhaps when we escape the Soviet Union, we could take him and his wife to Poland. At least then he would die among good people and not feel so miserable. For once in his life he would know the feeling of being free. These thoughts ran through my mind while I sat next to him pondering my response. I decided to offer a fishing trip with him the next day.

"Maybe," Mr. Petrovich answered.

Just then his wife came in, sat down in her chair, and with her usual fixed gaze, began to stare into space. It was time for me to leave his bedside.

The next morning, after Mother, Jurek, and Zosia left, I hung around the hut making as much noise as I could. I wanted to be sure Mr. Petrovich did not sleep until noon, as he had recently been doing. When he finally arose, it was still much later than was usual for him before becoming ill. He dragged himself out of bed and headed for the door, saying that today I could take him fishing.

We gathered our poles, dug up worms from the garden, and dragged the boat over the rough ground toward the lake. We had to stop at least ten times along the way. The old man was coughing and breathing heavily, and sweat poured from his forehead. Entering the boat, we shoved off as usual and he steered toward the middle of the lake, much farther out than we had gone before. We threw the lines in, sat, and watched, but no fish were biting. He was deep in thought and did not pay attention to the lines. He kept looking at me as if he wanted to talk. Then he asked me to promise not to tell anyone what he was about to say.

Chills went through my body. What could he want to say to a little boy like me? Still, I promised.

"You know I am a sick old man and probably will not live much longer," he began, "but there is something I would like to know that would make me happy before I die. Tell me about your country and your home. I think the Communists lie to us about everything. Is it much different in Poland than in the Soviet Union?"

I told Mr. Petrovich about the comforts of home, about my nanny and my friends. I told him about church, Easter and Christmas holidays, the snowmen, the sleigh rides with my father, the mushroom-picking excursions, the hunting expeditions, vacations to a peasant village, and my ducks, geese, and deer. I enjoyed sharing my memories with him. I also told him about the many books I had and the stories Father told me. Finally, I told him how much I missed my father and how proud I was of him for having fought in two wars already, and now in a third, against the Russians.

He listened in disbelief and interrupted me many times. I had to explain some things again and again. It seemed he either could not understand or could not believe that our home had a bathroom and toilet inside the house, and a dining room and a kitchen, and that every person had a bedroom to himself with its own heating stove. He seemed unable to imagine such comforts. He was especially surprised to hear that I had my own fairy tale books and that I had been taught to read and write by the age of six.

Now it was the old man's turn to talk. He told me that when he was six years old, he had to help out around the house and do chores outside. He never went to school and never learned how to read or write. "All I ever did in my life was hard work," he said. "First it was for the czars and then for the Communists. The czars were the rulers when I was young and they were blood-sucking leeches."

He paused, looking into the distance.

"No," he continued. "I never had any of the things you had, but at least the czars let us go to church. We observed our Christian holidays as you did."

His voice hardened. When the Communists took over, he said, they took away the churches and everything else that went with them. "By day, they called you citizen or tovarishch but at night, they murdered you," he said, adding that his wife had been out of her mind ever since the Communists murdered her family twenty years earlier. "So now she sits looking into space, and we both suffer," he said bitterly. "All our lives we have been dirt poor. The Communists tell us how Comrade Stalin gives us everything, how great he is, how great all our leaders are, how great Communism is, and how great the Soviet Union is. Nothing but lies! Stalin's a murdering son of a bitch. Some say he even murdered his own wife."

His voice had been rising steadily, and now he was nearly screaming. His clothes were wet from perspiration. I feared for my safety, thinking he might do something crazy. After all, we were in the middle of a lake and I could not swim. My feet were cold from the water in the bottom of the boat, and I was shivering.

"I'm sorry for you and your wife, Mr. Petrovich," I managed to say, hoping he would be calmed.

He seemed surprised by my remark. "You are sorry for us? I should be sorry for you because you and your family had it all and lost it."

I assured him that we would have it all back once we returned to Poland. I even offered to take the Petroviches with us when we left.

"May God bless you, Veslav," Mr. Petrovich said, regarding me ruefully. "Let me tell you something. Nobody gets out of the Soviet Union. Nobody. The Communists would rather kill you than let you go because they are afraid of other people finding out how we live. Then again, you, being a young boy, may not understand what I am going to tell you, but I want to die in Russia. Someday you will understand why a man wants to die in his own country, even if it is as bad as ours."

But I understood that already. Even when our lives were threatened by the fire on the steppe and I was overcome at first with the fear of dying, I knew somewhere inside me that if I had to die I wished to die and be buried in my own country. As for never getting out of the Soviet Union, that frightened me. But I knew that the old man had to be wrong. Why would Mother tell us that we would be free of our Soviet captors if it were not so?

The old man carried on about many different things. Much of what he said I did not understand. He talked about Lenin, the man I had seen on the posters, saying that the Communists called him "the father of their country." He kept calling them "liars, cheats, and murderers." His voice grew hoarser until I could hardly understand him, but he seemed unable to stop. He began to cough more, spitting blood, some into the boat, some onto his clothing. He kept wiping his nose on his sleeve. The longer he went on, the more emotional he became, and the more scared I grew. The water seeping into the leaky boat was getting ever higher, because we had been on the lake for a long time. I took the pail we always carried with us and began to bail, but the old man seemed not to notice.

"The Communists tell us how in Poland you have masters and slaves and how the masters kill the slaves any time they want. They told us how the masters force the peasant women to breast-feed puppies. Is that true, Veslav?" he asked.

I did not want to hear this kind of stupidity, but I could not blame the old man for asking.

"That is a lie, Mr. Petrovich! It is a lie! Polish people are good Christians, and they would never do that. I never saw anybody do things like that. To kill is a mortal sin. You can go to hell for killing," I answered, becoming angry myself.

"I know, Veslav, I know. The Communists are liars. I just wanted to hear all of these things from you because I know you do not lie."

He was right. I was brought up never to lie, and I did not. I was puzzled as to how the old man knew that, but I decided this was the wrong time to ask him. More water was seeping in and I was becoming too tired to bail it by myself. My fear increased with each passing minute. Earlier in our odyssey, the burning steppe in Sharmamulzak had awakened in me the fear of dying by fire. The winter had awakened the fear of freezing to death or being devoured by wolves. But drowning in a lake where no one could find me suddenly seemed even more frightening. The thought of lying on the muddy bottom with fish biting at my flesh sent shivers through my entire body. I had to say something to make Mr. Petrovich stop carrying on about the Communists and get us to the shore safely.

"Please, Mr. Petrovich," I implored, "I cannot swim and I am afraid of drowning. Can we start for shore?"

The old man stopped ranting, looked at me sympathetically, spat out some more blood, and started rowing toward the shore. "Do not be afraid, Veslav," he murmured. "Since you believe so strongly that one day you will go back to Poland, I have to get you to shore safely."

When the boat, now heavy with water, touched the solid ground, I thanked him one more time and reminded him not to say anything to my mother about our fishing trip.

CHAPTER 9

WAR AND SHORTAGES

By mid-August 1941, as the war between the invading Germans and the Soviets raged on, food supplies became ever tighter. People who had lived close to the front were especially endangered, but the fighting had increased the danger of starvation for everyone. The western and southern parts of the Soviet Union, which the quickly advancing Germans already occupied, were the most fertile and productive areas of the country. The Germans effectively cut off the USSR's major food source, located mainly in the Ukrainian provinces.

Incredibly, in less than two months the German armies reached Leningrad and Kiev and were moving rapidly toward Moscow. By August, the siege of Leningrad, the historic capital of Russia, began. It lasted for nine hundred days. The bravery shown by the city's defenders was unmatched. One million people lost their lives; six hundred thousand died of starvation.

As the Germans advanced, the Soviet government faced a major dilemma: how to feed the millions of people fleeing the Germans as well as the country's huge and growing army. Millions of Soviet citizens headed south and east toward our area and ate everything available along their route, worsening the food shortages already created by the loss of productive land to the Germans. These refugees also overtaxed the sanitary facilities, such as they were, leading to the spread of disease. Self-centered anarchy undercut civil safety.

From the beginning of the German invasion, the Soviet government employed a barrage of propaganda about German cruelty. Much was said about how the Germans were burning villages, hanging some civilians and burying others alive, and committing other atrocities. We did not know how much of this was true, but such news prompted many to flee the Germans. For us, hundreds of miles from the fighting, the situation became very difficult. Most available food was confiscated to feed the Red Army, and already scarce medicine became impossible to obtain. Workers on communes stole slop from the pigs to survive.

My father as a captain in the Polish Army
soon after Poland regained its independence, Cracow, Poland, 1919.

My mother, shortly before Zosia was born,
Sarny, Poland, 1926.

My father, Zosia, and me at the entrance to our apartment in Luck, Poland, 1939.

Zosia (*second from right*), our American cousin, Lt. Jean Siepak (*third from right*), and me (*second from left*) in Tehran, summer 1943. Jean, a surgical nurse with the 113th U.S. Army Hospital in Ahvaz, found us through the American Red Cross about nine months after our escape from the Soviet Union.

Jurek (*far right*) with Zosia and me, Tehran, 1943. Jurek was on furlough from the Polish Army in Iraq. The last time we met was in Turkmenistan the year before, when our mother was still alive. We would not be together again for five years.

Lt. Jean Siepak, U.S. Army Nursing Corps, Ahvaz, 1944. Jean was the daughter of Maria Adamczyk-Siepak, our father's sister who resided in Chicago.

Zosia, soon after arriving in Ghazir, Lebanon, 1946.

I am shown shortly after laying a wreath for my father during the international memorial service for Polish officers murdered in the Katyn Massacre. Members of the Polish-Ukrainian honor guard stand nearby. Piatichatki cemetery, Kharkov, Ukraine, 1998.

My American-born son George stands by the largest mass grave, which holds the remains of 1,025 Polish officers. Piatichatki cemetery, Kharkov, Ukraine, 1998.

This bell is part of a monument dedicated to the Polish officers who were murdered by the Soviet NKVD and buried in mass graves at Piatichatki cemetery. The bell, inscribed with a verse by Polish poet Adam Asnyk, is mounted partly below ground level to symbolize solidarity with the slain Polish officers. Kharkov, Ukraine, 2002. Courtesy of the Council for the Protection of Memories of Combat and Martyrdom, Warsaw.

Epaulets recovered from the mass graves of Polish officers during the 1995–96 exhumations of the site of the future Piatichatki cemetery, Kharkov, Ukraine. Courtesy of the Council for the Protection of Memories of Combat and Martyrdom, Warsaw.

СССР

**НАРОДНЫЙ КОМИССАРИАТ
ВНУТРЕННИХ ДЕЛ**

"___" марта 1940 г.
№ 794/б
г. МОСКВА

ЦК ВКП(б)

товарищу СТАЛИНУ

В лагерях для военнопленных НКВД СССР и в тюрьмах западных областей Украины и Белоруссии в настоящее время содержится большое количество бывших офицеров польской армии, бывших работников польской полиции и разведывательных органов, членов польских националистических к-р партий, участников вскрытых к-р повстанческих организаций, перебежчиков и др. Все они являются заклятыми врагами советской власти, преисполненными ненависти к советскому строю.

Военнопленные офицеры и полицейские, находясь в лагерях, пытаются продолжать к-р работу, ведут антисоветскую агитацию. Каждый из них только и ждет освобождения, чтобы иметь возможность активно включиться в борьбу против советской власти.

Органами НКВД в западных областях Украины и Белоруссии вскрыт ряд к-р повстанческих организаций. Во всех этих к-р организациях активную руководящую роль играли бывшие офицеры бывшей польской армии, бывшие полицейские и жандармы.

Среди задержанных ... перебежчиков и нарушителей гос-

т. Калинин - за
т. Каганович - за

С подлинным верно
Главный государственный архив
Российской Федерации

Р.Г.Пихоя

9.

Page one of a four-page execution order signed by Stalin, Voroshilov, Molotov, and Mikoyan on March 5, 1940, to execute 25,700 Polish POWs held in camps in the USSR.

Although we didn't know all these details as events were unfolding, we did feel their impact as food became harder to find. Fortunately, there were still some cucumbers and watermelons available to us, as well as fish, when we could catch them, which was less often because of Mr. Petrovich's poor health. Thinking ahead, we dried and salted some of our catch for the winter. Unfortunately, we were unable to do this often and, as the weeks progressed, I began to discover what it means to be hungry and, still later, how it feels to starve.

In order for us to survive, Mother had to trade her dwindling supply of smuggled valuables for the limited food that existed. As her jewelry supply shrank, she began to remove lace from her and Zosia's clothing and undergarments, valued decoration she had sewn on in large quantities back in Poland. She cut up our pillowcases and sheets, and she and my sister sat for days embroidering.

They also supplemented our provisions by telling fortunes for the local women in exchange for bread and flour. They drew on what they had learned from the gypsies who had told their fortunes back home. I listened as Mother advised Zosia to tell the women what they wanted to hear the most, which was that the war would be over and that their husbands and sons would come safely home. After hearing such good news, the women would be more inclined to seek such services again. I asked Mother what would happen if soon after her fortune-telling one of the sons or husbands was killed. She responded that for everyone's sake we had to hope nothing that bad would happen. For the time being, we had to do what we had to do.

Were it not for Mother's resourcefulness, we would have starved. The dark hour came much sooner than we expected. Though we ate the pieces of dried bread we had brought from Sarny only when there was absolutely nothing else, and then in very small portions, the three large bags we had carried with us were now nearly empty.

Almost the only food available in Semiozersk was yellow barley used in chicken feed. We could also get the husk of wheat, the dry outer skin of the grains obtained from sifting flour. It was pure fiber with no nutritional value beyond the tiny specks of flour dust that stuck to it. The government rationed the available bread, though the delivery of it and other supplies was often interrupted for days. When it did come in, it was black, heavy like clay, and gummy. The rationed amount was about one pound per person each day. Sometimes it would run out before the lines of waiting people could receive their allotted amount.

One day, after many hours of waiting in line, Jurek returned with the usual amount of black bread. That day the bread was noticeably heavy and smelled of mold. I asked him what the problem was. He answered that often the people who delivered or sold the bread would sprinkle it with water, making its total weight greater than the amount signed for in the bakery. Since bread was rationed by weight, the cheaters ended up with the excess, which they later sold on the black market or kept for themselves.

Bartering for food during the war was an illegal and therefore dangerous proposition. For that reason, Mother always sought out the Kazakhs, who were trustworthy people with sympathy for our plight. They had as little use for the Soviet regime as we had. From them, Mother was occasionally able to obtain rye flour. Having no eggs, milk, or butter to make noodles, she improvised by pouring flour into boiling water. Depending on how much was added, the resulting paste would range from watery to porridge-like. For this favor we often thanked the Lord for the Kazakhs' presence, and I had learned a valuable principle of life, which was never to prejudge a person by the color of his skin, the slant of his eyes, or the odor of his body.

Once when she returned home from bartering, Mother related a joke. A Kazakh had told her that the postage stamp issued by the Russians bearing a picture of Stalin would not stay on the envelope. She was puzzled and asked him why not. Laughing, he answered, "Because people spit on Stalin's face, turn the stamp over, and try to paste it on the envelope, but it will not stick." The Kazakhs knew that telling such derogatory stories was punishable by deportation to Siberia, but they trusted us and tried on occasion to cheer Mother up by sharing jokes with her.

Then a small miracle happened. For about six months, Jurek had been working part-time after school in a slaughterhouse. Most of the time he came home tired and withdrawn, but on one occasion he returned home in an upbeat mood. He greeted Mother and us, then set the bag with his schoolbooks on the floor by the bed. After resting a few minutes, when Jurek saw that Mother wasn't looking, he reached into the bag and pulled something out. Holding it behind his back, he approached Mother and announced that he had something for her. Then he presented her with a package wrapped in greasy brown paper. Mother looked surprised but said nothing. When she opened it, she looked at Jurek in disbelief and asked him how managed to get the meat.

Jurek replied that he stole it. Fear clouded my mother's features, and she reminded Jurek that he could be killed or sent to Siberia for stealing meat during wartime. She stood motionless, holding the meat but not knowing what to do with it. Jurek told her that he didn't want her to worry about him and that the survival of his family came first.

Mother set the meat on the table, then put both of her hands on Jurek's face in an imploring gesture, as parents sometimes do with a small child. She asked him to promise never to do it again, but Jurek would make no such vow. The only promise he would make was not to let her die from malnutrition or starvation as long as he could do something about it. "You risk your life for us by bartering, which is illegal," he pointed out. "You also try to give us part of your food even though you are malnourished and hungry."

She remonstrated with him. "You went to a Jesuit school. You know that stealing for any reason is a mortal sin."

"Mother," Jurek answered without wavering, "I am not in Jesuit school now, nor in Poland with civilized people. We are in a godless Communist country against our will. We are starving and you are in failing health. Mortal sin or not, I will do whatever is necessary for our survival. God should understand."

I could not believe that my brother spoke this way to our mother. But I was glad he did.

Mother started sobbing. Jurek put his arms around her, embracing her for a long time. Then he led her to her bed and helped her lie down, still holding her hand. In a subdued and gentle tone, he whispered, "Dear Mama, you pray to God every day that He will let us go back to Poland. For Him to help us, we have to help ourselves the best way we can. When there is only one way to do so, we have to take it. So please, understand. This is not the time for moral lessons."

Mother did not answer. How could she?

Listening to this exchange tore at my emotions. I felt deep compassion for her and absolute awe of him. It was like witnessing a parable being acted out before me, but with real people, both of whom I loved dearly.

Zosia, obviously shaken, still said nothing, hoping that Mother would calm down. She walked over to the stove, which was already lit, placed the meat into a pot of water, and set four soup plates on the table. Then she joined Jurek, who was still sitting by Mother's side.

Before long, the odor of cooking meat filled the room with an enticing aroma, teasing our taste buds while increasing the hunger pangs. Not having tasted meat for more than two months, I could only imagine how satisfying it would be to eat it. When it was done, Mother asked Zosia to set two more plates. Then she cut the meat into six portions, placed one in each plate, and poured over it some of the broth in which it had boiled. We sat down. Mother offered two plates to the Petroviches, who were in worse shape than we were and had been sitting quietly in their corner of the hut while the drama had unfolded.

Ivan came over to the table in disbelief at Mother's gesture of kindness. He stood, looking at each of us in turn, obviously wanting to say something but unable to speak. After a while, he uttered, "May God bless all of you." This was the first time my family heard the old Russian invoke the name of God. He picked up the two plates, handed one to his wife, and sat down in the chair by his bed to eat. His wife ate without saying anything; she only glared into space as if we were not there, as she always did.

Having calmed down from her initial shock, Mother thanked Jurek for this meal and asked Zosia and me to do the same. Evidently, she had not heard when we had thanked him while the meat was cooking.

Over the next few days, Mother pleaded with Jurek not to steal any more meat, trying to convince him how easy it would be for someone to catch him and report it to the NKVD. Jurek replied that he had "insurance." All his coworkers were stealing, even the supervisors. Their families were starving, too. In the Soviet Union, he said, if you do not steal food, you die.

How true this was. The locals said, "They steal from us and we steal from them."

A week later, when our bartered food supplies were nearly all gone, Jurek came home with another piece of meat in his school bag and nonchalantly handed it to Mother. After invoking God's protection upon Jurek, she began cooking the meat immediately. Jurek brought meat for us several more times as summer turned to fall.

I had learned a new, confusing lesson about life: that honesty ends where starvation begins.

CHAPTER 10

THE INTERROGATION

One evening toward the end of August, after saying our prayers, we all went to bed at our usual time, shortly after sunset. We went to sleep early and stayed in bed as long as possible to lessen the gnawing consciousness of hunger. Sleep came more quickly than usual as, once again, we had some protein in our stomachs and the tantalizing odor of meat lingered in our nostrils.

At some point in the night, we were jarred awake by a heavy pounding at the decrepit wooden door. My stomach turned as we all bolted from our beds.

"May God save us," Mother said. She went to the door. Although we all spoke Russian reasonably well by now, Mother still asked, "Who is it?" in Polish, as if she did not know who it would be in the middle of the night.

A man's voice answered in Russian, ordering her to open the door. He identified himself as an officer and representative of the National Commissariat of Interior Affairs.

My heart pounded. It was the same NKVD, the dreaded Soviet secret police force, that had pounded on the door of our home in Poland. They must have come to get my brother for stealing meat. Mother opened the door. An NKVD officer stepped in.

"Citizen Anna Adamczykova," he said, looking at Mother.

"Yes."

"Tell your son Yurii Adamczyk to dress quickly and come with us."

"But why?" she protested. "He's only a young boy. He has done nothing wrong."

"You are wasting our time," the official snapped. "Tell him to hurry."

Jurek was rushing to dress, trying not to aggravate a hopeless situation. We hugged and kissed him as if he would never return, which we knew was a real possibility. The man stood there watching, without a word as to why he was being taken away.

When the NKVD officer left with my brother and the door had closed behind them, Mother broke down in uncontrollable sobbing. There seemed to be nothing Zosia and I could say or do to make her stop. After some time, Mother cried out, "I pleaded with the boy, but he would not listen. Why wouldn't my own son listen to me?"

"Dear Mama," Zosia implored, "maybe it is not at all what you think. It could just be one of their routine Communist scare tactics."

Mother did not respond. Instead, she asked us to kneel with her in front of her bed while she led us in prayer. She asked us to pray for Jurek, and we did, in earnest. About an hour later, still kneeling, my bones began to hurt. I glanced at Mother a number of times to get her attention, but her eyes were closed with her head bowed. When I could not bear kneeling any longer, I interrupted her prayers to tell her how my knees hurt and how tired I was. She told Zosia and me to go to bed but would not go herself despite my sister's urging.

"I will pray for the three of us until my son comes back home." Mother's voice seemed to echo in the darkness.

What if he never comes back? I asked myself. She cannot kneel and pray forever. What then?

The minutes and hours dragged. Filled with anxiety and fear, neither Zosia nor I could fall asleep. My mind wandered over all that had happened to us since the night we were deported from Poland. As had been the case many times, I could not understand any of it. Nothing made any sense. Neither could I understand why Mother, sick and malnourished, would kneel for hours and pray for the same favor from God, again and again and again. If God hears our prayers the first time, as Mother had taught me at a very young age, there's no need to keep repeating them, is there? If he is all-merciful, as I was also taught, there's no need to beg him repeatedly for a little bit of kindness, is there? For the first time I consciously began to wonder whether Mother believed in something that did not exist.

Shortly before dawn, we heard another knock on the door. Mother stood up from her prayers and rushed to open the door. The same NKVD agent stood in the doorway, but I could not see anyone behind him. He stepped in and, looking directly at Mother, said, "Citizen Anna, if you know what is good for your son, you will tell him to join the victorious Red Army to fight our common enemy, the fascist German pigs."

I hated it with a passion any time a Soviet called my mother "citizen." It sounded like an insult, but there was nothing I could do about it without getting us in trouble. So I kept my tongue behind my teeth and did my best to bear it.

Evidently as stunned and confused by his statement as I was, Mother did not answer, asking instead where her son was.

"He is with us," the officer replied.

Surprisingly, the man did not say another word. He spun on his heel and went outside. We heard voices speaking in Russian. To our astonishment, a minute later, Jurek came in alone and closed the door. We swarmed around him like bees around honey. Zosia and I jumped up and down from the pure joy of seeing our brother alive. We were like two small children who had just received an unexpected Christmas present. Mother cried, but this time from joy as well. She put both of her arms around him and thanked the Lord for his return. After wiping away her tears, Mother asked Jurek whether he had been caught stealing meat.

"No," he said, adding that he would explain in a minute. "But first, I have very good news for us."

This was surreal. We had been praying for his life most of the night, terrified of what might happen to him, and now here was Jurek saying that he had good news beyond the treasure of his being alive. What a poor time to joke, I thought to myself. Mother warned Jurek not to tease the family at such a dreadful time, but he assured her that he was not joking. Then he told us that the Soviet government had given amnesty to all Polish people. As soon as the necessary papers were obtained, the family would be considered free citizens—free to move around the Soviet Union and free to leave the country.

Mother sat down in astonishment, while the three of us began jumping, hugging, kissing one another, and screaming with excitement. Then we grasped Mother's hands and the four of us began to sing the Polish national anthem: "Jeszcze Polska nie zginela / Kiedy my zyjemy. . . ." ("Poland has not yet perished / As long as we live. . . .").

Ivan Petrovich, who had stayed up with us through the night, remained silent. When we finished singing, he came up to us. Looking at my brother as if he were a ghost, the old man put his hands together in prayer, saying that he never thought he would see Jurek again. In a trembling voice, he asked whether the news was really true.

It occurred to me that the very thought of being free was beyond the old Russian's comprehension. I remembered well what he had told me in the leaky boat: "Nobody gets out of the Soviet Union. Nobody. The Communists would rather kill you than let you go."

Prompted by the excitement of the moment, I interjected a quick answer before Jurek could speak. "Yes, Mr. Petrovich, it is true. You do remember what I told you when we were fishing. Our mother did promise us from the very beginning that we would go back to Poland." In my joy I no longer cared about Mother's learning that I had spent some of my days in that rickety boat.

The old Russian put one hand on my shoulder and the other on my brother's. He told me he would never forget that promise. Then he turned to Jurek and told him what a lucky young man he was. A tear rolled down the old man's cheek, and he wiped it on the sleeve of his shirt. Then he went back to his corner. I did not know whether it was a tear of joy shed for us or whether it was a tear of sadness shed for himself and his wife. Deep in my heart, I felt it was a bit of each.

Although Mother was physically and emotionally exhausted from the episode, she was the first to ask Jurek the question puzzling us all.

"Jureczku, do you mean to tell me that the Soviet secret police woke us up in the middle of the night, dragged you off as if you were a criminal, scared you and us to death only to tell you the good news about the amnesty for the Polish people?"

"Mama, they had a devious scheme, trying a typical Communist scare tactic to make me agree to their demands," he replied.

"I am confused. What demands?" Mother asked.

"The NKVD wanted me to sign up with the Red Army."

The three of us were shocked. Zosia and I insisted on hearing everything that happened from the very beginning, convincing Mother that we were far too excited to fall asleep anyway. And despite his draining ordeal, Jurek was eager to tell us what had happened.

The NKVD agents had taken him to their headquarters and put him in a room that was draped with shiny red material. Oversized portraits of Lenin, Stalin, and other Communist leaders covered the walls. Without telling him why he had been brought in, they shone glaring lights on him and began their interrogation. Most of the questions were the same as those they had been asking us all along—centering on what he thought of Communism, the Soviet Union, and the Soviet people. For more than two hours he endured hundreds of questions about all phases of our lives, hoping all along not to trip himself up with some small, seemingly inconsequential answer that may have seemed to them to be a contradiction. If that happened, they could easily have accused him of being a liar, a common tactic during an interrogation.

To his amazement, they unexpectedly changed their tune, telling him what an exemplary student he was, able to speak Russian and German in addition to his native Polish. They commented on what a nice family he had and told him how the Poles and the Soviets had joined the Allies in Europe in "common brotherhood" to fight "our common enemy," the invading German fascist pigs. At the end of the interrogation, they told him how the brave Soviet soldiers and the "always victorious Red Army" were crushing the German aggressors and repelling them from Soviet soil.

With every word, especially the well-known Communist clichés, Jurek grew increasingly suspicious of the NKVD's intentions. First they tried to scare him. Then they were nice to him. It made no sense, though he recognized it as a routine interrogation tactic. What Jurek was most concerned about was the possibility that the NKVD might decide to use some of the other regular tactics well known to everyone: beating the prisoner, burning him with cigarettes, twisting his joints, interrogating him day and night under glaring lamps until the point of physical and mental exhaustion. If that did not succeed, kicking the prisoner in the groin and pulling out his nails would be the next step. Again, the most important thing was not to slip up, for this would lead automatically to the accusation of lying. That in turn could lead to the further charge of being an "enemy of the people," a spy, or some type of counterrevolutionary. Their logic for such accusations was based on the premise that a citizen of the workers' paradise had no reason to lie.

Fortunately for my brother, the worst he imagined did not happen. Instead the interrogators shocked him again by asking him to sign up with the Red Army and proudly offered him an officer's commission within a period of three months after joining. They probably expected that he would jump at such an unusual opportunity. But something did not add up, Jurek thought. Less than a year had passed since his family had been deported from Poland as "bourgeois spies, traitors, and the enemy of the people." Now Soviet secret service agents were spending most of the night trying to convince one young Pole to join the victorious Red Army. He figured that the Soviets were being badly defeated by the Germans and desperately needed fighting men. Calling the Red Army victorious was a ploy to induce him to sign up.

Zosia interrupted. "I hope you did not sign up with them!"

"Sister," Jurek answered, "Hell would have to freeze first for me to do that. They are our enemy, as much as the Germans."

Mother told Jurek what the NKVD agent said to her when they came the second time.

"That figures," he said. "Since they could not talk me into signing up with the Red Army, they tried to intimidate my mother."

"Why, then, did they let you go so easily?" Zosia interjected.

"They did not let me go so easily," he answered. "They kept me there most of the night and did not release me just because they wanted to. When I refused to accept the offer of an officer's commission in the Red Army, I was told that an amnesty had been granted by the Soviet government to Polish deportees and prisoners of war. Only after that did the NKVD inform me that a Polish army would be formed on Soviet soil."

The moment Mother heard about the amnesty of the Polish people and the POWs, her eyes lit up. She stood up and happily exclaimed, "Children, your father will be freed. We will see him again soon."

"Mama," Jurek broke in, "I will probably meet Father even sooner than that, because I am joining the Polish Army."

Zosia and I looked at poor Mother. After having only a few seconds to digest the thought of her husband being freed and being able to see him again, her firstborn son announced that he was joining the army. Spent with emotion, exhausted from the events of the night, she sighed.

"I knew you would. Your father will be proud of you and I will pray for you just as I have for him."

It was well past daybreak. We still had many questions but were too tired to continue. Putting work and school aside, Mother suggested that all of us lie down and at least try to get some rest. I woke up from a sound sleep in late afternoon to the whispering voices of my family discussing the amnesty. Mother called me to join in and promptly served all of us flour boiled in water.

Jurek told us what was going to happen in the months to come. Within the next few weeks, he said, the NKVD would inform him of the location of Polish recruiting stations. As soon as that happened and the necessary papers were issued, he would be leaving. His first priority would be to locate our father. Then, he hoped, the two of them would be able to help us survive by passing on to us any vital and timely information they received from the Polish Army headquarters. He promised that in the meantime he would gather an ample supply of wood for the coming winter and would do everything possible to barter with the Kazakhs for staple foods.

He cautioned that despite the amnesty, the possibility of our leaving the Soviet Union in the near future was still very bleak and that it would be foolhardy to think otherwise. To the west and northwest of us, war was raging between the Germans and the Soviets. To the north and northeast, stretching for thousands of miles, lay the vastness of Siberia. To the east was the huge expanse of Mongolia and China. To the south were other Soviet republics and, beyond them, the strange and foreign lands of western Asia; without money, resources, connections, knowledge of Asian languages, and travel protection, such a journey would end before it began. Moreover, Jurek pointed out, almost all of Europe was at war with the Germans. Because they occupied all of Poland and were waging war against the Soviets on Soviet soil, it would be suicidal to try to return to Poland. The alternative was hard to swallow, but at least it carried some thin hope of survival—to stay put and pray that the Polish Army command would save us one way or another.

Hearing this, I felt the elation of that morning deflate like a punctured balloon. I had been ready to leave immediately, even if it meant walking all the way back to Sarny. Now we had to wait for another opportunity, while our mother, with failing health, faced the burden of surviving another harsh Siberian winter with two children. At least if we had enough food to keep hunger pangs away, waiting for miracles would be much less painful. I was tired of waiting for miracles.

Throughout September, Jurek and I kept ourselves busy making trips to the forest, hauling and chopping wood. It was hard and dangerous work. Mother frequently cautioned us to be careful. But we both knew I needed to develop these skills if we were to survive. What if my brother had to leave in a week or two? Then what would we do? For the most part, Jurek let me chop small branches and stack the cut wood. Some went to the shed and some to our hut in preparation for the winter.

At the end of the month, the NKVD notified my brother that he could leave to join the Polish Army, which was now being formed in the Orenburg province, located where the Central Asian steppe meets the East European plain. His destination was an army camp near a town called Totskoye, twenty-five miles from the newly established army headquarters in Buzuluk, and our impression was that he would fight the Germans on the Soviet Union's western front. They gave him all the necessary travel papers. At this time we received only our "freedom papers," which Mother carefully stored away until we would be ready to leave ourselves.

The days before Jurek's departure were filled with anxiety and sorrow. In the short time remaining, Mother built up our food supply, trading to the Kazakhs handkerchiefs cut from old pillowcases that she and Zosia had embroidered. Poor Mother. This was the second time in two years that one of the men in her life was leaving for war.

When his time came to depart, Jurek looked sad and withdrawn. I could see anxiety in his eyes even before he told us how sorry he was to leave us. Then he gave us words of advice. First, he said that to receive a letter in wartime might take months; letters would be censored and their delivery unreliable. Next he advised us to stay in contact with other Polish people, to expect Polish Army plenipotentiaries to be sent to spread the news about amnesty developments, and to check constantly for news from the local authorities.

The NKVD was to drive him only to the railroad station. After that, he would be on his own, and only God knew how many weeks it would take to reach Totskoye. Mother gave Jurek travel money and some dried bread. She offered last-minute instructions for safe travel and told him to write to us as soon as he arrived. Our good-byes were emotional and painful. When the NKVD came to take Jurek to the station, Mother embraced him for a long time, kissing him on both cheeks while sobbing. "Go with God, Jureczku," she said.

"Why are you crying, Citizen Adamczykova?" asked the agent in charge. "You should be happy and smiling that your son is going to fight the German fascists to liberate our countries from their aggression."

Liberate our countries? I was sorely tempted to reply with some of the choice curse words and phrases I had learned from Mr. Petrovich but had yet to say aloud. Were it not for Mother's crying, I might have blurted out my true feelings. It was my good fortune to remember her admonition that God gave me teeth as a fence for my tongue.

Jurek and Zosia tearfully embraced. She wished him luck and repeated Mother's last words to him. "Go with God, Jureczku."

When my turn came, Jurek picked me up, gave me a brotherly hug, kissed me on both cheeks, and then whispered in my ear so that no one could hear, "Take care of your mother and sister." His words had a familiar ring to them, and I choked with emotion as the tears began to flow.

CHAPTER II

HOLDING ON

Jurek left Semiozersk for the Polish Army camp in Totskoye on October 4, 1941. His friend Mietek Kaminski and Mietek's father left with him. Heavy snow was already on the ground. The men wore traditional Russian padded jackets, matching hats and pants, and felt boots. We were to hear nothing from them for almost three months. Before then, however, news that did reach us by word of mouth told of the terrible conditions under which the newly forming army and the Polish civilians who followed it had to live.

As the days passed, we gradually learned that the formal agreement among the Soviets, the British, and the Poles was one thing but reality was something else. From the beginning, the Soviet government failed to live up to the amnesty agreement. It did not always issue permits for the now "free" Poles to leave or to travel as it had agreed to do, and many of those who did receive such permits were not given the promised assistance. Indeed, they faced dire prospects, with little or no money, no idea how to get to their destination, and no food or medical assistance along the way. Worst of all, they had to face an approaching winter without housing. Still others were not released from prisons, slave labor camps, and prisoner-of-war camps although the directive from Moscow purportedly freed them. When Stalin was challenged regarding this issue, he repeatedly answered that there must be a mix-up with local authorities and that he would deal with them. Many of those who were told about the amnesty were not told about the formation of the Polish Army. Others who were given this news were not told where the army was being formed.

Although the war raged to the west and northwest of us and the line of travel to Poland was completely blocked, many Polish deportees began to travel west from all over the Soviet Union in hopes of being closer to their own country. They were stranded and shunted aimlessly between train stations. Thousands of women with children followed the recruits to newly forming Polish Army camps out of sheer desperation. They had no money, food, or proper clothing for a harsh Siberian winter, yet they were willing to risk their lives simply to be close to the Polish soldiers. Promised nothing, they simply gathered their meager belongings and went, often traveling for months in confusion, many in the wrong direction. Thousands died from disease, starvation, and exposure to the weather.

Mother decided to stay put, primarily because she thought that leaving right away could jeopardize our being found by Father and Jurek. She hoped that by spring the situation would clarify itself and that it would be safer to travel. In Semiozersk, however, we were nearing the limit of our endurance. Cold weather and snow set in within days of Jurek's departure. There was no more meat, and our bartering supplies were dangerously low. Our very survival depended on them, and Mother did all she could to stretch them out. Meanwhile, the life we clung to dragged on. Mother worked whenever she was not too ill, and Zosia was in school whenever weather permitted.

Our situation was growing more desperate with each passing day, making me more depressed and miserable than ever before. With plenty of time to think, my nine-year-old mind was preoccupied with survival and death. To make matters worse, Father's and Jurek's parting words constantly echoed in my mind, but there was nothing I could do to improve our plight. I started wetting the bed, which caused me acute embarrassment. Mother kept changing and drying the sheet, saying only, "Do not worry, dear, it will pass."

Against my better judgment, but out of fear and frustration, I started smoking cigarettes. I made them out of dried leaves and tiny scraps of paper I found in the shed. These homemade cigarettes were only a touch worse than those made from *makhorka*, the cheapest tobacco available in the Soviet Union, which were not much more than the crudely cut stems, roots, and leaves of the tobacco plant. It wasn't long before Mother caught me. Thinking that she had justification to give me a solid spanking, I pleaded no contest and promised never to do it again. Mother gave me a stern lecture. At the end, she softened, saying, "These are hard times for you and for all of us. In spite of this, I expect you to use better judgment."

As winter approached, Mother spent months carefully sewing a coat for me from an old blanket to replace my padded winter jacket, which was now too small. While she sewed, I was busy making a pair of skis from two old boards found in the shed. By the time she was finished with the coat, I was ready to try out the only toy I ever had in Kazakhstan. She sternly warned me to take care of the coat; if I ruined it I would not get another one. But longing to have some fun, once outside I forgot her warnings, tied the two boards to my shoes, and took off. It was exciting to be sliding free, but before long I crashed into an old wooden fence and caught my coat on a rusty nail, ripping one side of it.

My fun was over. I was afraid to go home and face Mother. When my shivering body could no longer take the cold, I had to go back. I walked in sideways to hide the torn side of the coat, then took it off and placed it on a chair. Mother took one look at me and asked what happened. I tried very hard not to cry as I told her that I ripped my coat. She looked at me, and I could see the fatigue and resignation in her face. "Did you remember what I told you?" she asked.

"Yes, Mother," I answered, "I did remember, but . . ."

Zosia, shaking her head, said, "Wiesiu, how could you? You know that Mother has been ill and depressed about not having any news about Father and Jurek."

I knew all of this and felt bad enough without being reminded. I went to Mother and apologized, explaining that it was an accident. She put her arms around me as if nothing had happened and held me close for a long time. Without saying another word, she wearily sewed my coat up again.

After Jurek's departure and the arrival of the harsh Siberian winter, still with no news about Father, our spirits sank to the lowest point since our deportation. We believed that in view of the amnesty that had been granted, lack of news about Father was bad news. Still, living on hope, Mother made regular visits to the NKVD headquarters, though after long hours of waiting to see someone, she would come back always telling the same story. Like a broken record, the officers had answered her queries with "We do not know" or "He probably escaped."

Then, sometime in December, our prayers seemed finally to be answered. Just as I was beginning to lose all faith in miracles, something extraordinary happened to lift our spirits and fill our hearts with joy. One cold and snowy day, Mother entered our hut and without removing her heavy outer clothing ran up to us happy and smiling, something we had not seen since we left Poland.

"Children," she exclaimed, "I have unbelievable news for us. Your father has been found and he is in the same army camp as your brother."

She showed us a postcard from the Polish Army command headquarters in Buzuluk. On the top of one side was written in Polish:

I am sending you the address of
your husband; Adamczyk, Jan, Captain
in the Totskoye Camp.
Buzuluk, 20/ XI, 41

Mother was overjoyed, and Zosia and I cried tears of happiness. After
two years, we had found him! We could only imagine our reunion and
his joy in seeing us, even if it would be on the soil of our bitter enemy.
When the initial excitement subsided, Mother explained to us that this
card was a reply to a letter she had sent to the Buzuluk headquarters
shortly after we learned of the amnesty.

"Mother," Zosia asked, "if Father and Jurek are in the same camp,
why didn't we hear from either one of them by now?"

"Zosienko, my dear. Do not forget this is wartime. There could be
many reasons why we did not hear from either one of them sooner. Perhaps your father arrived in the camp late and they did not find each other
right away, or the Soviets censored the mail and delayed it, which you
know they are doing." This explanation satisfied my sister and me, and
we went on rejoicing about the best news we'd had since the war began.

CHAPTER 12

STARVATION AND VODKA

Our second winter on Soviet soil was much worse than the first. Bitterly cold temperatures, blizzards, and snowstorms immobilized man and beast. Lack of food drained whatever energy we still had to perform our simple daily chores. After months of a near-starvation diet, our gums bled, we developed boils, abscesses, and rashes, our stomachs were distended, and there were discharges from our eyes and ears. Jurek's share of the struggle to sustain us fell on Mother's shoulders. She had lost so much weight that she looked gaunt and frail. She was constantly depressed. Yet she always found the strength to take care of us, doing whatever she could for our survival.

For me, the lack of food was not only physically debilitating but also emotionally exhausting. Countless times I prayed for only a tiny portion of the food I had refused to eat back home in Poland. Watching Mother wither before my eyes was unbearable, and seeing Zosia so sickly added to my own suffering.

Zosia and I helped with the chores as much as we were able, standing for hours in lines for our ration of bread, firing up the stove, melting snow for drinking and cooking water, and emptying the buckets we used in lieu of the outhouse during blizzards or snowstorms.

Following one of the blizzards, Mr. Petrovich arose early with the intention of shoveling snow. He, too, had been growing sicker and weaker, often spitting blood into a small container he kept by his bed. He dressed slowly, stood up, and began to drag his feet toward the door. Seeing this, I stopped him.

"Mr. Petrovich, go back to your bed and rest," I said. "Zosia and I will shovel snow today."

"Thank you, Veslav," he whispered, spitting up more blood. "May God bless you and your family."

Somehow, it felt good to have been shown gratitude by this sickly old Russian. My motives were not totally altruistic, however. I sensed that he was about to die. He had the aura of death, and I was terrified. What if Mr. Petrovich went out to shovel snow in his condition, had a heart attack, and died? What would I do then? I would have no one to talk with when Mother and Zosia were away.

And what would we do with his body? The roads to town were often impassable owing to the heavy snowfall and high drifts. There would be nowhere to get a coffin, and even if we did, with the ground frozen solid we could not bury him. For a few days at least, his body would have to be laid out in our hut, and I had no intention, if I could help it, of exposing my mother and sister to sleeping in the same tiny room with his corpse. Life was hard enough for us without adding another traumatic experience. But that wouldn't be all. Later we would be forced to take his body out to the stable until he could be buried, and the starving wolves might easily get in through openings in its walls and eat his flesh. Although such a move would be necessary, the prospect seemed cruel and inhumane. I much preferred him to remain alive.

That day, Zosia and I took half-hour turns at digging us out and making a path to the outhouse. Toward the end of one of my turns, I stopped to rest while gazing at the horizon with what had become my usual melancholy. The sun was low, the brightness of its golden rays blinding as they were reflected in the clean white surface of the snow. The earth lay dormant, the only signs of life being the thin twists of smoke rising from chimneys and the treetops barely visible in the distance. There had to be life somewhere beyond the horizon, I thought, a better life than ours in this Soviet hell. I stood still, daydreaming, as I often had done on the steppe in Sharmamulzak, about the life my family used to have. Then my thoughts turned to how lonely I was and to my worries about Father. Was he alive? Would I ever see him again? And what of my brother, gone to fight the Germans? I wondered what fate awaited him.

A rumbling noise behind me broke the quiet of my thoughts. Two bearded Russians of middle age emerged from a nearby hut and stumbled their way through the snow, swaying as if the ground was moving under their feet, each with one arm on his companion's shoulder. Each held an empty glass in his free hand and a bottle of vodka in the other. They moved boisterously away from the hut, stumbling until, suddenly, as if united by a common purpose, they stopped. Releasing their hold on each other, they stepped apart, faced each other, and raised the glasses and their bottles toward the sky.

"Let us drink to the victory of our brave Russian comrades over the fascist German pigs," said one.

They lowered their bottles, filled the glasses, and banged them together in salute.

"To the victory," replied the second man. Bending their heads down to the level of the glasses, so as not to spill a drop, they began drinking, raising their torsos and tilting their heads backward until the glasses were empty. Then they scooped up some snow and swallowed it.

Their celebration was not over. Putting their arms around each other, they began to sing and dance, glasses and bottles firmly in hand, barely able to maintain balance. They both fell and disappeared in the snow. A minute or so later, their snow-covered figures arose, pushing and shoving each other like two playful polar bears. Another toast followed.

"To Stalin."

"To Stalin, our comrade," the other man responded.

Glasses were filled and emptied again, followed by snow to quench what had to be a burning thirst. The smaller of the two men began to wobble from side to side and then vomited on his clothing. The larger man took a step back, as if in disgust, and hollered, "Why can't you take your vodka like a true Russian, you motherfucker?"

"You say I am not a true Russian? You drunken bastard, I will show you who is a true Russian." The man was far more insulted by the charge that he was not a "true Russian" than by the insult to his mother. Clumsily, he attempted to straighten his body.

"Drink to Mother Russia with me, you no-good, lying thief," he stuttered in a drunken stupor.

"To Mother Russia," responded his comrade, his voice showing no sign that he was the least bit offended by the insults heaped on him.

This time, both men raised the bottles to their mouths, tilted back their heads, and drank to the last drop. They flung their arms skyward. The glasses and bottles went flying behind their backs, sinking into the deep snow. They embraced and began kissing each other on the cheeks in the traditional Russian style, vomit notwithstanding.

Just then I heard Mother calling from our hut. *"Wi-e-siu!"* Her tone of voice told me exactly what she was going to say. I started walking toward the open doorway where she stood just as Zosia was coming out to take her turn shoveling. Once I was inside, Mother closed the door, turned toward me, and whispered into my ear.

"Haven't I told you time and time again not to get close to the Russians, not to listen to their vulgarity, not to watch their vulgar behavior?"

"But, Mama, I was outside shoveling snow when they came out. What did you want me to do?"

"You know what you were supposed to do," she replied angrily.

Right or wrong, the better part of wisdom then was to keep quiet and not make the person who was guarding our lives feel any worse.

"Come, child, and warm up by the stove," she said, her voice apologetic. "I will fix you something to eat." Fix me something to eat? She used to say that at home. Here there was nothing to fix. This was surely a slip of the tongue. Even our dried bread was gone.

The heat radiating from the stove soothed me, warming my aching bones as I sat on a small wooden stool in front of it. Water was already boiling in a rusty cast-iron pot. Mother poured coarse brown flour into it and stirred the mixture. Minutes later, when the paste thickened a bit, she poured a portion into a soup bowl and set it on the old wooden table. I ate it very slowly to prolong the sensation of eating, which helped me feel that I had eaten more than I actually had. When it was all gone, I licked the plate as I always did in those days to salvage the remnants. Hunger pangs still gnawed at my stomach, but I could not ask for more because the rest of the flour paste was to be the only food that day for Mother and Zosia. There was nothing else to eat.

Mother told me to rest for a bit, and I lay down. My mind wandered for a while, but because I had just witnessed the drunken display of the two Russians, my thoughts turned to them and I began to reflect on our near-starvation diet. Something was horribly wrong.

"Mother?" I asked, sitting up.

"Yes, Wiesiulku," she answered in an endearing tone of voice. Her anger with me never lasted more than a few moments, and now she patted my forehead.

"I would like to know why the Soviet government can make enough vodka to drown in, but they cannot make enough food to feed themselves."

She replied that she was too tired to talk about it just now, but I persisted, knowing that sooner or later, she would give in. After making me promise not to ask any more questions, she agreed to explain. She sat beside me on the bed and began, choosing her words with care.

Long before my siblings and I were born, she said, the Russians had a revolution, and the Communists seized power. Since that time the Communists have murdered millions of their own people and starved millions of others to death. Soviet citizens were treated like prisoners in their own country and controlled like puppets on strings. They had nothing to look forward to, so the Communist government fed them vodka to give them some momentary pleasure and a feeling of escape from their miserable existence. Mother explained that when people drink they often forget their troubles, and if they drink enough, they sometimes forget even their own families and their own names.

It still didn't make sense to me. Wouldn't it be smarter to make food rather than vodka? I wondered aloud. How long could a person keep drinking to forget he has an empty stomach? Mother reminded me of my promise not to ask any more questions and said that she would not say anything further because it was a very dangerous subject. Then she paused. "I want you to know that the Communists are not smart enough to know what's good for them," she said. "To cover up their own mistakes over the past twenty years, they have executed people who had better ideas and those who criticized them. This is the end of our discussion. By now you should understand why I want you to stay away from these people. Now, lie down and get some rest."

Suddenly the fear of dying a horrible death by starvation overcame me. Any other way, even being shot by a bullet, would have been preferable.

"Mama, I do not want to die. Do you think the Communists will also starve us to death?"

"My dear child," she replied, tears beginning to flow from her eyes as she leaned over and took me in her arms. "I pray to Almighty God every single day to let us survive and to lead us out of this hell."

Her tears dripped onto my face. To see my mother crying and not be able to do anything for her added to my own misery, but at least at that moment, I felt safe and secure in her arms. That night Mother, Zosia, and I would again pray for a pittance of food to eat tomorrow. There was little more we could do.

When I suffered from hunger pangs, sleep did not come easily, but when it did come it shortened the time I suffered. When sleep was not possible, I closed my eyes so as not to see anything around me. One evening my reveries carried me to our home in Poland. It was Christmas Eve. The tree glittered with lights, ornaments sparkled with mesmerizing colors, and white cotton snow covered the branches, which seemed to hover protectively over many beautifully wrapped presents. Our angel sat majestically on top, looking down at our happy faces, happy because all of us were together.

The Christmas table was set with fine china and gleaming silver. The first of the traditional twelve Christmas Eve courses was awaiting us, and it was time for wishing each other well. Mother and Father carried the

Holy Wafer to share with every person, hugging and kissing them while wishing them good health, happiness, and whatever else their hearts desired.

I felt someone pat me on my head and kiss me tenderly on my forehead. I opened my eyes. The room was in semi-darkness. Mother was sitting next to me on the edge of the wooden bed, holding my hand. She looked old, with wrinkles on her face and dark shadows under her eyes. Where was her happy, radiant face, the one I had seen moments earlier?

In confusion, I pushed myself up and looked all around. In the opposite corner, Mr. Petrovich and his wife were sitting slumped over in their chairs, gazing aimlessly at the earthen floor of the hut. Zosia lay curled up in her bed.

I saw no Christmas table, no father or brother, no happy faces, no Christmas tree, no presents. There was no Christmas at all, only the flicker of yellow flames from burning wood. The hut was silent.

CHAPTER 13

TUTORING

As the dreadful winter passed, we often sat for days in our dungeon trapped by snow. Mother was unable to go to work, nor Zosia to school. Even the NKVD did not bother anyone at these times. There was no need to. Only the starving wolves visited, returning again and again to howl outside our hut as if trying to discover whether we were still alive. The snow was piled so high that we could not even take the stinking buckets of waste outside to empty them.

Mother became progressively weaker and spent most of the time lying down and resting. The hardships she had endured from the time we were deported were beginning to greatly affect her health. We did not know exactly what was wrong with her and were afraid that she might die, yet there was no place we could go for help. My sister and I sat by the wooden table, watching the flames flicker in the stove and talking to keep ourselves from going crazy. We reminisced about the good times in Poland, our father, family, and friends. We dreamed aloud about being back at home. When it became too painful to compare our wretched existence to the good life we'd had, we changed the topic to our regular lessons in the Polish language, Polish history, arithmetic, and geometry. With no books, no paper, no pencils or pens, all we could do was transfer information from Zosia's memory to mine, just as people had done thousands of years before us.

When we tired of the repetition, we talked about the progress of the war, matters that might affect us, and the living history of which we were a part. I asked her about the things that she heard when she was at school or out on errands. Most of my questions concerned the people and events I understood the least about. Zosia would tell me in frustration that I was asking questions that were too difficult to answer. Still, I came back to the same subject again and again. What puzzled me most was why the Germans and the Soviets attacked Poland in the first place and caused all this misery to themselves and others. Time and again, Zosia would tell me there was no justifiable reason that any civilized person could accept, but, justified or not, they had done so. I insisted that there had to be an answer.

On one occasion, visibly annoyed with my persistence, she snapped back, "Why? You really want to know why? The only answer I can think of is that both the Germans and the Soviets, just as their Russian predecessors under the czars, are warmongers. It is in their blood."

"But why are they that way?" I insisted.

"It is because of hatred, greed, obsession with power, or some combination of all those things."

As I continued to prod her with questions, Zosia grew increasingly more upset, just as Mother did anytime I pinned her down on a subject she did not wish to talk about. She announced that she was tired and tried abruptly to end the conversation.

"Yes, dear teacher, I know you are tired, but the real reason you don't want to answer me is that you, like Mother, do not want to admit that we belong to the same race as these savages. Both of you are ashamed to admit it and it hurts, doesn't it?" I asked, knowing she would not respond.

She did not.

Every time I got close to having some of my questions answered, the adults would become evasive. I was told that they didn't want to talk about the subject, that I was too young to talk about it, or that they would talk about it some other time. This became more and more frustrating. In due time I began to believe that adults sometimes have a harder time facing the truth than children do.

I stood up to tend to my daily chores. The red glow of the burning wood was getting dimmer. Now and then, a yellow flame appeared to jump from log to log as if trying to remind me that it was time to add fuel to the fire. My glance fell on the motionless bodies resting in their beds, faintly outlined in shadows against the dark wall of our mud hut. Zosia walked toward the corner of the hut and stepped behind the waist-high white curtain that blocked the waste bucket from the rest of the room. The curtain, which looked like a crippled white ghost suspended in the darkness, was what remained of a bed sheet. How bizarre it was, yet it served many purposes well. Later it would be cut up into small pieces, embroidered, and bartered for food when needed.

I fed the fire, and when Zosia was finished we went to the door and together opened it very gently so as not to collapse the wall of packed snow behind it that towered over our heads. With great care, we filled two buckets with the pure white powder for drinking water. We put some on to boil, then went back to the wooden table and sat quietly, watching the fire glow. Perhaps tomorrow or the next day, my sister and I would face the bigger challenge of digging ourselves out.

Mother, who had been listening to our conversation, pulled herself up from her bed and joined us but did not take sides. "Maybe one day, after we get out of this inhuman land, you can write about the seldom spoken part of history, the one with a human face," she said. "Tell the world a human story of what it takes in blood, tears, pain, and suffering to live through war. Maybe then someone—somewhere—will take heed. Maybe someday there will be no more wars, no more Hitlers, no more Stalins. I pray this for you, your children, and your grandchildren."

A tear rolled down her face. She stood up and went to the stove. With an air of futility, she poured three cups of nearly useless grain husks into the boiling water. We drank the concoction in resigned silence and went to sleep starving. Someplace beyond the horizon, battles raged between the Germans and the Soviets. In my mind I could hear shells exploding and see men dying. Outside the hut, the wolves howled.

CHAPTER 14

THE CULTURE
OF COMMUNISM

We survived the winter of 1941–42, hoping that in the spring our hardships would ease. Nearly two years had passed since we had been deported to the Soviet Union. Ivan Petrovich, perhaps to vent his own hatred of Communism, continued to describe to me the evils that I did not witness myself. This only increased my fear and hatred of those who had created the culture in which we were forced to live.

Even after Jurek left for the army, the NKVD continued spying on us. The amnesty had already been granted, and technically we were free citizens with the right to leave the country. Why, then, could they not leave us alone? Most of the time they came at night, once or twice a month, and asked repetitious questions about members of our family and about other Polish people. *Where do we go? What do we do? What do we think about the Soviet Union? What do we think about the Soviet people? What do we think about the Communist system?* On and on and on. It made no sense to us.

For me the worst thing about the visits by the NKVD was the fear that at any time they might do something terrible to us. There was nothing to stop them from doing so. When I asked my mother why they continued to come back again and again to ask the same questions, she answered that they could be looking for a reason to detain us in the Soviet Union in spite of the amnesty. Or they might be concerned that we had started telling the local people about life outside the Soviet Union and what we knew of the persecution of the citizens within it.

The spying was a constant reminder of the fear, oppression, and degradation under which we lived. Even sleep provided no respite, for my dreams would be filled with real-life images of our having to wait in long lines with other desperate people hoping to buy ordinary goods that for the most part were not there; of people spitting and blowing their noses with their fingers in public, even defecating in public; of people speaking in loud and vulgar ways as they drank themselves into a vodka-soaked stupor to drown their sorrows. I saw sad, scared, and degraded people oppressed by brutal force, deprived of freedom, frustrated and hopeless. I heard the lies they told one another to stay alive and the lies their government told them in order to stay in power. I heard gloomy Russians speaking in their own code, concealing their thoughts out of fear of punishment for telling the truth.

A well-known anecdote illustrates the cynical atmosphere in which Soviet citizens lived. A visitor asks a Russian worker laboring on a government farm, "How is life in the kolkhoz?" "It's good, very good," replies the worker as he breaks down in tears.

Disgusted by the failures of the system yet resigned to their fate, Soviet citizens resorted to ambiguous aphorisms, bitter humor, and vulgar curses to express the misery they felt. Ask an old Russian who had lived under the czar why the Soviet methods of farming were so bad and he would reply, "God is far above, and the government is far away." Soviet citizens knew that the central government in Moscow had no understanding of the problems facing local communal farms scattered throughout the Soviet Union. Perhaps the government didn't care.

Downtrodden citizens were often able to find common cause in bitter jokes. A disgruntled citizen waiting in line all night for a piece of bread would be comforted by another who said, "Do not forget, my friend, that we went to war with Finland because the bread line in Leningrad crossed the Finnish border." Those who dared secretly joked that NKVD stood for Neisvestno Kogda Vernioshsya Domoi ("You never know when you will be allowed to go home"). Such dark humor was the only way of hinting at the truth that everyone knew but could not say publicly for fear of being denounced as a traitor, a capitalist agitator, or a saboteur and sent to prison.

By far the most common outlet for expressing the misery of life in the Soviet Union lay in vulgar cursing, indulged in by men and women alike. The vilest of curses would be directed against anything and anybody except, of course, the true objects of their scorn—Joseph Stalin, the NKVD, the Communist Party, and the entire Communist system.

A friend of my sister's, Krystyna Ziemlo, who was deported from Poland to Siberia at age nineteen, later told us a poignant anecdote about her experience with the Soviet habit of cursing. She had been assigned to haul wood with a horse-drawn wagon. Her reward for meeting her daily quota was a meager ration of food. Failure to meet the quota meant less food and eventual starvation. Her problem was that the horse, also malnourished and tired from excessive labor, eventually refused to pull the heavy load. No matter how she tried to encourage the horse, nothing worked. A kind Russian peasant noticed her dilemma and told her that she must speak to the horse in Russian. He took the reins and said, "Trogai! Yebat tvoyu mat!" ("Move! Fuck your mother!") Only then did the horse begin to pull the load. From that day on, Krystyna cursed the horse in Russian and thanked the Lord for small miracles. She never again missed a quota.

At first I did not know the meaning of such talk; not only was I just beginning to learn the language, but I never before had heard anyone speak of such matters. Only over time, as my Russian greatly improved, did I come to have a sense of what was being said. No less did it surprise me to realize that such crude language was not always spoken out of anger or viciousness.

Whenever we heard such talk, Mother would always remind me not to listen but to walk away. But that policy was futile, because this was how the Soviet men and women all around us spoke. It was a natural part of their everyday conversation, and I could not plug my ears every time I went outside. Even in cordial greetings it was common to hear two people say to each other, "How are you, you motherfucker?" or "Hello, you cocksucker! How's it going?" It did not take me long to realize that the main reason for such vile cursing was the fact that it was recognized as a rare instance of freedom of expression.

From the time of our arrival in the Soviet Union, I had noticed something that didn't seem to fit with the rest of the drab and primitive surroundings we encountered. Practically everywhere you looked, both inside public buildings and outside, throughout the various towns and villages, there were large, spectacular posters in full, vivid color, most noticeably red. When I asked my family why there were so many of them, I was told that this was how the government portrayed life in the Soviet Union to its own citizens. The answer only puzzled me more, as I wondered why Soviet citizens couldn't see for themselves how they were living.

The pride and joy of the government were the public portraits depicting the leaders of the Supreme Soviet; these were by far the most frequently seen. Larger than life, many of these posters featured Lenin and Stalin, the liberators and protectors of the workers. There were also posters showing young, happy, healthy children laying flowers at Lenin's tomb or handing flowers to Comrade Stalin, who always wore his hat with the red star in the middle.

Other posters depicted the Soviet pilots, sailors, and soldiers as not only the bravest in the world but the ones who never lost a battle or war. The question of bravery aside, even I knew at age nine that such posters were outright fabrications. I well remembered Father telling me that in the War of 1920 the Bolsheviks attacked Poland as part of their plan to take over all of Europe and convert the continent to Communism. Not only did they lose the Battle of Warsaw, but they also lost the war.

Some of the posters depicted the Soviet doctors, engineers, and scientists who, they proclaimed, had invented almost everything. The truth, also well known to the Poles before the start of the war, was that most of these ideas and products were stolen from the West, copied, and passed off as Soviet inventiveness. Even when a Soviet invention was a total failure, the posters deceitfully extolled its successes. Still other propaganda posters presented what amounted to elaborate fictions about Soviet science and research. One proudly claimed that Soviet agricultural engineers had invented methods to grow certain crops even in the cold, snowy Siberian winter. We wondered how the government could make such wild claims and expect people to believe them in view of the constant hunger and starvation.

Other posters glorified the working people. One of the most memorable depicted a huge man holding a hammer and sickle, his sleeves rolled up to display his bulging muscles. His gleaming eyes were turned to the sky, looking toward the glorious future that only Lenin and Stalin could have provided. Standing beside and slightly behind him was a woman also bursting with good health. She wore a multicolored scarf on her head, her bright eyes shone with a blissful expression, and her smiling cheeks were full and rosy. To this day I remember clearly the glowing contentment of this couple, who were fortunate enough to live under Communism. Happy and healthy, the man and woman personified proletarian perfection. Seeing this poster, I wondered where such people could be found in the vastness of the USSR.

Another striking poster depicted a *kolkhoznik,* a person working on a large collective farm, who was shown driving a huge modern tractor. He was neatly dressed with a new leather jacket adorning his splendid body, and he wore a popular Communist hat with a visor. The red star on his hat, identical to that of his comrade Stalin, glittered in the sunshine. The suggestion that this was typical of workers and machinery on a communal farm was effectively directed only at people living far from the farms, especially the townspeople, who were not allowed to travel and see for themselves what conditions were really like.

Other posters glorified women, picturing them at labor but always smiling. From what we could see, women's plight had significantly worsened since they gained "equality" after the revolution. Many were forced to do backbreaking labor, cutting trees and hauling heavy timber, digging ditches along roadsides, carrying large loads at railroad stations, and doing much of the other heavy work that only men had done previously. Pregnant women were expected to work right up until childbirth, thus maximizing their contribution to the common good. Having by this time outgrown the stork theory of delivery, I understood that for a woman to be expected to have many children and to work until delivery could not really serve the good of anyone. My childish comprehension was stretched to the limit trying to figure out why the state gave medals to women as a reward for having a lot of children yet at the same time put to death millions of its own citizens.

I had already learned that in the Soviet Union "common good" meant the good of the state, even if it meant taking the life of an individual falsely accused of a crime. I often awoke in the middle of the night shaking with terror, thinking that I had heard a knock at the door. Even imagining that sound put fear in the hearts of millions of people living within the reach of the NKVD, which extended throughout the whole of the country.

The night the Red Stars knocked on the door of our home in Poland continually preyed on my mind. Two years later, I could still hear the NKVD captain screaming that Russia was a great country and had everything one could want. "Everything! Even matches!" Only on a few occasions since that night had I seen a match. Most of the time, we had to spark a smooth stone with a steel rod against dried moss, cotton, or dried wood shavings. Or we borrowed some burning wood from a neighbor, carrying it in a clay pot.

The boastful Russian had also lied to me about the toys in this great country of his. All I had were sticks and stones to play with. Even then, I had to be very careful about which stones I picked up, because smooth round ones were a highly sought-after substitute for toilet paper.

PART IV

Escape to Freedom

Uzbeks and camel caravans seen along our escape route from the Soviet Union to the Caspian Sea through Uzbekistan and Turkmenistan, USSR, August 1942

CHAPTER 15

THE ESCAPE PLAN

During the winter of 1941–42, news of the amnesty and information about the mobilization of the Polish Army traveled at a snail's pace. Often, by the time we heard that something was going to happen, it was already history. The official sources of information in the town were the single radio in the Palace of Culture, the NKVD office, and occasional newspapers. But because the Soviet government controlled the news media, no information from these sources could be relied on. Further, although the NKVD had been directed by the Soviet leaders to tell the Poles about the amnesty and issue their papers and give assistance, in many parts of the country they failed to do so. Some Poles were never told of the amnesty. Others were told that only men were eligible.

Meanwhile, as late as December, most of the Polish Army troops that had gathered near the towns of Buzuluk, Tatishchevo, and Totskoye still wore an assortment of tattered civilian clothing not suitable for the winter. More than half had only rags to cover their feet. They lived in unheated tents, and their rations diminished over time. We heard that when the would-be soldiers or their civilian camp followers died of malnutrition or from exposure, they were buried in graves circling the army camps. By February, those who survived had moved to southern Kazakhstan and Uzbekistan. The army, still untrained and underfed, had not been provided with uniforms, equipment, or ammunition, yet it was expected to go to the front lines to fight the Germans. The Polish Army command, convinced that this was a ruse to disguise genocide, refused. At this point, the British agreed to help. Because Stalin did not want a well-equipped and well-trained Polish army on Soviet soil, he backed an agreement that half of the Polish forces would leave for the Middle East. There they would be placed under British command to fight the Germans in northern Africa and southern Europe. Stalin also agreed that thousands of their civilian relatives could also leave for the Middle East, a plan the British at first resisted. They were interested only in getting fighting men. It was only due to the insistence of General Wladyslaw

Anders, commander of the Polish Army, that civilians were allowed to leave with the army.

The first evacuation of Poles from the USSR took place at the beginning of April, but we heard of it too late to take part. For a brief time we envied those who had been brave or desperate enough to follow the army, but our feelings changed when we learned that thousands had died in the southern Soviet republics from diseases caused by the squalor in which they had to live.

W ith the advent of spring, our lives became more bearable. When the snow melted, it was easier to move around again in order to barter with the Kazakhs. Later the lake ice thawed and warmer breezes came. We had survived another winter thanks to Mother's perseverance, and I went back to carp fishing with Mr. Petrovich to supplement our meager diet.

Mother remained alert for every piece of reliable news that might come our way, and in July her diligence paid off. We learned that the remaining Polish Army troops and their families would be allowed to leave the Soviet Union for Persia (present-day Iran). The news came from one of 136 plenipotentiaries sent out by the leaders of the Polish Army, who realized they could not trust the Soviets to spread the word to the twenty-six hundred places in the USSR to which Poles had been deported. The troops were to leave from the port of Krasnovodsk in Soviet Turkmenistan, on the Caspian Sea, roughly twenty-five hundred winding miles from us by train. Mother was determined to leave at all costs. The day after we heard the news, she went to the NKVD office to request the necessary documents to supplement the "freedom papers" that we had received before Jurek left. Those papers stated that we were free citizens allowed to move within the USSR and that we could leave the country, but they did not, in themselves, permit us to travel. For that, we also needed written permission from the NKVD to buy railroad tickets, papers stating the exact point of our destination, and a certificate stating that we had been disinfected.

The Soviet government had given the NKVD clear instructions nine months earlier to issue all necessary papers to Polish deportees. By now, these should have been ready on demand, but when Mother asked for them, the NKVD told her to come back in a week. Predictably, when she returned the papers still were not ready. The agent told her to come back in yet another week. Mother returned home stricken with panic, surer than ever that this would be our last chance to leave the Soviet Union. As she walked in the door, I heard her tell Zosia that the Communists were liars and cheats. I feared that we might not be able to leave after all but would be sentenced to live forever in this terrible place.

That evening and in the days that followed, Mother and Zosia spent a great deal of time talking together in whispers. I knew that something important was brewing, and my curiosity only increased as they remained secretive. I did my best to eavesdrop inconspicuously, and gradually I began to put the pieces together. What I heard convinced me even more that my mother was a very smart and brave woman.

The two were apparently devising an escape plan. Mother told Zosia that because the NKVD did most of their devious work in the middle of the night, they probably would be less likely to suspect people during the day. Moreover, travel routes were likely to be filled with Polish refugees trying to reach the Polish Army camps and Soviet refugees escaping the fighting at the front, and the confusion would work to our advantage. The connection between these observations and her plan for escape began to jell.

Mother had decided to leave even if the travel papers were not ready the next time they were promised, though she well knew that leaving without the necessary documents would be running a dangerous risk. Everyone in the Soviet Union, natives and deportees alike, needed permission from the secret police to do just about anything: to move from house to house, to change jobs, to congregate, to talk in certain places, to make speeches, to write articles, and most of all to travel. To be caught by the NKVD doing any of these things without proper authorization could be very costly or even deadly, especially in wartime, because it could prompt accusations of spying. This weighed heavily on Mother's mind. As for me, I couldn't care less about such accusations; I was ready for an exciting adventure, especially if it meant a chance to leave. I was confident that the NKVD couldn't get any information from me if they tried. All I had to do was pretend to know nothing. Then they would get tired and leave me alone, just as they did with my brother.

Mother thought there were two main reasons why we were not issued the necessary travel papers in a timely fashion. First, Jurek had refused to join the Red Army. Second, the Communists had a fixation about the "upper classes," and they were aware that Father was a Polish officer who had fought the Bolsheviks. The NKVD knew that if they withheld permission to travel we might miss our last chance to leave the Soviet Union. In their minds it would have been a fitting punishment for our sins.

The next week Mother went again for our travel permits, and again she was told that they were not ready. The die was cast, and her plan went into effect. Mainly I feared what might happen to her if we were caught. As a rule, the Soviets, unlike the Nazis, did not shoot children. They thought nothing, however, of sending women to Siberia for hard labor after taking their children away.

The only reasonable way to travel toward the Caspian Sea, where the Polish Army was congregating for departure, was by train, and the train station was at least a day's walk away, close to the town of Kustanai. Mother knew that borrowing a wagon was out of the question, so her hope was that someone would pick us up somewhere along the way. She made a crucial decision. We would leave our hut with only the clothes on our backs so as not to arouse suspicion. That precaution alone was not enough, however, because a mother walking out of town with her children would still attract attention. The second element of her plan was that we would split up. She would leave first and go to a prearranged spot an hour or so away where Zosia and I would join her.

Mother still did not want to reveal the escape plan to me, but from what I had been able to overhear, I had formed a fair idea of it. The night before we were to leave, I was nervous and excited and did not sleep much. For some reason, neither did Mr. Petrovich. Every time I opened my eyes, the old man was sitting on a chair, constantly moving, as if something were on his mind. Could he have overheard something? Did he know we were about to escape? Would he want to leave his crazy wife behind and escape with us? This would be his only chance for freedom, and I did promise him that when we left, he could leave with us. Then I recalled what the old man had said to me: that every man wants to die in his own country no matter how bad it is. Still, I wanted to ask him one more time, but I knew that I could not. Torn between genuine affection for Mr. Petrovich and jeopardizing my family's safety, eventually I fell asleep. When I awoke soon after sunrise, the old man was gone. It was strange. For the entire winter and spring, he had struggled with his health and seldom arose before noon.

Mother left first, telling me only that I should not leave my sister's side. An hour later, Zosia asked me to go out with her for a walk. I went along, pretending to know nothing about the scheme. We left our hut without saying anything to Mrs. Petrovich. Outside, looking one last time around the hut that had been our home away from home, I noticed immediately that the door of the old barn was open. The boat was gone. Then I spotted it floating in the middle of the lake, but there was no sign of Mr. Petrovich. I stopped and stared at the boat anxiously, hoping to see some movement. After all, I knew this was the last time I would ever see him. He was a good person who had helped lighten some of my lonely hours, and I suddenly felt terrible leaving him behind. At least I wanted to give him a wave of my hand, although he might not know until later that it would be good-bye.

Zosia began to pull me by the hand, but I kept looking back at the boat, hoping that Mr. Petrovich would sit up. The last time I looked, there was still no sign of anyone in the boat. I wanted to stay a few more minutes, but Zosia dragged me on.

"You are acting strangely today, Wiesiu," she said. But I was not in the mood for talking. I was already anxious about our attempt to escape, wondering about its chances of success and by now scared for our lives. And not seeing the old man in his boat sent fear through my body. Yet there was nothing I could do. I felt remorse for not being able to keep my childish promise to take Mr. Petrovich and his wife back to Poland with us when we left. Our journey was just beginning, but I knew in my heart that for him the journey had ended. Perhaps his heart had finally given out, or he may have committed suicide by jumping overboard. My last image of Semiozersk was of an empty boat in the middle of a lake, symbolic of the empty life of a good human being trapped in the midst of Communism.

Zosia and I walked along a country road of dried mud. The going was difficult because the uneven road was scarred by horses' hooves and the tracks of wagon wheels. But I didn't mind, because with each laboring step we were moving closer to freedom. At last!

When we met Mother, she embraced us. I could feel the sweat on her body. She turned to me and said, "Wiesiu, listen carefully to what I am going to tell you. If we meet anyone on the road, I do not want you to talk to them, no matter who they are or what they want to know, even if they speak Polish. Do you understand?"

"Yes, Mother. I do."

"We are going to town to buy some potatoes."

She still did not tell me about the escape plan, and I restrained myself from telling her that I knew what we were doing.

"Yes, Mother. We are going to town to buy some potatoes."

How clever, I thought. We, like most other people from Semiozersk, had not even seen a potato in the past eight months. Naturally we would need to go a great distance to try to find them.

"Come, children, it is time to go," said Mother. We held hands to keep from stumbling as we resumed walking. Soon every stone, every bump, every hole, and every crevice became torturous. Bits of hardened mud and tiny stones entered through holes in my shoes, and my feet began to blister and bleed. After we had walked for about two hours, we met a Russian peasant with a horse-drawn wagon heading in the same direction. Mother greeted him in Russian. He greeted us and stopped the horse.

Mother asked if he was going to the next town, where there was a marketplace, and if so, whether he could take us there. He replied that he was and motioned to us to get in. Once we were aboard, he shook the reins and resumed his trip. The malnourished horse, pitifully reduced to skin and bone, did not walk much faster than we could have. With its extra burden, the animal labored over every bump and hole, but at least we were able to rest.

No one spoke as we went along. The only sounds came from the horse's hooves and the wheels crushing the clumps of dried mud. Now and then the exhausted horse whinnied. I let my legs hang over the back of the bouncing wagon. My thoughts wandered back to Mr. Petrovich, and I quietly said a prayer for him. Mother heard me and asked whom I was talking to. Nobody, I answered.

After many hours, which included a number of stops to rest the horse, we came to Kustanai. We got off near the marketplace so as not to make the farmer suspicious. Mother thanked him and gave him some money. He said good-bye and drove off without looking back.

Sitting near the marketplace, Mother finally told me we were escaping Semiozersk, hoping to join the Polish Army by the Caspian Sea. She was surprised to learn that I already knew what we were up to. She cautioned me in no uncertain terms about giving any information to anybody. I promised.

"Nothing," she said for emphasis. "No matter who talks, just say, 'I know nothing.'"

"Mama," I answered, "why are you so worried?" Then, for a joke, I added in Russian, "Ya nichego ne znayu, grazhdanka Adamchikova" ("I do not know anything, Citizen Adamczyk").

Mother's eyes widened. She looked at Zosia and they both started laughing. She turned to me and said in jest, "So you, too, have learned how the Soviet people are forced to talk! My own little son calling me a grazhdanka. Wait till I tell your father and brother about your sense of humor. Maybe one day instead of becoming a poet, you will become a comedian, so that we can all look back and laugh a little for a change."

Then we walked to the railroad station and took our place in line. When we reached the ticket agent, he told us, as Mother had expected, that he could not sell us tickets unless we had the proper papers. She leaned forward and, talking softly to him, pushed a small package into his hand. Mother had come prepared to bribe him with some of her remaining jewelry. Without registering the slightest surprise, he gave her three tickets. Having satisfactorily completed the illegal transaction, Mother told us that the agent was overselling the available room on the train and that we should find a spot on the platform close to the track so that we would be near the front when the train arrived.

After making our way to the platform area, the first thing we saw was excrement and urine stains all over the platform. Without toilets in working order, as with most public facilities in the Soviet Union, travelers were left to tend to their needs as best they could. We had to pick our way carefully to avoid getting the waste on our shoes. One could not take two steps in any direction without stepping into a mess, and the stench was horrible.

No one knew when the train would arrive. Even the ticket agent admitted that the posted schedules were useless. This left Mother, Zosia, and me with no choice but to stand on the platform amid all the human waste, as close to the rails as possible. We didn't dare lose our place for fear of being left behind when the rush came for the train's doors. There was a chance that the NKVD was looking for us, in which case missing the train could prove disastrous.

The southwest-bound train arrived late in the evening. No one knew how far it would go, and we had no idea when or where we would have to change trains before we would arrive at the port of Krasnovodsk. To make matters worse, because the station had no maps we were left with no idea how to plan our journey. The only thing we knew for sure was that to meet up with the Polish Army we had to travel south through Kazakhstan to Uzbekistan and then west through Turkmenistan to the Caspian Sea. When we scrambled aboard, there was barely room left to stand. After the rest of the passengers had crowded in, the train slowly started moving. Unlike my previous journey by rail, this one made me happy to hear the spinning and clicking of the wheels. And though we had eaten nothing since that morning, it hardly seemed to matter, because the train was picking up speed in the direction of freedom. Suddenly this word acquired a new meaning and was no longer something we could only talk and dream about. I felt it well up inside me, and my heart pounded with excitement that we might be free.

We lay down on the cold steel floor, cuddling each other for comfort. How I wished we had taken heavier clothing with us when we had left that morning! Despite the heat of the day, I was now cold, shivering and coughing heavily, and my entire body ached. My feet were covered with dried blood and whatever had made its way through the holes in my shoes during the day. Before she lay down, Mother warned me not to take my shoes off because someone would steal them. I removed them anyway to ease my discomfort and quickly fell asleep between Mother and my sister.

When I awoke my shoes were gone, and I had to tell Mother what had happened. It was useless for me to try to explain how I couldn't believe anyone would stoop so low as to steal a pair of shoes from a little boy. I could see pain and frustration in her eyes. "Didn't I tell you not to take your shoes off?" she said. "I knew someone would steal them. What are we going to do now?" I could not look at Mother for guilt. Standing on the cold steel with my feet swollen, cut-up, and bruised, I was miserable. And the prospect of having to travel barefoot only added to my misery. I knew that finding a pair of shoes would be next to impossible, and we could be in transit for weeks.

After traveling all night, the train stopped at a station for three hours in the morning. While Zosia held our spot on the floor of the car, Mother took me to search for a pair of shoes, hot water, and food. We had not eaten in twenty-four hours. She approached people with children my age and asked about buying a pair of shoes from them. They looked at Mother in disbelief for asking such a question and ignored us. About an hour later, we came across a malnourished Russian boy begging for food. He was older than I and wore torn shoes much bigger than my size. Mother approached him and whispered something in his ear. Without hesitation the boy took off his shoes and handed them to her, while she discreetly put something in his hand. Then he gave her a part of the old newspaper in which his few possessions were wrapped. I put the shoes on and Mother stuffed them with newspapers to keep them from falling off. We wished the boy good luck and walked on to look for water and food.

When we came upon the building where hot water was supposed to be available from spigots in the wall, we were told that the boilers were broken and there would be no hot water. Inside, in the eatery, there was no food other than flour paste. Mother was able to buy three portions of paste and three wooden bowls for cash. She also bought a tin can for drinking water on our journey. Leaving the building, we walked farther away from the station toward a yard with steam locomotives. One of the engineers agreed to fill our tin can with hot water, though it smelled of rust and machine grease. We started back, eager to bring food and water to Zosia.

About halfway back, I saw from a distance a woman lying on a bench with two young boys who seemed to be playing with her. As we came closer, I realized that the woman was dead. To my horror, the two boys were pouring sand into her mouth while gouging her eyes out with sticks and laughing. People passed by without seeming to pay any attention. Mother's hand tightened as she pulled me away. For the second time in two days, I was overcome with guilt, this time not because of what I had done but because of my powerlessness to do anything about the misery and callousness surrounding us.

"Mama, aren't we going to do anything about it?" I asked, feeling nauseated.

"My child, if I interfere with local children and cause a commotion, the NKVD will be here in no time, and we will be finished. I cannot afford to risk our freedom even though I would like to do something about it."

After a few days and many unannounced layovers of varying duration, we changed trains. This occurred in an area away from any town, and we had no idea of where we were. Luck was with us, however. The train we boarded was a passenger train, so we grabbed a bench seat for the three of us and kept it all the way to our destination. During the stops, Zosia and I guarded the seats while Mother searched for food and water. With so many desperate people on board, it was hard to avoid confrontations with potential claimants for our seats, and our space was frequently threatened.

As the train traveled southward, the percentage of Poles among our fellow travelers increased. Many were refugees fleeing from the NKVD just as we were, hoping to reach freedom. Not everyone would make it. In the days that followed, we often saw teams of oxen pulling wagons filled with dead bodies picked up along the roads and at railroad stations. These people had died of disease or starvation, some after traveling aimlessly for months.

Whenever the trains stopped somewhere in the barren countryside of Kazakhstan and Uzbekistan, some people, particularly women and girls, would crawl under the cars behind the train's wheels to relieve themselves, attempting to preserve some semblance of modesty. Mother would never let us do this because of the danger. The trains often started without notice, and more than one unfortunate person was crushed to death. Others who for modesty's sake had gone a short distance away to relieve themselves were left behind, unable to catch up with the moving train. Many children and mothers were separated in this way, never to see each other again. It was said among the Poles that some of the Soviet engineers intentionally took off without blowing the whistles merely to add to the travelers' misery.

Northwest of us, the war still raged. The siege of Leningrad continued, and many Russians who had the connections and the money to flee were clogging the rail routes as they escaped southward. Our trip to the Caspian Sea was also slowed by the frequent layovers needed to make way for military transports of personnel and supplies heading toward the war zone and for returning transports laden with the wounded. With troops, supply trains, and civilians going in every direction, chaos reigned at each railroad station. In these places many people became separated from their families—little children stood crying and alone while parents searched frantically for their lost children. Almost everyone had one thing in common, however. They were desperate for passage on a southbound train.

Chaos was exactly what Mother had counted on; much the same situation had been described in the accounts of the Russian Revolution that she had read. Although we saw NKVD uniforms and local militia at every station, not once were we stopped and questioned. Indeed, thousands of travelers were able to hop on trains with neither travel papers nor tickets because the crowded conditions made it impossible for the NKVD to keep a watchful eye on everyone. It was the only time during our imprisonment in the Soviet Union when those feared agents were not alert to our every move.

As our journey continued through Kazakhstan almost due south, the weather grew hotter. With no ventilation in our train car, the smell of unclean bodies, some with diarrhea and dysentery, was overpowering. Crammed together in such conditions, we realized how easy it would be to catch a disease. In a relatively short time, my body broke out in boils and abscesses. One abscess on my left arm became as large as a lima bean, full of pus and very painful to the touch. Mother wanted to lance it when it first began bothering me, but I wouldn't let her. When it grew bigger yet, she insisted that it must be broken but told me that we must wait for sanitary conditions. The only prospect was to hold off until we could seek out one of the Soviet nurses whom we had sometimes seen offering aid at railroad stations. Their services were provided free of charge by the government.

Hours later the train stopped at a platform, fortuitous in itself, because more often than not it stopped either past the station or in the middle of nowhere. Mother and I stepped out on the platform and waited for a nurse to walk by. Twenty minutes later we saw one and showed her my abscess while I suspiciously looked her over. She was round-faced, short, and stocky. The skin on her big hands was cracked, and she had wide, dirty fingers with long, unclean fingernails. She wore peasant garb with a white apron that was spotted all over with what seemed to be dried blood and other bodily fluids. The only clean part of her clothing was the nurse's cap she wore. She held a rectangular container of medical supplies: a bottle of dark liquid, cotton, and used bandages, also spotted with blood and other fluids. The nurse looked at my abscess, then turned to Mother and, speaking in Russian, offered to lance it for me.

I looked at Mother and said in Polish that I would not let her do it.

Mother pleaded with me, but I insisted that I would not let the nurse, with her dirty hands and fingernails, come near me. "Will you please do it?" I asked.

Seeing my determination and anguish, Mother agreed. She explained to the nurse in Russian that I was nervous and that she would prefer to lance it herself if she could use the nurse's supplies. The woman nodded. Mother told me to stay with the nurse while she went to fetch some hot water. When she returned, she took some cotton and soaked it in the dark liquid, which could have been permanganate solution, and swabbed the abscess. She was ready for the procedure.

I closed my eyes, clenched my teeth, and held my hands together. I felt a shooting pain and everything went dark inside my head, then stars exploded. The nurse poured warm water over my open wound to clean it out, and Mother again applied the cotton with the stinging liquid. She ripped off a piece of her slip and tied it around my arm as a dressing. I wanted to cry, but I didn't.

During another of our layovers, I was witness to what I have ever since carried with me as a vision of hell. As we sat there, another train pulled up carrying Polish children, most of whom were orphans. Some had become separated from their families while traveling and had fended for themselves for months before being grouped with other children. Others had been told to find their way to the Polish Army camps by dying mothers who were too sick or weak to go on and pleaded with them to take what little they had left to trade for food. Still others had either escaped from or been thrown out of Russian orphanages and put on the nearest train to travel toward the Polish camps. These children, most older than I was, were among many thousands from all over the USSR and had been traveling aimlessly for weeks or sometimes months.

The orphaned children were led off the train to get what fresh air they could in the blistering heat. All had shaved heads, sunken cheeks and chests, and bulging eyes. Most had puffed-up eyelids that were closed over their eyes by infection or disease. Pus dripped down their faces. Flies and bugs crawled over their bodies. Some were infested with vermin. Some of the boys had testicles swollen to the size of small oranges that protruded from their shorts. I saw these poor children stand up, relieve themselves, then lie down again next to their own waste and lapse back into sleep. Others without the strength to stand up on their own relieved themselves where they lay.

As I sat watching from the train window, I asked Mother why no one was taking care of them. She explained that the few women in charge of them were exhausted and needed to rest during layovers, so they were left by themselves. Mother paused deliberately, then warned me not to stare at the poor orphans and, above all, not to go near them. I looked out the window confused and sorry for these children. I could not stop staring at them—not out of pity but out of compassion. What if I were lying there among them? What if I were an orphan? Who would take care of me?

"Mama, how much longer do I have to close my eyes or not look at the world around me?" I asked.

She took my hand in hers but did not answer. I continued to look outside and after a few moments of silence asked another question that for some time had been forming in my mind.

"Mama, is God blind too, like these children?"

Mother became visibly perturbed. "Wiesiu, it is a sacrilege to talk like this," she admonished me. And I remained silent.

Our journey continued. At some stations, the Soviet authorities sold small amounts of food on a rationed basis. The fortunate travelers ate fish soup or flour mixed with water. Those who were more fortunate, the ones who had enough money or luck or personal belongings to trade with the local population, sometimes fared better. Those who ran out of items to barter starved and were reduced to begging, depending on the kindness of others for survival.

The Soviets made the so-called fish soup by putting small fish into boiling water. If you were hungry enough, you would eat it, even if some of the fish were still alive. At one stop, I saw through the train window a man with five children sitting around a bucket of this soup. The fish, about the size of sardines, were still swimming around and jumping. His starving children reached in with their hands, caught the fish, and ate them. Then the man and children drank the hot liquid.

Our lot was with the more fortunate. In some way, Mother always seemed to find out about the long stops and take advantage of them to search for food among the enterprising locals, who in turn were seeking to make the bargains of their lives from trapped and helpless victims of circumstance. Now and then, she returned clutching a small wooden bowl that had something in it that looked like flour paste. For the first time since we were introduced to it, I was happy to see the paste; it was better than fish wiggling in boiling water. At other times she brought us dried pumpkin or sunflower seeds. If there was a way to survive, she would find it. Zosia told me that Mother had been preparing for months to make this journey by sewing valuables—Russian money, small items of value, and her remaining jewelry—into the hems of her and Zosia's dresses and undergarments.

When we neared the southernmost point of Kazakhstan and the USSR, the train turned almost due west to Uzbekistan. Eventually we passed the cities of Tashkent and Samarkand. At some point we were about 125 miles from Afghanistan and 375 miles from China. The train then continued through Turkmenistan, passing the city of Ashgabat. After about three weeks from the time we left Semiozersk we arrived in Krasnovodsk. It was mid-August. The train stopped near the transit camps, one for members of the Polish Army and an adjoining one for civilian Polish deportees. All those gathered there, like us, were lucky to have so far survived the journey toward freedom. Now everyone was waiting anxiously for transportation across the Caspian Sea and out of the Soviet Union, still filled with fear that the Soviet government would abruptly change its mind about letting us leave.

As we got off the train, we prayed that our ordeal was coming to an end. We felt indescribable relief at being near the Polish Army, though we were still on Soviet soil. Being in a community with other Polish people was comforting beyond measure. Our exhilaration was promptly tempered by the readily apparent disorganization and by the news that hundreds of soldiers and civilians were suffering and dying daily from malnutrition and combinations of diseases such typhus, typhoid fever, dysentery, malaria, scurvy, pellagra, scarlet fever, and night blindness.

Still, as hard as the journey had been, we knew we were very lucky to have made it this far. We arrived toward the end of the second evacuation and, though weary and hungry, were better off than many of those who had tried to be part of the first or those who had come months too early for the second. Thousands had died traveling in January and February, when conditions were much harsher than those we had faced. Many of those who managed to survive but had missed the first evacuation had been dispersed among hundreds of government-owned farms, where they clung to life. Others were sent back to the places in the Soviet Union whence they had come.

CHAPTER 16

JUREK'S ORDEAL

On our arrival at Krasnovodsk, we were assigned a tent just big enough to provide the three of us with shelter. Then we registered with the Polish Army for evacuation. Mother warned Zosia and me not to go any place other than to get food or use the latrine. We were surrounded by thousands of soldiers and civilians, all anxiously awaiting the chance to board the ships to freedom.

Mother set out to find Father and Jurek. The task she was tackling was far from easy. Here chaos worked against her, as thousands of people arrived almost daily from throughout the USSR while others left from the port of Krasnovodsk to travel across the Caspian Sea to Pahlevi (present-day Bandar-e Anzali) in Persia. Understandably, record-keeping was difficult and communication between various Polish Army camps in the USSR was extremely slow. Thousands of soldiers and civilians were looking for their relatives. There was no way to determine quickly where a soldier was stationed or whether he was alive. It was not possible in a short time to determine whether any one soldier was still in Uzbekistan or Turkmenistan or had already crossed the Caspian. The best Mother could do was search the existing records and go from one company to another, asking the commanders whether her husband, Captain Jan Adamczyk, or her son Jerzy were with his unit. No one she spoke to had heard of Jerzy Adamczyk, though some told her that they thought there was a Sergeant Jan Adamczyk somewhere in the camp. It was also possible that neither of them had yet arrived in Krasnovodsk. When she exhausted the list of commanders and had visited all the companies present there without success, Mother turned to the last possible place either of them could be.

Near the camp was a Soviet field hospital that had been pressed into service for critically ill people. Mother made her way there but was told by the nurses that they knew of no patient by the name of Adamczyk. She pleaded with the staff to let her look through the admittance books to see if by some chance her husband or son had been hospitalized there. They reluctantly agreed. Mother pored over the records for hours. Then to her utmost joy Jurek's name jumped out at her. She had found him! She immediately made arrangements with the Polish Army command to have him transferred to a field hospital in the camp, where she could take care of him herself. Mother stayed with Jurek until he was transferred.

After he was placed in the army field hospital, Mother returned to the tent, crying and distraught, to check on us. She stayed only minutes, telling us that Jurek was suffering from extreme malnutrition and exhaustion. A Polish doctor at the field hospital had told her that unless he had something of substance to eat quickly, he could die.

"I must try to save him," she said, hurrying to leave again.

She turned to Zosia and told her to look after me, because she did not know when she would be back. Mother paused briefly and said that there was a Sergeant Jan Adamczyk somewhere in camp. "More than likely, it's not Father, unless there was a mix-up in the paperwork. I will find out, but first I must attend to Jurek." She reminded us again not to wander around.

After Mother headed back to the hospital, Zosia and I were left with only a sliver of hope. We understood that there was only a remote chance that this Jan Adamczyk was our father. But it was a chance! Mother's caution notwithstanding, the news left us dreaming up reasons why Father would want to disguise himself as a sergeant. One of the reasons was factually plausible. When the Soviets attacked Poland in 1939, they often executed Polish officers on the spot. Many officers therefore tried to hide their identity by cutting off their lapels and insignia or by changing uniforms. We hoped that Father had successfully been able to do something of the sort. And for the next three days, Zosia and I lived on such hopes.

The overflow of civilians created severe hunger in our camp, and no extra food rations were available. Mother therefore resolved to take her search for some substantive nourishment for Jurek to one of the local villages. This was very dangerous. Apart from the Polish deportees, there were thousands of starving people in the vicinity as well as gangs of marauding Russian hoodlums. It was not a safe place for a lone woman to either search for or carry food. Undaunted, after spending the night at Jurek's bedside, Mother arranged to have two Polish soldiers go with her. They walked for hours until she eventually found a local peasant who was willing to exchange a live chicken and half a loaf of bread for a gold watch. Apart from a pair of earrings and her wedding ring, that was the last of her jewelry.

Mother returned to the field hospital with the chicken, the bread, an old pot, and camel dung for making a fire. Then she prepared chicken broth. She nursed Jurek for three days, and gradually he regained some of his strength. When the doctor told her Jurek was out of immediate danger and well enough to have visitors, she came to get Zosia and me. Unfortunately, she also brought the bad news that Sergeant Adamczyk was not our father. Moreover, there was no information about Father at all.

But this was not the worst of it. Mother was told by the camp headquarters that of thousands of Polish officers, including many generals taken prisoner by the Soviets in the fall of 1939, only a few hundred were accounted for. General Anders, commander of the Polish Army, and his high command pressed the Soviets to explain what had happened to more than fifteen thousand Polish POWs. The amnesty had been granted by order of Stalin a year earlier, and the Polish Army desperately needed the leadership of experienced officers. Stalin told Anders that he did not know what had happened to them. He also said that they might have escaped to Manchuria. But the terrible question was how the Soviet Union could lose more than fifteen thousand POWs with the NKVD watching their every step. The conclusion drawn by most Poles was the worst imaginable: that the Soviets had murdered them.

We were stunned, knowing what the lack of news about a prisoner in the Soviet Union meant. When Mother repeated to us the rumors of a possible mass murder of Polish officers, she started crying and took some time to compose herself. Then she looked at us with desperation in her eyes and asked us to pray that Father was safe and that he would return to us. And for the thousandth time, we prayed that prayer. But our hearts were broken upon hearing of this horrible possibility, our torment much deeper because we were on the way to freedom. I asked Mother whether the Soviets were capable of committing such a crime.

"Child, I pray to God that they did not commit this crime. If they did, God will repay them," she answered, avoiding my question.

Despite our circumstances, our reunion with Jurek was a happy one. To see our brother again when many around us were dying was a gift from heaven. On Mother's advice, we delayed hugging and kissing him in greeting because he had so recently been exposed to many people dying from communicable diseases, but we gladly settled for the joy of seeing him alive. All of us were eager to hear what had happened to Jurek after he left for the army.

From Semiozersk the NKVD had taken him only as far as the train station, after which he was on his own when it came to food and other needs. His trip to the Polish Army camp near Totskoye, southeast of the fighting between the Germans and the Red Army, had taken more than a month, from October 4 to November 11. The trains on which he had traveled were often sidetracked for substantial periods to permit the passage of army personnel and war materiel. Delays were also caused by the hundreds of thousands of people who were fleeing the fighting.

Jurek described his surprise at seeing at railroad stations the striking contrast between the Communist elite, who wore fancy clothes and fur coats, and their comrades, who wore common clothing and the typical padded jackets. But all of them were equally caught up in the chaos that reigned while searching for mostly unavailable food. He also saw Soviet soldiers and their officers coming back from the front lines. They were wounded and disheveled and begged passersby for food, water, and cigarettes. Toward the end of his trip, when it was bitterly cold and snowing heavily, Jurek also noticed trains coming from the war zone carrying German prisoners. The Soviets had loaded some of them onto open flatcars, where Jurek could see the stiff, uniformed bodies frozen to the beds of the cars.

Hungry and cold after a five-week journey, Jurek arrived in the army camp to find conditions there abominable. Many of the new recruits were better off in the miserable places from which they had come. He confirmed all we had heard about Polish troops having inadequate clothing for the bitter Siberian winter. Worse, he said that they had to survive the winter in tents raised on frozen ground, each of which housed twelve men.

On many nights, he would awaken with his hair frozen to the ground or to the tent. To keep from freezing to death, the soldiers dug ditches about a yard deep in each tent, running lengthwise from its entrance to its back. At the end of the ditch farthest from the entrance, they built a makeshift stove of loose bricks in which they burned wood twenty-four hours a day, each man standing a two-hour vigil to keep the fire going. The edge of the ditch provided everyone a place to sit, for there were no chairs or beds. Because the Soviets failed to supply promised means of transport to the Poles, the soldiers were forced to carry wood on their shoulders from a forest about six miles away.

When Jurek first arrived at the camp, the daily rations supplied by the Soviets consisted of two slices of frozen bread, two cubes of sugar, and one cup of hot soup, which was usually no more than hot water with a little barley or some other grain floating in it. As time went on, the rations allowed by Stalin were reduced. When the thousands of civilian deportees began arriving, the Polish soldiers voluntarily reduced their meager rations even further to help feed the many who were starving. Faced with such conditions, a few bold men organized highly risky night-time raids on nearby government farms. First they would lead a cow quietly away from the farm. When they had gone a safe distance, they would butcher it and bring the meat back to their tents. The wolves would clean up any traces before dawn.

Jurek told us that when the army was first being organized, he and the other men were told they would fight the Germans on Soviet soil. Almost from the beginning the Soviets failed to live up to their agreement with the British and the Polish governments to provide food, clothing, arms, and ammunition. Their official explanation was that they were short of these items for their own army. According to Jurek, most of the soldiers in the Polish Army believed that the reason the Poles were not armed was that Stalin was afraid they would turn against the Red Army. In any event, Jurek described how some of the troops trained with make-believe wooden cannons and toy rifles and bayonets. Stalin's unofficial recommendation was that if the Polish soldiers wanted to fight, they could go to the front lines and pick up rifles from soldiers who had already been killed. The Polish command was appalled by this suggestion and took a firm stand against it.

The brutal conditions of winter, combined with the lack of military equipment and food and the absence of sanitary conditions, made training of the newly forming army almost impossible. By February 1942, the Polish Army had been moved to the southern Soviet republics, mainly Uzbekistan, where the weather was dramatically milder but conditions for military training were still deplorable. By April the temperatures rose as high as 95 degrees, and malaria, typhus, and dysentery were rampant.

Masses of desperate Polish deportees followed the army, gathering around it for protection and hoping to share its food supplies. Their most fervent wish was that the Polish Army would lead them out of the Soviet Union to freedom. With the coming of spring and then summer, the civilians in particular suffered from the desertlike heat. Sanitation was lacking, medical care was poor or nonexistent, and food was scarce. Contagious diseases started to spread, with people dying in such numbers that they had to be buried in mass graves. At times coffins could not be built quickly enough and were used again and again to carry bodies to the burial site.

Jurek went on to describe how, by the beginning of 1942, the Soviets were gaining the upper hand over the Germans in the battle for Moscow, reducing Stalin's need for support from the Polish troops. The Soviets, the British, and the Poles agreed that the Polish Army would serve much more effectively by fighting the Germans in Africa and southern Europe. For Stalin this meant that he would no longer face the danger of having a well-equipped and well-trained Polish army on Soviet soil. For the British, it swelled the number of fighting men under its command that could be deployed in the Middle East and Africa. General Anders was pleased with this agreement because he knew that this would be the only way to get as many Polish civilians as possible out of the USSR.

This chain of events opened the way for some of the Polish soldiers and their families who were on site to leave the Soviet Union in March for Persia. Jurek had been worried that it might be the first and only transport, and we were not on it. He had previously written us two letters advising that we come to Uzbekistan, but we never received them. In July 1942, the Soviets, British, and Poles agreed that the rest of the Polish Army would move into the Middle East, be equipped and supplied, and serve under British command. They also agreed that the soldiers' families would be allowed to go with them.

After such a long narration, Jurek had grown tired. When we stood up to leave, he turned to Mother and said, "Mama, thank you for your prayers and for everything you have done for us."

"I only did what any mother would do for her children," she answered with her usual modesty. Zosia and I bid him a tearful farewell, wishing him a speedy recovery and pleading for him to look for us in Persia. The next day the three of us would board a Soviet freighter and cross the Caspian Sea. We did not know when Jurek would be leaving. Unbeknownst to us, he would be carried aboard the same ship on a stretcher, but a year would pass before we would see him again.

CHAPTER 17

ABOARD THE
KAGANOVICH

The sun shone brightly the morning of our departure. The Soviet freighter *Kaganovich* stood at the dock ready to receive us. In a small brown paper bag, Mother had the few items we had collected since leaving Semiozersk and the small pot in which she had boiled the life-saving chicken broth for my brother.

Representatives of both the NKVD and the Polish Army stood by the gangplanks checking lists of names; the Polish military was under orders to give women and children priority. Mother had made sure that we were on the Polish list to board the *Kaganovich,* just in case we were not on the NKVD list. As it turned out, we would be among the last to board, and as we inched our way forward a commotion broke out as people who were afraid to be left behind pushed and shoved toward the boarding areas. Mother instructed us to hold hands tightly, stay close to her, and keep moving toward the gangplank no matter what happened. The next thing I knew, we were walking up toward the ship. As I took my first step onto it I glanced back momentarily and without losing a step said a prayer for my father, still somewhere in the Soviet Union.

By noon, we were ready for departure. The *Kaganovich* carried almost forty-five hundred Polish soldiers and civilians, dangerously exceeding its tonnage capacity. This overcrowding, which could easily have caused the ship to sink in rough seas, was uncomfortable but strategic. The Polish military leaders and the evacuees were desperately afraid that the Soviet-controlled transports would be abruptly discontinued. For that reason, the army command encouraged loading as many civilians on board as possible. To get all those who had already reached Krasnovodsk out of the Soviet Union was of paramount importance. Although Mother, Zosia, and I, like the others, were afraid that the ship might sink, we were willing to accept the risk. After living in fear for our lives for more than two long years in the Soviet Union, the fear of going down with the ship in the Caspian Sea was a small price to pay for a chance to reach freedom.

We found a spot on the front deck of the ship where we could lean against its smokestack. Hours later, for the first time in my life, I watched from a moving vessel the beauty of the sun setting over the sea. Old Mr. Petrovich's warning—"Nobody gets out of the Soviet Union. Nobody. They would rather kill you than let you go"—had at last been proved wrong.

The freighter had an open cargo bay amidships, on each side of which were steps from the bottom of the bay that also gave access to the raised decks at the front and back of the ship. Use of the toilet facilities was re-served for the crew, and the evacuees had to use cordoned-off sections on the side of the ship. Heavy rope was hung across the railing for a person to hold onto while urinating and defecating over the rail. This was espe-cially treacherous for the old, the young, the sick, and hundreds weak-ened by diarrhea. Within the first few hours after we set out, a number of people fell overboard and were lost at sea. The freighter made no ef-fort to rescue them because, being so overloaded, it ran the risk of capsiz-ing unless it kept moving, especially if the weather turned bad.

Although physically and emotionally exhausted from our ordeal, Mother hovered over Zosia and me like a hen over her little chicks. Af-ter she heard about the drowning, she gave us strict orders. Mine were that under no circumstances could I go to the cordoned-off area to relieve myself. She took out the little pot and told me I had two options. One was to use the pot and the other was to wet my pants. When I heard this, I cringed. There was no way that I was going to wet my pants, nor could I relieve myself with so many people standing around, most of whom were women and girls.

Sometime later I told Mother that I had to urinate and could not wait any longer. At first I asked her to take me to the cordoned-off area, but then I realized that having to weave through and step over hundreds of people meant that I would not make it in time. I had no choice but to uri-nate in the little pot in front of all those people while Mother shielded me as best she could. Then she went to the side of the freighter and dumped the urine overboard.

When night came and I again had to urinate, I noticed that Mother and Zosia had dozed off. Most people, having no place to lie down, were sitting up and talking. I could not face repeating my earlier experience, so I started to walk across to the cordoned-off area on the other side of the ship, weaving my way through the crowd and stepping over people. I made it down the steps of the cargo bay and had just crossed it when I realized I could hardly control my bladder. I decided I could not go on and had better go back to use the pot after all. In desperation, I retraced my steps across the bay, straining to contain myself, and had climbed halfway back up the stairs when I felt my pants getting wet and urine dripping from my legs onto the soldiers sitting and sleeping below. They screamed at me, recognizing from the smell and the warmth what was raining down on them. Mortified, I hurriedly made my way back to the smokestack, where Mother and Zosia were still sleeping. I prayed that my pants would dry before they awoke in the morning.

The following day, I realized how unique my experience must have been. During the night most people simply headed for the railing closest to them to relieve themselves. As a result, both sides of the ship were soon covered with urine, excrement, and blood from those who had dysentery. Many who were too sick to move were lying in their own excretions, covered with flies. To make matters worse, we ran out of drinking water, and the heat became more intense as we continued southward toward the port of Pahlevi.

The voyage took almost two days, and when we arrived, the *Kaganovich* was not allowed to enter the port. Because the deck along both sides of the ship was covered with human waste, the Persians feared that it would spread disease. So we anchored offshore and boarded British naval barges for the last part of our voyage. At that moment, the Polish escapees from the Soviet Union entered the protection of His Majesty, the King of England. I saw a British uniform for the first time, and my heart was filled with awe and gratitude.

Mother, Zosia, and I stepped onto the golden sands of the beach at Pahlevi. The clothes we had worn since leaving Semiozersk were tattered, filthy, and stinking. Mother, her hair disheveled, her face looking wrinkled and old, clutched the small paper bag and the all-purpose pot. Suffering from extreme exhaustion, she labored with every step. Yet one thing about her never changed. Her eyes glowed with love and hope. That was what had kept all of us alive.

PART V

The Bitter Taste of Freedom

Mother's ultimate sacrifice for her children's freedom. Anna Adamczyk died on October 18, 1942, and was buried in Dulab cemetery, Tehran.

CHAPTER 18

THE BEACH AT PAHLEVI

As it turned out, some time would pass before we actually saw anything of life in Persia. Still, as we stepped down from the British barge on that hot, sunny day in late August 1942, we felt safe for the first time since our deportation.

We arrived with little more than our unwelcome baggage of lice, bugs, and disease. We were stripped naked and sent through special showers with disinfecting and delousing sprays. People found to have lice and nits had their hair shaved off. What we had been wearing was burned, and we were issued new clothing. A quarantine of at least two weeks was required for everyone. We did not have to travel far to our temporary quarters. They were right on the beach, a few hundred yards away. We were awaited by sand for our beds and palm-leaf mats strung overhead on poles to shield us from the scorching sun. Each shelter accommodated between fifty and sixty people, who would sleep in two rows, head to head. We were close enough to the sea that the sound of the waves washing up on the beach lulled us to sleep.

A little more than a mile away was the town of Pahlevi, where the Persians met us with exotic food and drink. They looked in disbelief at our emaciated condition and asked question after question. Why were thousands of Poles leaving the Soviet Union, and what were they doing there in the first place? Why were so many dying and so many others suffering from disease? Why and how did we leave our own country? Why were there so many orphans? The Persians were horrified when we told them about our imprisonment and starvation in the Soviet Union, which was plainly attested to not only by our physical condition and the diseases we brought with us but by the number of people who died shortly after arrival. Six hundred and fifty people who escaped did not live to enjoy it. They were buried in a Polish cemetery in Pahlevi.

The Soviet government, meanwhile, countered with a perfidious public relations campaign, blaming the Germans for the condition of the Polish evacuees and claiming to have saved the Poles by taking them in at great sacrifice and expense. The incongruity of such assertions was transparent, and we wondered how the Soviet leaders could think the world so gullible.

Our exhilaration at being free was soon tempered. When the rains came, the palm-leaf cover overhead failed to block the torrential downpour. Worse, our crowded living conditions allowed dysentery, typhus, typhoid fever, and various rashes to flourish. Many of the evacuees were so weakened by illness that they could not make it to the latrines and defecated in or close by the temporary quarters. Though many were trucked to camps near Tehran daily as they finished their quarantine, the numbers on the beach seemed to grow in the first days we were there.

It is difficult for me to remember how many days we were on that beach before Mother became ill. A doctor examined her and told her that she must go to a communicable disease shelter. I will never forget the afternoon when the army trucks came to pick up the sick people. Mother was the last to climb aboard, and as the truck pulled away, she looked over at Zosia and me and waved. She continued waving until the truck was out of sight. I knew why she had delayed getting on the truck. She wanted to be at the back so that she could have the longest chance to wave and to look at her children. As the truck slowly disappeared in the distance, we cried as I held my sister's hand and she held mine.

Some time later, I became extremely ill and soon afterward lapsed into unconsciousness. I was taken to the children's section of the makeshift hospital on the beach a couple of miles away, which was staffed by Polish doctors and nurses. After more than a week, when I had recovered somewhat, I asked the nurses where my mother and sister were, but no one could give me an answer. I had awoken to find myself on a Persian beach with other sick children and with no clue as to my family's whereabouts. As soon as I had the strength, I sneaked out of the tent and started walking in the direction of the camp where we had been quartered. I found only tattered palm-leaf mats, poles, and wet sand. Not a single human being was left in that camp. I stood on the beach staring at the barren sand, the endless sea, and the sky. At first, I choked back my tears. Then I cried and cried, my tears flowing onto the sand. I thought about how only a few years earlier, I had had everything a child could want or need. Now my father was missing and my mother was sick and perhaps dying. I had no idea where my brother and sister were. I felt so alone and so abandoned that it seemed even God had forgotten me.

I had no choice but to go back to the hospital. When I returned, my eyes swollen from crying, I asked the nurse to tell me what happened to all the people in the camp. She said that the quarantine was over and that the people were evacuated to camps in Tehran. She also told me that the entire children's hospital would be evacuated in a few days. I was devastated. What was to become of me? Would I ever see my family again?

CHAPTER 19

THE AIR FORCE HANGAR

When the time came to take us to Tehran, I had to face another journey, this time without my mother and sister. We were transported to the city in British Army trucks, which were driven by Armenians or Persians and guarded by Polish soldiers. Our Persian driver, with a Polish soldier sitting beside him in the cab, drove us through the Elburz Mountains, which separate Tehran from the Caspian Sea.

As the truck climbed higher, the ravines became deeper and the precipices more pronounced. Known as the Hammadan Route, the road we traveled was carved out of rock and in most places wide enough for only one vehicle. Hundreds of feet below lay crushed vehicles and skeletons. The wheels of our truck often rode the edge of the road, and our driver drove much too fast. Before long, everyone was terrified. Some passengers asked the driver to slow down. He ignored their requests, and they began to notice a strong smell of alcohol on his breath. Something had to be done, but I knew that if the driver would not listen to the adults, he certainly would not pay attention to me.

I recalled the way Mother analyzed the NKVD in coming up with our escape plan. They did not want to listen to her, so she fooled them. It occurred to me that if the driver became worried for his own life, perhaps he would be more careful. I sat right behind him, where a steel grate separated the cab from the truck bed. Looking around, I found a small piece of metal that I used to scratch the grate when we began to pass a dangerous drop. It made a dull, cracking noise as if something were breaking. The driver stopped the truck and went out to inspect it. He found nothing, and I breathed a sigh of relief. I repeated the scratching a number of times whenever we came upon a dangerous ravine. The driver became more suspicious with each incident and began to interrogate everybody.

When my turn came to be questioned, I looked the man straight in the eye and said I knew nothing. I knew I should never lie but figured it was necessary this time for our survival. The other people, who by now must have been aware of what I was doing, also said they knew nothing. The driver began to drive cautiously and even slowed to a crawl in dangerous places.

After crossing the mountains, the adults on the truck thanked me for tricking the driver into slowing down. They told me that they, too, had feared for their lives and those of their children.

Upon arriving in Tehran, we were driven to one of five Polish camps located on the outskirts of the city. Those who arrived last, including my transport, were taken to a huge Persian air force hangar nearby, which served as a temporary debarkation point. We were told to find a space for ourselves in the hangar until we could be transferred to newly built barracks as they became available.

There were already hundreds of people sitting or lying on the cement floor. Looking around, I could hardly see any space in which to lie down. A woman saw me standing in confusion and asked me if I was alone. I heard myself acknowledge aloud for the first time my own misery and loss.

"Why don't you join us?" the woman asked kindly. She had three children of her own, all near my age, and only two blankets, so the five of us spread out one blanket on the cement floor. The other we used as a cover.

The cooking area was located a short distance away, but it was close enough for one to smell the putrid odor of fatty mutton boiling in huge open-air kettles. The very thought of eating it nearly made me sick to my stomach. Nevertheless, I joined the lines and awaited my ration. When my turn came, I stepped up to the kettle, my nostrils filling with the steamy, acrid smell of rendered fat. An old, matronly-looking woman prepared to pour a greasy mass of barley and mutton into my mess kit.

"May I please have less mutton and more bread?" I asked shyly.

She looked at me somewhat surprised, poured me about half of my allotted portion, and gave me three extra slices of bread instead.

"Remember, son, after the Soviet Union, you must eat more meat than bread to gain weight and strength," she advised me.

I thanked her politely, then went to find an available place to sit on the ground. When I had finished eating, I walked over to a barrel of boiling water to wash my utensils. A boy much bigger than I came up and pushed me aside. I almost fell, causing some of the hot water to spill on my left hand.

"Move over, skinny bones," he said. "Can't you see I want to wash my utensils?"

My hand hurt, but my feelings were even more wounded. Taken by surprise, I was confused and frightened by the boy's behavior and did not know what to do. People next to us were watching, but nobody said a word. Not wanting to get into a fight with him, I walked away.

The following day, the confrontation occurred again. People watched but didn't say a word. Nobody would stand up for me. Enough was enough. I asked the bully, "Did your mother ever teach you to be nice to other people?"

"No! But at least she did not desert me like your mother did," he answered, laughing.

Anger raged within me, but again I walked away. The following morning, however, I awoke determined to take care of things myself, in whatever way I needed to. Though my stomach was in knots, one way or the other I had to make sure that there would be no more bullying. When the time came to go to the designated area to eat, I was ready. After finishing my meal, I started walking back holding my eating utensils in my left hand. Once again the bully showed up, blocking my way and spewing insults. I looked directly into his eyes as my right fist tightened. My adrenaline pumped. I struck him with all my might, right on his mouth and nose. One of his lips split open. Blood gushed from his nose and lip onto his face and clothing. He placed his hands over his mouth, then looked at his bloody hands and ran.

The people around me began to applaud—the same people who did nothing when I needed help. For the second time in three days, I stood in front of them not knowing what to say. I wondered what my parents would have done if they saw me applauded for such behavior, so contrary to my upbringing. But from that moment on, I was a different person. I had learned my first real lesson about surviving on my own. There were no more confrontations with the bully and no more insults.

A kind nurse from the camp clinic took care of my hands. The bruises on my right hand were worse than the few tiny blisters on my left. With compassion in her voice, she asked what had happened, and I replied that I had had an accident. She looked at me and asked, "On both hands at the same time?" Tears welled in my eyes, but no answer was forthcoming. She waited for a few seconds, and then continued. "You may go now, but I want to see you in two days. By then you should feel better and maybe you will tell me what happened."

I did not go back.

One evening, about a week after I arrived at the hangar, the camp authorities scheduled a party with a large bonfire, speeches, and the singing of patriotic songs to celebrate our freedom. Thinking this could be a good opportunity to look for my mother and sister, I attended. For most of the evening, I walked around the ring of people sitting four deep around the fire, stopping only long enough here and there to see who was near me. I persevered, though trying to find two people in the dark when all had their backs to me seemed futile.

It became late. The singing stopped, the bonfire was dying, and I was growing weary from my search. When the crowd began to thin I moved closer to the fire to rest my feet for a while and watch the remaining glow from the spectacular blaze. As I prepared to sit down, I suddenly heard a familiar voice. Whirling around, I listened for a moment, and then called out, "Zosia?" My sister turned and gasped in disbelief.

"My God! Is it really you, Wiesiu?" she exclaimed.

Before I could answer, we were hugging each other with the pure joy of discovery. I told her that I had been looking for Mother and her at the bonfire for hours, only to find that she had been looking for me as well. She told me that she had been looking every day for our mother and me, not knowing whether we were still in some hospital in Pahlevi or in Tehran. She described how difficult it was to find one person in that constantly shifting mass of people. More than seventy thousand people had crossed the Caspian Sea in a three-week period, and officials had been hard-pressed to keep track of them. Although the camp authorities had supplied some limited means of transportation, Zosia had searched the hospitals and widely scattered camps mainly on foot. It was a slow process, and she rejoiced that we had found each other and could join our efforts to find Mother.

Because it was so late and the barracks where she was staying were so crowded, we decided it would be best for me to return to the hangar for one more night. The following day, Zosia made the necessary arrangements with the Polish authorities running the camp, and I was transferred to her barracks.

The barracks were divided lengthwise by a wall, on each side of which was a continuous row of elevated boards for sleeping. Zosia and I were assigned a narrow space only wide enough for us to lie down. Under the boards was space to store our few belongings. An aisle ran alongside the outside wall. There were no dividers separating families. Total strangers slept on each side of us. Men, women, and children lived and slept side by side. Each person was allotted two blankets, one to lie down on and one to use as a cover.

Women, changing their clothes under the blankets in the interests of modesty, had a more difficult time than men. There was a humorous side to this as far as men and boys were concerned. Now and then an embarrassed female had her blanket slip off in the process of changing her undergarments, exposing her naked body and prompting boys' indiscreet laughter. I must confess that I also laughed at these incidents. Nature, however, had its own equalizer. In the morning, one could hear girls and women giggling at the evidence of men's erections under the blankets.

Outside the barracks, greasy mutton and barley were cooked in huge kettles. This and a portion of bread made up our daily rations. Not having eaten fruit for more than two years while in the Soviet Union, many people could not resist the temptation of helping themselves to mulberries, figs, dates, and pomegranates, which flourished in the Persian climate. But Zosia explained to me that the worst thing starving people could do was to consume food or drink that they were not used to, because doing so could result in serious stomach ailments or death. I followed her example by eating nothing but bread and strained barley and drinking nothing but boiled water.

Within a week of my moving into the barracks with Zosia, classes began for children of all ages. The Polish camp authorities were determined to provide some semblance of a normal life to the intellectually and physically deprived youngsters. There was no shortage of teachers, for Polish educational professionals had been prime candidates for deportation to the Soviet Union. So, at nine and a half years of age, I began my formal schooling. Almost all the children in my class had also missed two or more years of school, but their experience was different from mine. Many of them had been sent with their parents or a parent to the northern reaches of the Soviet Union or to Siberian work camps, where no schools existed.

The teachers spent the first several days asking hundreds of question about a broad range of topics. They were trying to learn how much elementary knowledge their students had in order to determine what and how we should be taught. To my surprise and delight, I raised my hand to answer almost every question, but I noticed that only a few of my fellow students did likewise. It took me some time to realize that many of my classmates suffered from the trauma of their experiences and were withdrawn as a result, especially in the presence of adults. The effects of deportation from their homes and the horrors endured in the Soviet Union were evident in their behavior: they sat quietly in class, not wanting to talk or learn or participate in class activities; some did not even want to play outside the classroom.

Boy and Girl Scout troops were organized for the children, and participation was mandatory. Zosia encouraged me to attend the Sunday Masses that were held in the open air to give everyone the chance to participate in religious activities, which had been forbidden in the Soviet Union. Tacitly I began to rebel. Not to disappoint my sister, I did attend one service, but only for a short time. Standing at the back of a huge crowd, I watched as the faithful dropped to their knees on the Persian sand in prayer, their hands and eyes raised to heaven. But I could not understand why all these people, who had lost their homes and their country and in some cases lost their loved ones to murder or disease, would praise the Lord. It only increased my confusion and inner turmoil about the human race and God.

M any of the Polish refugees became afflicted with dysentery, which causes great loss of blood and other bodily fluids and can be fatal. Malnutrition made us all prime candidates for contracting it, and the unhygienic conditions surrounding us only compounded the problem. Within the first few days of using the large public latrines I acquired an unforgettable first-hand observation of what dysentery is like. Early symptoms include severe stomach pains, fever, and a constant need to defecate. In the tormenting advanced stages, the victim excretes bloody feces but has little to pass and answers the constant pressure to excrete by passing bloody slime or bile, which gives off a terrible odor. Seeing so many people suffering in that way was very different from having seen people relieve themselves on the decks of the ship, where the waste could be washed overboard and out of sight. For a short while I was forced to watch the poor afflicted people literally drag themselves to the latrines. Most of the time, they could not make it and excreted the mess all over themselves. Flies swarmed all over. A few days' exposure to this suffering was all I could tolerate, and I stopped using the public latrines. Instead, I walked a good distance outside the camp to relieve myself. Having survived our imprisonment in the Soviet Union, dying from dysentery or some other contagious disease was not my idea of how I should depart from this earth. Yet my biggest fear was not so much catching a disease as dying before we found our mother.

CHAPTER 20

THE DARKEST HOUR

Every day, Zosia searched for Mother from early morning until midafternoon, but without success. The search consumed her. The authorities were unable to determine whether our mother was still in a hospital in Pahlevi or whether she had been transported to one of the refugee camps near Tehran or to a hospital nearby.

Despite my pleading, Zosia never allowed me to join her. The main reason for her refusal was not based on the fact that I had begun attending camp school. Rather, she explained, many refugees were dying each day from contagious diseases and there was no need for me to be exposed any more than I already was. "One of us looking for Mother is enough," she would say firmly.

Because I could not accompany her, I made it a point to await her return every day while anxiously praying for good news. One afternoon, about the time she usually returned, I stepped out of our barracks to watch for her. The sun beat down, and hot air seared my lungs. Two, three, and four o'clock came and went. Yet Zosia was nowhere in sight. To escape the direct rays of the sun, I took long breaks inside the barracks, where it was still hot but at least it was shady. Why would Zosia take so long?

It occurred to me that her delay could mean good news. Why would she stay hours longer than usual unless she had found Mother? As time went on, my frustration gradually turned to expectation. I went out again and saw my sister in the distance, walking slowly and holding something in her right hand. Eager to hear that Zosia had found Mother, I ran toward her, but even after seeing me her demeanor and pace did not change. I began to feel uneasy and frightened. As we approached each other, the object she carried became recognizable. It was a pair of boots, our mother's boots. I knew them well. It was the only pair she had left. At that moment, I sensed what had happened and came to a halt. It seemed forever before Zosia reached me. Her dark hair was disheveled, her eyes puffy from crying. She spoke to me in a low, barely audible voice.

"Wiesiu, our mother is dead." It was October 18, 1942. Mother was forty-five years old.

Zosia reached into the pocket of her blouse and pulled out a pair of Mother's earrings and her gold wedding band. She continued, with tears streaming down her face, "Other than these worn-out boots, these are the only earthly possessions Mother had when she died. I will keep them for us." She paused. Though only fifteen at the time, she announced, "I want you to know, little brother, that from this moment on, I will be your adopted mother." Her words spun in my head, leaving me standing speechless and confused. Zosia took my hand. I managed to answer, "Thank you, Zosiu."

We went inside the barracks and sat together on the wooden boards that were our assigned piece of the world. We cried together for a long time. Gathering my courage, I turned to my sister with the questions that I needed to ask.

"Zosiu," I began, "did you have a chance to talk to Mother and to comfort her before she died?"

"No, Wiesiu. Mama died about an hour before I found her. I am so sorry." A sob escaped her.

"What did Mother die from?"

"The doctor told me it was dysentery, malaria, a weakened heart, and general exhaustion."

Her efforts to keep us alive and bring us to freedom had caught up with her. She had sacrificed her life to save ours, and we had no way to repay her. If only I could have been with her in her dying moments.

"Zosiu, do you think Mother's soul went straight to heaven?"

Zosia took my hands in hers and looked at me tenderly. Her eyes were so like Mother's.

"Dear Wiesiulku," she tearfully whispered. "You know the answer to that question. Mother's soul is already in heaven, and you can take comfort that she will be looking after us from above, just as she did on this earth. Her spirit will guide us the rest of our lives."

I sighed deeply. "Thank you, Zosiu. I believe that, too, but I wanted to hear it from you."

Mother was buried the following day. Neither Zosia nor I had any decent clothes to put on. We still had only the clothing given to us after we were deloused. I wore wrinkled khaki shorts, a short-sleeved shirt, and beat-up sandals, and Zosia did not look much better. We were sad and ashamed to go to our mother's funeral looking like beggars, but we had no choice. Between the two of us we did not have a broken coin and could not even buy a small bouquet of flowers. Mother would understand. Our pockets were empty, but our hearts were full of pain and sorrow and love.

When it came time to leave for the ceremony, the Polish authorities took us in trucks to the recently opened Polish section of a Persian cemetery outside of town called Dulab. I have little memory of the trip. All I could think of was Mother's dying and being buried in Persian soil. After we had been standing at the graveside for about half an hour, trucks arrived piled with wooden caskets. I walked up and asked the man in charge if I could see my mother one last time, because I had not seen her for two months. He told me that the caskets were all nailed shut and that they could not be opened for fear of spreading disease. Broken up inside and helpless, I started to walk away. After a few steps I stopped and went back. Maybe the man did not understand me. It was my mother I wanted to see for the very last time, and I did not care about catching some disease.

"Please, mister," I begged. "Do it for me if only for a brief moment so that I could say good-bye to my mother face to face. Maybe she could still hear."

He hesitated for a moment.

"I am very sorry, young boy, these are my orders," the man answered, and he tried to comfort me.

I wiped my tears with my hands and went back to the graveside without saying a word to my sister. We stood in silence and watched as Mother's casket was put into the ground. I wondered what dying is like, the last hours, the last minutes, and the last seconds. What happens to a person? Did Mother still remember to the very end that we loved her? Did she die peacefully? Was Mother's spirit still with her? Could she hear us? We knelt and prayed. I thanked Mother for her kindness and her love. I thanked her for leading us to freedom. Then, while wiping my tears, I thought about my father and brother. At least they were spared this day of suffering, though I wondered how I would ever be able to tell them that Mother had died and that we had been unable to find her in time to be with her in that dark hour. We would have no explanation to give other than that we had tried. I felt guilty for being alive.

When all the burials were over, people began to board the trucks, but I did not want to leave. I felt it would be like deserting Mother at the worst possible time. Zosia put her arms around me just as she did in Poland when the Soviet soldiers were taking us away.

"Come, Wiesiu. You cannot stay here forever."

I stood up, still looking at the grave. Zosia took my hand. I lifted my eyes to hers. Together we walked past dozens of mourners, who knelt with hands outstretched to heaven and prayed for their departed loved ones. We left the cemetery and walked to one of the waiting trucks to begin a new journey alone. The skies were dark as the truck pulled away, taking us to face a new world on our own.

Soon after Mother's death, Zosia and I made an important decision. Orphans were generally shipped to orphanages or given the option of joining cadet groups being formed for boys and girls to be run by the Polish Army in Palestine. Either prospect could mean separation, which we wanted to avoid. Zosia had already spent a lot of time working with the camp administration to keep us in Persia as long as possible. We wanted to be closer to Jurek, who was stationed in Iraq, and closer to Poland.

Possible destinations were a constant topic of discussion among the refugees. For some months now, refugees had been leaving for eastern and southern Africa and India. Many of us felt that because Tehran was closer to home than any other place that was offered, staying put made more sense in view of our hopes for eventual repatriation. But we soon learned that there were risks in doing so. Polish authorities were told by British intelligence that there was a good possibility of Soviet occupation of northern Persia, in which case we would be in grave danger. It was for this reason that efforts had been made to quickly take as many Poles out of the area as possible. Zosia and I, after discussing the matter for days, decided to stay. Neither of us wanted to end up in a distant jungle with snakes and wild animals. We gambled that with the presence of the British and the Polish Armies, the Soviets would not dare make a move against us.

Shortly after Mother's death, Zosia became ill with a contagious disease but would not tell me what it was. She was moved to a hospital, and I stayed behind in the camp alone with strangers once more to await her return. Learning how to survive as an orphan was painful. Each day since that day on the beach at Pahlevi, I had been forced to learn to take care of myself without depending on others. A sense of pride was molding me into a loner. I was beginning to do things for other people and desperately trying to be self-sufficient. This helped me hide my loneliness. Zosia returned many weeks later. Despite the embarrassment of having her head shaved and having to wear a headscarf for the next three months, she focused her efforts on comforting me.

CHAPTER 21

AN UNEXPECTED
VISITOR

One day in April 1943, Zosia's and my classroom routine was interrupted by a visit from the Polish camp commander, who told us to come to his headquarters to meet a very special and unexpected visitor. He gave us some time to go back to our barracks to clean up and change into our Scout uniforms, our nicest clothes at the time. We pleaded with him to tell us who the visitor was, but he refused. All he was willing to say was that we would be very pleasantly surprised.

We prayed that our father had escaped from prison in the Soviet Union and finally found us. I believed that a miracle was about to happen. After all, we knew of no one in Persia who would generate so much fuss. It could not have been our brother because Polish soldiers were coming from Iraq on furloughs routinely to visit their families. It could not be anyone other than our father.

With great anticipation, we prepared to greet him. Zosia even put some animal grease on my hair to flatten it out. She parted my hair on the left side and told me how good I looked. My hopes of meeting Father for the first time in more than three years were growing. At headquarters, the camp commander and his assistants met us in a small waiting room with great fanfare. All this fuss convinced me even more that our visitor had to be our lost father. One of the assistants left to bring in the visitor. The few moments we waited seemed an eternity. My heart was ready to jump out of my chest. The door opened. I gasped in disbelief. It was not our father but a total stranger. My hopes were shattered.

In the doorway stood a distinguished woman. Tall and beautiful, she was dressed in the uniform of a lieutenant in the U.S. Army Nursing Corps. We were surprised that this was our visitor and shocked when she spoke to us in fluent Polish. She introduced herself as Jean Siepak, our cousin from the United States, the daughter of our father's sister Maria. Seeing our surprise, she tried to jar our memory.

"Do you remember my sister Gerry who came to visit you in Poland right before the war?"

Stunned by the events of the day, at first my memory failed to recall someone I'd met five years earlier, when I was not quite six years old. It did not matter. Zosia flew into her arms. The two women hugged each other for at least a minute and then burst into tears.

"Auntie from America!" Zosia exclaimed and hugged her again. I heard my sister continue, "Please take us to America. We cannot stand it any more."

"I promise to do the best I can," Jean answered. Then she turned toward me with tears still streaming down her cheeks. She hugged and kissed me, while I clung to her for comfort, lost for words.

It seemed to me that Providence had guided Jean to us. Of all the thousands of refugees from the Soviet Union who had already been sent to Africa, India, Australia, and other places, we had stayed behind. Lieutenant Siepak could have been sent to any number of hospitals in the war zone. How incredible that she found us! Given all the refugees who needed help and comfort, I realized that even after all we had been through, my sister and I were the fortunate ones. Perhaps miracles really did happen. Zosia and I were given permission to leave the camp with Jean for a few days. She was on leave from her assignment as a surgical nurse in an American army hospital located in a desert near Ahvaz. Her leave was short because of the constant flow of wounded servicemen arriving from the fronts. When we left the headquarters, we found an American Red Cross station wagon with two American soldiers and a Red Cross representative waiting for us. It was all so unexpected. The soldiers took pictures of Zosia and me with Jean, and we asked a passerby to take pictures of all of us standing next to the station wagon. Then we left for Tehran, where Jean was staying in a luxurious hotel.

When we reached the city, the driver took us directly to the shopping district. Along the way, we marveled at the modern buildings, elegant shops, and well-dressed people. Men wore European suits, white shirts, and ties; most women wore chadors. The driver stopped in front of a store where Jean took us to be outfitted with new clothes. We were treated like royalty and served coffee in a demitasse with fine Persian pastries. Following our novel shopping experience, dressed in our new finery, we went to eat at the hotel restaurant. For us, the meal was more of a banquet. Having starved for two years in the workers' paradise and then lived on fatty mutton and barley in Persia, I could not satisfy my appetite and had to loosen my new belt three times. Jean later wrote her mother that she could not believe how much food a little boy put away.

During the dinner, she described the 113th U.S. Army Hospital, part of the Fifth Army, where she was a surgical nurse, and told us about the thousands of wounded American soldiers who came there from the war zones for treatment and recuperation. Jean asked many questions about our deportation from Poland, life in the Soviet Union, our escape, and Father, Mother, and Jurek. We asked her about America and about all our relatives. Zosia and I were both very interested to hear how Jean had found us.

The search for us had started almost immediately after our deportation. Father's sister Stasia, who had lived near Cracow, wrote a letter to her sister Maria in Chicago about what had happened. After receiving it, Maria began a search with the American Red Cross and the Polish consulate in Chicago. She even wrote letters to the Soviet Union and the Polish government-in-exile in London. Sometime in the late summer of 1942, Maria was informed that there had been an evacuation of Polish people from the Soviet Union to Persia in March of that year, but our names did not appear on the list of those evacuees. Months later, she also learned that there had been a second, bigger evacuation to Persia. By the time her daughter Jean joined the U.S. Army Nursing Corps and left for Persia, Maria still did not know whether we were among the refugees. Upon arriving in Ahvaz, Jean immediately began her search for us by contacting the American Red Cross. It was not long before they found us, and Jean came as soon as she could arrange leave. To our surprise, she also told us that she had already made arrangements with the Polish authorities to ensure our passage to Mexico on a transport ship at the end of April. We almost jumped for joy to hear this news.

We spent the next few days getting to know each other. When her leave was over and she had to return to Ahvaz, Jean drove us back to camp and repeated her promise to do whatever she could to help us. She gave us some money, her address, and the address and telephone number of her parents in Chicago. When the time came for Jean to leave, our parting was difficult. The address of Jean's mother and father—1906 North Kedzie Boulevard, Chicago, Illinois—became a source of hope that Zosia and I always carried with us. While we dreamed of going to the wonderful world Jean had described, we knew that with war raging in Africa and Europe, it would be a long time before we could hope to take our first step on American soil.

CHAPTER 22

SHATTERED HOPES

When Jean returned to her nursing duties in Ahvaz, our lives fell back into the camp routine. During the day I went to school. In the evening I studied. We still were served mutton, barley, and bread. At night, we spent a good deal of time fighting off bedbugs. All the while, I grieved for Mother but tried hard to keep the grief to myself.

Shortly after Jean left, the camp headquarters notified us that the first ship to take refugees to Mexico was scheduled for April 30, 1943, and thanks to arrangements made by Jean, we were expected aboard. This was great news, because from Mexico Aunt Maria could easily bring Zosia and me to the United States.

But fate was against us. As we prepared to leave for the Persian Gulf to board the ship, I fell ill. My face became flushed and my temperature rose. Zosia took me to a doctor, who looked at my throat and tongue, and seeing them covered with red dots, ordered me to go straight to the hospital. My condition was confirmed as scarlet fever. Most of the first week, I was delirious from high fever, so I do not remember what happened. All I recall is having a rash all over my body that led to my skin peeling. I was in quarantine for a month with other children.

On June 27, 1943, another ship left for Mexico, but this time I came down with malaria. Though it was extremely hot inside the hospital, I lay shivering under a pile of blankets. Once more, we could not go. We did not learn it for a long time, but the ship with Polish children on board that left for Mexico on June 27 was the last one. Additional ships were promised but never arrived.

Scarlet fever and malaria were not the only diseases to afflict me. Hardly anyone who arrived in the Middle East escaped being prey to one serious illness or another. In this respect I was lucky. In three years in Persia, I only came down with malaria twice, scarlet fever, mumps, measles, and some other disease while on the beach at Pahlevi whose name I cannot recall. Of these, malaria was the worst to endure, but scarlet fever was the most dangerous.

Although I avoided the public latrines so as not to catch any of the deadly diseases, I could not escape the malaria-spreading mosquitoes. My first symptoms were a loss of energy, headache, and stomach pains. Then came uncontrollable shivering, which led to extreme shaking of my body and chattering of my teeth. The day I was first hospitalized with malaria, I lay on a hospital bed under a stack of blankets, curled in a fetal position, trying to keep warm and wishing that my mother were with me. Except during the worst chills and fever attacks, I slept constantly and do not remember how many days I was hospitalized. I do remember taking the terrible-tasting quinine for a long time during the hospital stay and afterward.

In the midsummer of 1943, Zosia received a letter from Jurek, who was stationed in Iraq. He said he would be coming to visit us on his furlough. We rejoiced at the prospect of seeing him. Although I looked forward to our reunion, I was faced with a dilemma. In my mind, I heard the echoes of Father's and Jurek's last words to me before their departures to the army: "Take care of your mother." How would I ever be able to tell my brother that I did not do anything for her before she died? I was convinced that somehow I should have been taking better care of her, though I was only nine years old at the time. Such thoughts haunted me, and my hopes of enjoying our reunion with Jurek were tempered with anxiety.

Jurek arrived, looking a hundred times better than when we had seen him last in Krasnovodsk. He was handsome in his British uniform with Polish insignia on his sleeve and a black beret. He looked like the brother we knew in Poland. Our meeting was emotional. At first we were searching for words, and soon it became obvious that no one wanted to bring up the subject dearest to our hearts and the most painful. Jurek took us to Tehran for a change of scenery and a chance to talk in private. Until late evening, the subjects of our missing father and our mother's death were not broached. Then Zosia told him about everything that had happened from the time we stepped on the beach of Pahlevi to the day when she found Mother in a hospital, already dead. Jurek was vividly shaken and at a loss for words. Though he had tears in his eyes, he tried to conceal his emotions and to comfort us, but it was difficult for him to talk. I could see my otherwise eloquent sister grappling with words, and I feared that I would cry if I tried to say anything. After that evening, we did not talk about Mother's death.

For the rest of the time Jurek was with us, we talked about what we were doing and what we would like to do when the war was over. He told us what had happened to him from the time we left Krasnovodsk and about his training in Iraq as a tank driver in the armored division. We told him about our cousin Jean and the missed opportunities to go to Mexico. The days before Jurek's departure were especially difficult for me. I dreaded the day of parting and wished he did not have to leave. In a way it seemed like only yesterday since my father had told me good-bye, and I hadn't seen him since. Would saying good-bye to my brother, whom I also loved, be the same? What if Jurek never returned? When the time came to see him off, I told Jurek that I loved him. Zosia and I wished him good luck in the war, and we all promised that we would meet again soon. Yet deep inside I knew that promises of this kind were no more than wishes in disguise. Our brother left for the war, and we were left with hope that our wishes would come true.

In the meantime, news spread quickly through the Polish camps that the Germans had discovered a mass grave of more than four thousand Polish officers in the Katyn Forest, near the town of Smolensk in the Soviet Union. The Germans announced to the world that the Soviets had murdered the Polish POWs. They promptly invited international observers and a team of forensic experts to investigate the crime. This devastating news awakened our deepest fear—that Father might have been murdered. As the news filtered in, we learned that the bodies of the officers discovered in the Katyn Forest were all from the Kozielsk camp. Because we knew that our father was imprisoned in the Starobelsk camp, this information gave us hope that he might still be alive. Eleven thousand other Polish POWs imprisoned by the Soviet Communists were still unaccounted for, and the Soviets were still indignantly silent as to their whereabouts. We waited for every scrap of information that might reveal whether at least some of the missing men were alive. One of them could be our father.

By sheer coincidence we found a reliable source of the most recent information concerning the massacre and the missing officers, but the news was not encouraging. Zosia had become acquainted with a Polish girl in her class named Iwona Gronkowska, who had just escaped with her mother from the Soviet Union. Iwona's father, Leon Gronkowski, had been chosen by the Polish embassy in the Soviet Union as one of the plenipotentiaries who traveled the country informing Polish deportees of the "amnesty" granted them in 1942 and offering assistance. When the Soviets forbade such activities, Mr. Gronkowski received a

new assignment from the embassy. He was placed in charge of distrib-
uting various kinds of assistance to Polish centers spread throughout
the Soviet Union for people who were left behind; in this group were
most of the Polish deportees. In the course of his two assignments and
through his contacts with the Polish embassy and officials of the Polish
government-in-exile in London, he gathered mountains of information
and was willing to share that which was most pertinent to us. He told us
that after the departure of the Polish Army and civilians from the Soviet
Union in August 1942, the relationship of the Soviet government in Moscow and the Polish government-in-exile fast deteriorated. The primary
reason was the insistence of the Polish government on an explanation
from the Soviets as to the fate of the thousands of Polish officers taken
prisoner in the fall of 1939. They should have been released after the
amnesty to join the Polish Army.

Matters grew worse once the Germans discovered the massacre at the
Katyn Forest. When the initial forensic investigation proved conclusively
that the murders occurred in the spring of 1940, when the Polish officers
were in Soviet hands, the Polish government demanded that the International Red Cross perform its own independent investigation. The
Soviets refused, blaming the Germans for the crime and accusing the
Poles of being tools of the Nazis and the Western capitalists, who wanted
only to tarnish the good image of the Soviet state. To demonstrate their
outrage at being accused of the massacre, the Soviets severed relations
with Poland despite the fact that they were both part of the Allied war effort. The Soviets gave the members of the Polish embassy in Kuybyshev
three days to leave. This chain of events boded poorly not only for the
Polish deportees left behind in the Soviet Union but also for any immediate chance of discovering the fate of the other eleven thousand missing POWs.

There was no new information about the massacre for months. Then
late in the year we learned that the Red Army had pushed back the Germans and occupied the area of the Katyn Forest. Some time later the
Soviets organized their own forensic team and began again to open the
mass graves. They now claimed to have proof that it was the Germans
who were responsible for the crime. None of us believed it; we knew that
all the evidence of the massacre pointed in their direction. As time went
on Zosia and I still searched for any glimmer of hope that Father could
still be alive. The day came for us to leave Tehran. Once more we boarded
trucks, this time to travel 350 miles to another refugee camp.

CHAPTER 23

AHVAZ

In December 1943, Zosia and I were transported to a transit camp less than two miles from the city of Ahvaz. The camp was set up by the British in 1942 to transport the Polish Army to Iraq and the Polish refugees from the Soviet Union to their various destinations around the world. Their stay there generally varied between a few days and a number of months, depending on the availability of ships leaving the Persian Gulf. Because the gulf ports of Khorramshahr and Basra were only about ninety and one hundred miles away, respectively, the Ahvaz site served its purpose well. Refugees now could be shipped on short notice.

Ahvaz is an ancient city, one of the oldest in Persia, and the capital of Khuzestan, a region composed mainly of desertlike lowlands. For centuries it was an agricultural and commercial center. It straddles the muddy Karun River, one of the biggest in Persia, which flows into the Persian Gulf. Ahvaz has long been home to a diverse range of people: Arabian, Persian, Kurdish, Turkish, Bakhtiari, and others, although most of the Bakhtiars live northeast of Ahvaz in the mountains. During our time there, most of the residents by far were Arabs. The city was divided into two sections: the newer European area had wide streets lined with palm trees, hotels, shops, restaurants, and cafes; the older section was rather shabby and unsafe for Europeans.

As soon as we arrived, Zosia and I were assigned to our new quarters, which had originally been built as a camel stable sometime around World War I. Each family was assigned a small area next to wooden bunks and given enough blankets to hang on ropes to screen their compartment, but we did not receive mattresses or pillows. The bunks were placed along each side of the stable, by the mangers. Although overall sanitation facilities were poor, showers were available. The camp was designed to hold two thousand people in the summer and three thousand in the winter, but on occasion it housed many more.

Once we were settled, the first thing we did was notify our cousin

Jean, who was stationed at a nearby American army hospital. During the year or so that followed until her tour of duty ended, we visited often at the camp and, more frequently, at the hospital and the nurses' quarters. Jean made arrangements each time for an army jeep to pick us up and bring us back. The American soldiers were delighted that they could help and obviously enjoyed meeting two young survivors of Soviet imprisonment, Zosia in particular. They also liked me, and I liked them. They gave me money, candy, and chewing gum. They also taught me dirty words in English. When Jean introduced me to her fellow nurses, I proudly tried to impress them with my newly acquired English vocabulary and could not understand why everybody broke out in laughter.

The visits did, however, generate some jealousy in the camp, which I made an effort to defuse by sharing the candy and other things I received. I was, however, uncomfortable wearing clothing tailored from U.S. government uniforms.

During our first visit to the hospital, we saw soldiers with missing legs and hands, some blinded, others with part of their face or their genitals shot off—all lying helplessly in their beds. Zosia was so horrified by what we saw that she eventually broke down and cried, and I felt sick to my stomach. We asked Jean to call it quits for that day, earlier than we had planned. But the next time Jean visited us she related that the soldiers we had met talked to her about us. "When are the orphans coming back?" they kept asking. Jean told us that we reminded these soldiers of their own younger siblings, and of home.

We often returned to visit the wounded and disfigured American soldiers, and each time I prayed that nothing so horrible would happen to my brother. Our visits left many of the soldiers with smiles of appreciation. Even the severely wounded were happy to see us. Those who were able shook our hands.

A number of the wounded Americans were of Polish origin and spoke Polish fluently. They asked what we were doing in Persia, so far away from Poland. We would stop by their beds and talk about America and freedom, which cheered us all up. They promised us that soon the Germans would be beaten and we would be able to go home. Some, who had learned that Zosia and I were orphans, asked whether they could do something for us. We could not imagine how those who had lost a limb or their eyesight could be moved to ask whether they could help.

On our second visit to the hospital, Lieutenant Jean introduced us to an army major who was one of her favorite patients. To this day, I remember him as the Major. He was a big, strapping fellow who was recovering from surgery, having sustained multiple wounds all over his body. Jean acted as a translator, because he did not speak Polish, but his natural humor and friendliness made up for our difficulty in communicating. We took an instant liking to one another. Through Jean, we learned that he was soon going back to his cattle ranch in the western United States. After about fifteen minutes, Jean felt that she had to move on to visit the rest of her many patients. The Major thanked us for our visit and gave us some American candy and some Wrigley's chewing gum, my recent and irresistible discovery. While we shook hands, the Major insisted that we come to visit him again. We promised.

About five days later, a hospital jeep pulled up to the camel stable. A Polish-speaking American soldier brought us a message from the Major inviting us for lunch in the hospital cafeteria at noon the coming Saturday. The driver told us he would pick us up at 11:15 A.M. He spent another half-hour flirting with Zosia, while I made myself comfortable in the driver's seat of the jeep and tested all the buttons and knobs on the dashboard. Having just received from the driver a large package of chewing gum also made by Mr. Wrigley, I managed to put five pieces in my mouth all at once. Then I stuck my left foot out over the side of the jeep, as American soldiers did, leaned back, and watched a small group of curious boys gather around. I was a hero just for sitting in the driver's seat of the jeep. How proud I was! Much too soon, the driver announced that it was time for him to go back to the base. The boys all pleaded with him for a ride.

"Five minutes. That's all I have," he said.

The boys quickly piled in and screamed with laughter as he drove us around the entire camp, bewildering spectators with all the commotion. When we returned, all of us jumped out of the jeep and gathered around the driver, pleading with him to come back again. "Only if you help me improve my Polish," he answered. He waved at Zosia, giving her a big smile. She blushed and waved back. The young soldier revved up the engine to a roar and, to our delight, spun the wheels of the jeep in the sand so that it peppered us all over like pellets from a shotgun. We stood in awe and waved as he drove off. The boys were ecstatic and marveled at how well the Americans knew how to drive.

On Saturday morning my sister, noticeably anxious, did not let me go out and play with my friends. She told me to shower, clean up well, and stay in our cubicle until it was time to visit the Major. Meanwhile, she tried on all her dresses but was unable to decide which one to wear, though she did not have much to choose from. By eleven o'clock, she was

ready. We went out and waited by the cavernous door of our stable. At
11:15 sharp, the jeep pulled up with the same driver and Lieutenant Jean.
We greeted her affectionately. A swarm of women surrounded us and
begged Jean for information about relatives in Poland and children who
had been lost while leaving the Soviet Union. As always, she took their
names and promised to do the best she could but cautioned that during
wartime some things were impossible. The most touching requests were
those by weeping mothers looking for children they had lost somewhere
in the Soviet Union. They would kneel down on the ground before Jean
and kiss her hands as if she were a miraculous savior with the power to
rescue their children from a certain death. She did not pretend to have
such power, but neither did she say anything to lead the women to give
up hope.

We boarded the jeep with heavy hearts. This time there was no revving
up the engine for a fast take-off. When we were out of the camp, Jean
turned to us and said that it broke her heart to see mothers so desperate
to save their children. Nor could she tell them the awful truth that the
movement of Poles from the Soviet Union had ceased and that the Soviets were not willing to cooperate with anyone searching for Poles left behind in their country.

We arrived at the main entrance of the American field hospital, which
was located a reasonably short distance from our camp. The driver
helped Zosia out of the jeep as I jumped out. He saluted our cousin and
was requested by her to meet us back there in two hours. A corner table
had been reserved for us in the cafeteria. We were greeted by an orderly,
who told Jean that he was assigned to assist us throughout our lunch.
Minutes later, the Major arrived in a wheelchair holding two packages in
his lap. We all greeted each other in two languages, attracting the attention of people sitting close by who were not used to seeing civilians,
especially children, in an army hospital. Having made himself comfortable, the Major placed a small package in front of my sister and a bigger
one in front of me, saying something in English with a big smile. From
this point onward, Jean served as translator. She told us how happy the
Major was to have met us and that the packages were small tokens to
commemorate the occasion. Zosia received a silver Persian bracelet and
a matching set of earrings. I received a big stamp album filled with thousands of Persian, American, and British stamps. We were overwhelmed
with excitement at receiving such generous and unexpected gifts. Zosia
and I stood up to thank the Major. I shook his hand while Zosia, in her
girlish exuberance, gave him a kiss on the cheek. People came up to our

table curious to see what all the excitement was about. After brief introductions and conversations, we ate a lunch that was a thousand times better than our usual fare. We were offered an assortment of pancakes, fried potatoes, Spam, corned beef hash, eggs, muffins, butter, milk, orange juice, bananas, figs, oranges, various flavors of Jell-O, coffee, tea, and cookies. We tasted almost everything. I marveled at how Americans could deliver and prepare all this food for their soldiers in the middle of a desert.

Soon after we began eating, the Major described life in the United States. He concentrated on his cattle ranch, located in a state with such a strange-sounding English name that I forgot it almost immediately. He told us all about how a modern ranch operates, describing the state-of-the-art equipment, the herds of cattle, and the wild mustangs that grazed nearby. He told us how he and his friends went to the mountains to hunt for deer and elk and to fish for salmon. He asked me if I would like to live in such a place. Would I? After all we had been through, there could be no other answer. Simply to see such a place would be wonderful enough, but to be able to live there was beyond imagining.

Then came the bombshell. Jean told us that the Major would like to talk about adoption. Adoption? Not in my wildest dreams had I expected that the adoption of Zosia and me would come up today or ever, especially from a near stranger speaking a foreign language. I was immediately confused and my emotions were in turmoil.

The Major continued to talk about the good schools and universities in America, the lifestyle, and the popular sports for young people and gradually turned to a different subject. He explained that he and his wife had always wanted to have children but could not. They had considered adopting but, when the war broke out, delayed any plans to do so. He went on to say that he would love to adopt both of us, but that it probably would not be in Zosia's best interests. The war should be over soon, and because she was almost eighteen, he imagined that she would likely be more interested in returning home to marry a Polish boy, while our brother would settle there as well. I, on the other hand, being only eleven, would still need a lot of care and many years of education, which the Major and his wife would be happy to provide. He thought that this plan would be best for everyone.

I was at a loss for words. What was I to say now? How could I express my gratitude to the Major for his kindness without hurting my sister's feelings? The Major told us that he would be leaving for the States in two months and would have to have my decision within three weeks in order to make the necessary arrangements. He was confident that if I accepted, we would be able to go there together. His last advice was to think it over thoroughly, visit him as much as we wished, and ask any questions that we had. Zosia expressed our deepest gratitude to him for his kindness. I shook his hand, searching clumsily for the right words to say, but could not find any. So I said, "Thank you, sir. We will see you soon." The three of us walked him to his ward and said good-bye until the next time.

Our driver was waiting. Jean, who was in a rush to go back to her quarters to get ready for duty, hugged us good-bye and encouraged us to think carefully about the Major's offer. We climbed aboard the jeep. Not interested in talking, I let my sister sit in the front seat by the driver. Not surprisingly, it took him twice as long as usual to get back to camp, giving me time to start thinking about all that the Major had said. Upon our arrival at the camp, Zosia and I went to our cubicle in the stable. I lay down on the board, facing away from my sister, confused and depressed. Zosia sat down next to me and, putting her hand on my shoulder, asked me what was the matter. I told her that although at first I had been happy about the Major's offer, now I felt just the opposite.

Zosia pointed out that going to America would be for my own good. I knew this was true, but I also knew that I could not leave my sister behind. Did we not promise each other when Mother died not to separate, at least until the war was over? I was not going to go back on that now, for better or for worse.

"Do you think for one second that I could leave you all alone in a Persian desert, not knowing which camp or foreign country you would be transported to while I am on the way to a good life in America? Do you really think that?" I asked.

"You are so adamant. Are you sure, Wiesiu, there is no other reason you want to tell me about?"

Even if there were another reason, there was no point in talking about it. I repeated that I was going to keep our promise never to separate until the war was over. Zosia leaned over and gave me a hug and a kiss. "Thank you, my brother, but we will talk about it later."

I had not lied to my sister, but neither had I told her the whole truth. I felt that to agree to adoption would be to betray the love my parents had shown me from the first breath I took. Could I do this for the sake of improving my circumstances? My mother had saved my life and that of my sister and brother. Could I voluntarily call some other woman Mama, no matter how nice and loving she might be? Never. And what about Father? We did not know for sure whether he was alive or dead. What if he arrived at our camp a day after I left for America and asked Zosia, "Where is Wiesiu?" Could she reply, "Your loving son, thinking that you were murdered, left for a better life in America with a new father?" That would surely break his heart. No, I could not do that, either. There was another aspect of adoption that bothered me. It was a matter of pride. To be adopted is to lose one's own name. I remembered how my father taught me as a little boy to be proud of my ancestors and proud of who I was. One day, I thought, if I wanted to, I could still go to America for a better life, but with my own heritage and my own name intact.

In the following weeks, Zosia and Jean spent much time trying to convince me to accept the Major's offer and give myself a good start in life. I was tempted but could not be persuaded. I dreaded the moment when I would have to face the Major and tell him my decision. When the day came, the three of us went to visit him. We asked Jean to convey to him our gratitude for his kindness but that we had decided to stay together to honor a promise we had made to each other when our mother had died. We wished him the best and promised that should we ever come to America we would visit him. The Major accepted our decision graciously, but we could see the disappointment in his eyes. The one thing he asked was for us to visit him as much as we could before he left. We did that.

At the same time, we visited Jean often at the nurses' quarters where she lived. Her room was in a round compound with only one entrance that was strictly off limits to men. Jean told me, however, that because I was just a boy, the nurses living there agreed to make an exception. She cautioned me, however, that during the hot summer months there would be nurses walking naked on the way to the showers. She didn't tell me what I should do if I saw a nurse with no clothes on, nor was I going to ask. The first time it happened I was completely flustered. A young woman crossed my path holding a towel in one hand and a bar of soap in the other, with sandals on her feet and only the sun's rays covering her body. She gracefully walked by, in no hurry at all, looked at me, said hello, and kept going. This was the first time I ever saw a completely naked woman in my life. My voice choked a little and I barely managed to answer in Polish, "Good morning, ma'am." My eyes remained glued to her breasts until we passed each other and thereafter I kept my eyes averted, trying to be a gentleman.

Later, after many similar incidents, I was surprised that none of these women tried to cover up—not much, that is. For reasons I did not understand at the time, the frequency of my visits to Jean increased, as did my appreciation of women. I thought their bodies were beautiful and exciting. For the first time in a long time, I began to look forward to the next day.

Living in the camel stable in the desert environment was a trying experience. The conditions in the camp were harsh. The overwhelming stench at the latrines attracted swarms of flies, while bloodsucking bedbugs paid us nightly visits. These nuisances, however, were the least of our many hardships. Malaria-carrying mosquitoes were so thick in the air during the rainy season that it was difficult to talk without swallowing them. At night we slept under mosquito nets while the jackals howling in the distance lulled us to sleep. Poisonous snakes and deadly scorpions were another constant threat. In order to avoid being stung by the scorpions, we had to shake out our clothing and shoes before putting them on. There were also thousands of bats that lived in the top section of the stables in cavelike crevices. At night, they flew about at eye level or lower, making whistling sounds as they searched for food. They fluttered by within inches of us, and their scary appearance gave us a creepy feeling of being among evil spirits.

Daytime heat during the summer often reached such intensity that the unwary suffered sunstroke and brain damage. An egg dropped on sun-exposed cement would fry in an instant. Daily salt tablets were a must during hot and dry months. Conversely, at other times, when heavy winds blew in from the Persian Gulf, they brought with them so much salt that our bodies were constantly covered with deposits of it, requiring frequent showers each day. For relief, a few friends of mine and I would often sneak out of our camp to the old Arab section of town to swim in the forbidden muddy Karun. Fearing deadly attacks from the sharks and the swordfish that swam up the river from the gulf, we would indulge ourselves with swimming only when the Arabs did likewise. We assumed that they somehow knew when it was safe.

Sandstorms occurred a few times during our stay in Ahvaz. According to the stories we heard from the Arabs, unsuspecting travelers in the desert or others who strayed away from their habitat were often found buried and suffocated in the sand after such storms. Upon our arrival we were warned of them and instructed in what to do if caught in one. Having already experienced many blizzards during our time in the Soviet Union, both Zosia and I wanted to see how it would feel to be in a desert sandstorm, at least for a short while. One typically clear and scorching day, with the sun directly above us, my friends and I were playing outside the stables. Just as we were going to call it a day because of the extreme heat, I observed dark clouds forming on the horizon and moving fast in our direction.

"A sandstorm is coming!" I screamed.

We ran for the stables at full speed. Once inside, we put fluffed cotton in our ears and noses and wrapped ourselves in bed sheets, leaving only a small opening in front to look through. Then we quickly stepped outside. In the far distance the sky was very dark, almost black. As the storm came closer and the wind whipped up the sand in front of it, the clouds' appearance changed from very dark to gray, to grayish red, and then to bright red. When the sandstorm descended upon us, the sky above turned bright orange-red as the rays of the sun reflected off the golden grains of the airborne sand. It seemed as if the earth itself had turned into a ball of fire. The clouds of sand whirled furiously around us, pounding our bodies and penetrating the protective covering we wore. We had sand in our mouths, ears, noses, and undergarments. Fearing that the worst was yet to come, Zosia and I ran back to our stable, though we could barely make it out amid the clouds of orange-red dust. Sometime later we came out again to take another look at nature's fury, only to see the orange-red turn into red, then to reddish gray, to gray, and finally to dark gray and almost black. The sky then cleared and brightened, and the sun's rays beat down as before. No matter how hard we worked to be rid of it, there would be sand in our clothes and in the living area for days.

CHAPTER 24

DESERT GAMES

British troops and those of other nationalities were temporarily stationed near our camp while they were in transit. The English were the coolest and most aloof, whereas the Hindu troops from India were the friendliest and most likable. It was not long after our arrival that my friends and I became acquainted with a few men from the Hindu Special Forces, the world-famous Gurkhas. Their specialty was hand-to-hand combat using large wooden-handled knives with razor-sharp blades. These warriors were greatly feared by their enemies because they could crawl up silently at night into enemy positions and slit the enemies' throats without producing a sound. The knives were also thrown to kill someone at a distance. The Gurkhas did so with astonishing precision.

Some of these men came to the stables a few times a week to play with us. They always brought candy and chewing gum. I remember them distinctly—their black hair, black eyes, and dark complexions, their immaculately pressed battle-green uniforms and bright white turbans. The elegant appearance and kind demeanor of these men belied the nature of their work.

The best part of such visits was learning how to throw the knife. We would mark a spot the size of a coin on a wooden post, and the Gurkhas would send their knives twirling through the air, always hitting the marked spot with its sharp point. It was fascinating to witness. Time and again they showed us how to throw the knife, never losing their patience. After what seemed like hundreds of tries, I finally stuck the knife into the wooden post with a throw. It was a thrilling moment not only for me but also for my teachers, who were happy for me. My lessons ended abruptly, however, when my sister learned of my new fancy. A week later, the Special Forces left for Italy to fight the Germans. My Hindu friends came to say good-bye, bringing small gifts for us. All we could do was wish them good luck in Polish, hoping they would somehow understand. After shaking hands, each made a crisp about-face and left.

Because the camp was designed to be strictly a transit base, organized recreation was practically nonexistent. To make matters worse, by the time we came to Ahvaz, Zosia had begun watching me like a hawk, even more than Mother had. To my chagrin, my ability to run around loose was curtailed as Zosia tried to live up to her responsibility as my adopted mother.

On occasion my friends and I were invited to the hospital theater by my cousin Jean to watch American movies about cowboys and Indians, or sometimes the Arabian Nights, the stories I had been told so many times as a little boy. The mysterious Arabs, the sultans and the sheiks, their imaginary flying carpets, their famous Arabian horses, their jewels, their sword fighting, and their beautiful women came to life on the screen true to the memories of my childhood, inflaming my desire to see them in real life. There had to be such exotic places and people not far from us. Out of curiosity, when the movies were over, my friends and I would search in the forbidden Arab section of Ahvaz for validation of our fantasies. What we found instead was the true picture of Arabian nights and days enveloped in abject poverty.

Generally toward sunset at the end of each day, my sister and I joined many other Polish refugees who would sit outside for hours and watch American army convoys heading for the Soviet Union from the Persian Gulf. The line of trucks stretched like a serpent from one edge of the horizon to the other. According to the American soldiers, these trucks were loaded with enormous quantities of war materiel to aid the Red Army. It was America's contribution to the combined war effort.

With many idle hours and eager for news of the war, I sometimes engaged in long conversations with the adults in the camp. We talked about countrymen who had been left behind in the Soviet Union and whether they would ever again see freedom. We speculated as to the impact Germany's attack would have on Poland's future, whether there would be a Soviet takeover of Poland, and whether we would see our homeland again.

Around that time I began to invent war games for distraction and recreation. My first game involved trying to shoot down vultures, pretending they were Soviet and German warplanes. It took a lot of planning to decide how to shoot them down, how to design and construct the weapons, and where to get the powder and ammunition. I also had to recruit soldiers for my army and find a suitable place to construct and test the weaponry without being detected by the adults.

To make guns, we gathered scraps of wood and copper pipe about the thickness of a cigarette. Then we found a secluded place outside the camp in an empty, dilapidated building to construct and hide our weapons and ammunition. Using small saws and pocketknives, we cut each piece of wood into the shape of a handgun. When this was done, the copper pipe was cut to size, pounded closed on one end with a hammer, bent to fit the handle of the gun, and firmly attached with wire to the stock. Then a very small incision was made where the powder would be ignited with a match. The American soldiers were kind enough to provide us with gunpowder. For ammunition, we collected tiny pieces of metal.

One Saturday afternoon, six boys aged nine to twelve met at the secret place where the weaponry was stored. We loaded the guns with powder and the projectiles and proceeded into the desert with matches in hand. The vultures could always be seen gathered over some carcass not far from the camp, but they would never allow us to come too close before flapping away. Frustrated at having to chase them from one place to another, we decided to test our weaponry from a distance. On command, each one of us lit a match and placed it by the incision in the copper pipe. The guns went off with a bang almost simultaneously, scaring away the vultures. Satisfied with the success of our invention, if not with the hunt itself, we returned to camp in high spirits. The next Saturday could not come soon enough. We again went into the desert in pursuit of our imaginary Soviets and Germans. But this time, two of the weakened copper barrels backfired, and the loaded shrapnel injured the boys' hands.

Shortly after we returned, the entire camp knew what had happened. Although unscathed by the gun, I received my first and only real spanking from my sister. She was enraged by what I had done and gave me a stern lecture on how childish it was of me to play such a dangerous game, how I could have lost one or both of my eyes, and how it could have affected me for the rest of my life. She reminded me that I was the ringleader, and that if something happened to the other boys I would have been blamed. The commander in chief was then grounded, and our expeditions to the battlefield came to an end.

For the next few weeks I did my best not to offend my sister or get into any more trouble. Remembering Mother's advice about always seeking to expand one's knowledge, however, I devised another war game that I hoped would be, if not less dangerous, at least less likely to be discovered by the adults, and, I hoped, less painful on my behind if it became known. This time there would be no homemade guns. We switched to catching deadly scorpions, which was much more dangerous. I proudly became the ringleader again; it gave me a feeling of satisfaction to be in control of a dangerous situation instead of being dependent on the whims of adults and being at the mercy of unpredictable circumstances. It was a practical way of learning how to take charge of others and myself.

Playing war games with scorpions was a very different kind of challenge from the vulture game. In the Persian desert, the vultures were huge and looked menacing even from a distance. We knew they did not kill but only picked at the bones of the dead. Scorpions, in contrast, were small, hence harder to notice, and they killed by injecting venom. Although we only pretended that the scorpions were Hitler and the Germans or Stalin and the Soviets, the actual games we played were now full of real danger. If one of us were to be stung, he would likely die, because we were not close enough to the camp to get immediate medical assistance.

Having studied the behavior of scorpions in the desert, I knew that they feared water and fire. Armed with this information, we set about gathering our supplies—a can of water, a small can of gasoline, matches, and two empty cans to capture and hold the scorpions. I obtained the gasoline and matches from my American soldier friends. The problem was where to hide this equipment from my sister and others who might tell her about it. Since the camel stable was full of people, storing it there was out of the question. We decided to hide the cans in the public latrines, where no one would ever bother looking.

The scorpion war game had two versions. One was to catch the German and Soviet soldiers, the followers. The other was to catch Hitler and Stalin, the venomous leaders. The rules for each game were very different. Catching scorpions in a desert was easy if one knew how, and it did not take us long to learn. Because the surface of the desert was relatively flat, the holes that the scorpions made were highly visible, about the width of a man's finger. All we had to do was find the hole in the sand where a scorpion lived and pour in a small amount of water, then wait a few seconds for the scorpion to pop out.

When our goal was merely to capture soldiers, we could catch up to six of these poisonous creatures in an hour. We would carefully slide them into the prisoners' can without losing the ones already caught and start marching our prisoners back toward the camp. Shortly before arrival, we would let all of them loose and run as fast as we could, never killing a single one.

Capturing Hitler and Stalin was different. We let these creatures decide their own fate, just as they decided the fate of others. Once we found a scorpion hole, we would pour a circle of gasoline around it about a yard in diameter and apply a match. Because of the size of the circle, the fire from the burning gasoline would never hurt the scorpion if it stayed near the circle's center. Then we would pour water into the hole and the scorpion would rush out. It would go about four inches from the hole and would begin to explore the circle of fire in search of a safe route of escape. It would never go back into the hole because of the fear of drowning. In each case the scorpion would make a complete circle around its hole in search of a break in the fire, but never more than once; then it would stop, raise its tail, puncture its back with its stinger, and die from its own venom.

We watched this extraordinary ritual again and again but could not figure out how the scorpion knew when it had completed exactly one full circle in its search for escape, only to decide at that moment that all was lost and turn its stinger on itself. It became clear that unlike other animals, the scorpion would not fight to the death or retreat to safety; instead, overwhelmed by fear, it followed some programmed imperative and simply killed itself.

A s we were fighting our desert war games against the scorpions, the Allies were marching toward victory. We waited anxiously for each day's news as the Red Army pushed into our homeland. We heard about the home army in France, which joined the advancing Allied troops to fight the Germans, and hoped that a similar opportunity awaited our own underground force, gathered in Warsaw.

Our hearts soared when we heard in early August 1944 that Polish resistance forces, encouraged by radio appeals from the Soviet Union, had risen up against the German troops who had occupied our capital for the past five years. Then we were crushed to hear that the Soviet forces had stopped east of the Vistula River, where they waited while the Polish resistance fighters in Warsaw were ruthlessly defeated by the departing Germans. As many as two hundred thousand Poles, many of them boys my age, died during the sixty-three-day battle, after which a vengeful Hitler ordered Warsaw's destruction.

The Soviet troops, ordered by Stalin to wait until the Germans had destroyed the remnants of Polish resistance, then moved into what was left of Warsaw, flushed out the remaining Germans, and proclaimed themselves liberators of the city and of Poland. With the Red Army's occupation of Poland, it became clear to us that an Allied victory would come on

Soviet terms and at Poland's expense. It now seemed unlikely that we could ever return to a free Poland in our lifetime.

Toward the end of 1944, when the camp in Ahvaz was almost empty, Zosia arranged for our transfer from the camel stable to the barracks. There we would have a room to ourselves, two army cots, a desk, and two chairs. The room was painted white and was illuminated by a single light bulb in the center of the ceiling. Our new quarters were a great improvement over all the other places we had lived since being deported. I was looking forward to enjoying the privacy of a room as well as the comfort of sleeping on something other than wooden boards. The thought of not having my sleep constantly interrupted by the voices of other people or by the bites of bedbugs made me feel better about our situation than I had in a long time.

The move to our new quarters was simple. We gathered our blankets, our pillows, and our two suitcases, and ten minutes later the move was completed. Zosia and I talked about how nice it would be if we were instead returning home to enjoy all the comforts we once had. Yet we were thankful for having a room to ourselves.

That evening we went to sleep late, but the new surroundings kept me awake. My mind wandered aimlessly. Just before I fell asleep, I felt a tingling sensation on my neck and my spine. A short while later, the sensation moved on to my arms, legs, and crotch. The tingling increased and suddenly my body went into a brutal shiver. Was it my dreamy imagination or a reality? Half asleep, I got out of bed and stumbled to the light switch. It was not my imagination at all. Hundreds of bedbugs were crawling all over my bed sheets, the walls, and my body. Awakened by the light, Zosia jumped out of bed not realizing what had happened. She was standing with her white garments spotted with moving red dots.

"Bedbugs!" I screamed. Both of us began to frantically shake loose the slimy creatures, watching them scamper back into the crevices of our beds and behind the walls to their safe haven of darkness. Even in the camel stable, there were not nearly so many of them.

The next day we washed the cots with scalding water. Then we set all the wooden legs of the cots in cans filled with water, hoping that the bedbugs would not be able to swim to their hunting grounds. After that, we stuck Mr. Wrigley's chewing gum in as many wall crevices as we could. For a few nights, our efforts seemed to pay off. Our sleep was still disturbed, however, because our fear of the bloodsuckers kept us awake for hours.

Our success at keeping the night raiders away was short-lived. They eventually outsmarted us. One night I woke up feeling again the tingling sensation all over my body. I jumped out of bed and quickly flicked the light switch on to see where they could possibly be coming from this time. There they were on the ceiling directly over our beds, from which vantage point they could drop down on us. There seemed to be no escaping them. In the daytime, they never came out. They were afraid of the light and of being seen and killed. Some nights I would try to sleep with the light burning above, feeling its security and hoping that the attackers would be fooled. But even then sleep was not always possible because of my suspicion that the red creatures were quietly preparing to mount their next attack.

Some nights, while trying to fall asleep, I would lie in bed not stirring, listening quietly for the sounds of thousands of small feet marching across the walls, the floor, the ceiling, my bed, my covers. I would imagine them all over my body and, convinced they were on the brink of an attack, would rush to the light switch and with one flick of a finger change darkness into light and watch the night raiders rush for cover. I was desperate to hide from them—to find someplace, anyplace, to crawl away and not be seen or found. But there was no place to hide. Night after night, the bedbugs attacked. Our only option was to consider moving back to a nearly empty camel stable. At least there, the bedbugs would not drop down on us from the ceiling.

One evening, before trying to sleep, I told my sister that I was at the end of my patience and that we would get revenge by killing as many of them as we could. She was not happy about the prospects of having their blood, which was our blood, squirted all over the room and us. But exhausted from sleepless nights, I no longer cared about the squirting blood of the little devils. I wanted revenge. After failing to dissuade me, Zosia agreed to do it only to pacify me.

I went to sleep with my shoes on and a pair of sandals next to my bed. After being awakened in the middle of the night by the bloodsuckers, I woke up Zosia and flipped the light on. Hundreds of the slimy creatures ran in every direction. I went on a rampage, stamping them with my shoes, hitting them with my sandals on the walls and beds. Zosia stood watching me as if she were in a state of shock.

"Kill them!" I screamed at her.

By the time she was able to make a move, the survivors of my vengeance had escaped. The slimy red ooze of decomposed blood was smeared all over the floor, the beds, the white walls, and my shoes and legs. A putrid odor filled the room. We opened the door to let in fresh air and began a grisly cleanup. When we were done, Zosia asked me if I wanted to move back to the camel stable.

"No, but tomorrow morning I am going to sign up with the Polish Army to fight the Germans. At least the bedbugs won't get me!"

She laughed but did not comment.

In early 1945, our cousin Jean's tour of duty ended. We parted with tears but hoped to meet again soon in America (Jean's letters to her American relatives appear in the appendix). After she left, the departure of Polish refugees from our camp accelerated. It gradually came to look like a ghost town, but I did not mind. For the first time since our escape from the Soviet Union, it was a relief not to be surrounded by thousands of people at every turn. Soon there remained only a handful of refugees; except for the administrators, we were almost alone, but only for a short while.

CHAPTER 25

THE ORPHANAGE

With Jean gone and the refugee population in Ahvaz reduced to a handful, Zosia and I faced the realization that it was unlikely that there would be another ship to Mexico. We were in limbo. If we were to stay in Ahvaz, our prospects for an education would be limited to what we could learn on our own. Hearing that she was eligible for nursing courses in Tehran, Zosia applied for them, and both of us were transferred back to the tent camp north of Tehran where we had lived before. Only a handful of Poles remained there, and not a sufficient number of children my age to fill a class, so the problem we then faced was what to do with me. Zosia solved the problem by finding an orphanage in Tehran for Polish children where I could stay. It was the best solution at the time, but I was not happy about going. To me, the orphanage was more than a place for children who were orphaned. I felt it was a house for children who were the "debris" of war. I did not want to be labeled as such because I still hoped that our father and brother would come back and we would be a family again. But despite my feelings, Zosia convinced me that it was only a temporary solution and the best she could do for the time being.

From the outside, the orphanage compound appeared forbidding. The building was surrounded by a tall brick wall, and even the small window of the entrance door to the compound was closed. A huge locked gate with no windows stood almost as tall as the gates in our camel stable in Ahvaz. It was big enough for a camel to pass through. This gave me the impression that a wealthy Persian had lived there before the house was converted to an orphanage. I entered with trepidation, not knowing what to expect.

The brick house was about three times larger than most houses in Tehran. From the inside, the surrounding brick wall seemed to be twice as tall because not a single house on the outside—not even a rooftop—could be seen. The garden was filled with tall trees, and a long, paved path ran alongside the house all the way to the gate and the adjoining door. Even before being shown where I was to sleep, I was overpowered with the feeling of being a prisoner. It was a feeling similar to the one I had when the Soviets had imprisoned us in Rowne. But then I had my family with me for comfort. Now I was alone.

Two Polish women dressed neatly in blue blouses and white skirts covered with white aprons greeted me politely. They showed me to my bed near the biggest window on the first floor, overlooking the garden. The room was filled with beds all the way to the other side, where the smaller children slept near the two attendants. There were no windows at that end, so it was much darker. I could often hear the youngest cry for their mothers or fathers. I felt more sorry for these young children than for myself.

Through the window, I could look at the tall trees—and plan one day soon to climb one of them and escape over the wall. I wanted to be free again. If Mother could lead us to freedom from the Soviet Union, I should be able to find a way to escape from this place.

Everything else about the orphanage has faded into the dark corners of my mind. Was there a dining room, a playroom, a washroom? I remember nothing. Two scars remain as unwanted souvenirs from my having run into rusty nails on the tall gate while racing another boy as we played outside, where I spent most of my time.

Zosia visited me frequently, and one day in early 1945 she told me she planned to visit the British embassy in Tehran to see if there was any recent information about our father. A week later she was back, her expression grim and bitter. Without greeting me in the customary manner, she proceeded to inform me that Father had been murdered by the Soviets and buried in a mass grave. The horror of those words has never left me. I began to cry.

Zosia refused to recount the most gruesome details of how the victims were killed, but she did confirm much that we had heard two years earlier. The British embassy informed her that Father's name was on the list of more than fifteen thousand murdered Polish POWs held prisoner in the Kozelsk, Ostashkov, and Starobelsk camps. Nearly forty-two hundred, almost all officers, were identified in the Katyn Forest. About eleven thousand other POWs were still missing, their graves not yet discovered. But how, then, did the British know for sure that our father was one of the victims? Did they know something that no one else knew or was willing to talk about?

"Then is there some hope that Father is still alive?" I asked.

"There is always hope, no matter how small," she answered, though not convincingly. She continued by telling me that only a few hundred of the people stationed in those camps, those who had become puppets of Stalin or regarded as sympathetic to the Communist cause, had been seen or heard from since April 1940. My soul was torn between the longing to see my father again and the weight of the facts about his probable fate.

As Zosia finished speaking, I railed against the inhumanity of it all. "God is cruel!" I blurted out.

"Wiesiu!" she said sternly, just as Mother used to. "You know very well that to talk like that is blasphemous. Do not ever forget that you were brought up in a good Polish home. I do not want to hear you talk like that ever again." But I was no longer willing to be silent. I had to explain to my sister that God was cruel for allowing the horrors of the last five years to happen. She asserted that it was not God but people who should be blamed.

I had had my fill of listening to adults talk like this. Every time something good happened, people dropped to their knees, raised their hands to heaven in gratitude, and gave thanks to God for his goodness and his mercy, I told her. But when terrible, cruel, and inhuman things happened, it was always people who were blamed rather than God. Zosia reminded me that people had free will and thus did not have to do evil things. But so did God, I pointed out. "He, too, had a choice at the beginning to create only good people or bad people or both kinds, with or without free will. He had a choice as well whether to allow misery on this earth or not. He did create evil people, and he did allow misery and suffering on this earth. Why? For what purpose?

"Another thing we were taught at home was that God has created people in his own image," I went on, not waiting for her reply. "That has to include evil people as well, doesn't it? If you are going to believe this, then you must also believe that if God exists, he is not all good."

"Wiesiu," my sister said angrily, "we'd better stop this conversation because I see that I am not going to change your mind today." Then she started crying. What Zosia did not know was that she would be unable to change my mind that day or any other day. But the harshness of my own words shocked me.

"We cannot understand God's motives," she whispered, holding me close. "We have lost both our parents to war, and there is nothing we can do but be reassured they are together. We still have our brother and should be thankful to God for that. We should pray for Jurek's safety and a quick end to the war."

Zosia and I spent the rest of the afternoon together. When it was time for her to return to camp, we parted with deep sorrow in our hearts. After the huge wooden gate closed behind her, I went back to my bed in a room filled with other orphans. I was now truly one of them. I covered my face with a sheet to hide the tears flooding from my eyes and hoped no one would ask me what happened, especially the younger ones.

As the days went by, I grew more depressed. The tall brick walls that encircled the orphanage and the locked gates were oppressive reminders of my situation. Most of my waking hours were spent thinking of what I had lost, of my parents and the happy days in our home in Poland. Being confined to an orphanage full of sad, lonely children only deepened my sense of deprivation.

I felt driven to tell my sister that I was not going to stay there any longer, but I saw no need to wait until her next visit. When the main gate was opened for a delivery of food, I was gone.

CHAPTER 26

THE SILVER CASE

Once I was outside the wall, my spirits rose. Hidden in my shoes were my entire worldly possessions, the remainder of the money our cousin Jean had given me when she left Ahvaz to return to the United States. Though I did not speak Persian, walking alone in Tehran did not scare me. I took comfort in knowing that the Persians were a friendly people. Since I did not know when or if buses ran to the camp, I decided to rent a bicycle and follow the route with which I was somewhat familiar. I had never ridden a bicycle, and something told me I had better rent one for the entire day to allow for possible delays. Guided by key landmarks and the position of the sun, I set out toward the camp.

While within the confines of the city, I walked the bike to avoid the embarrassment of being seen falling off. Walking gave me ample opportunity to look in the display windows of the exotic shops filled with beautiful merchandise. There were Persian rugs, pots, copper goods, and artifacts from India and Africa. But the most striking of all were the numerous jewelry shops filled with the most magnificent bracelets and earrings I had ever seen. The display of such treasures brought back memories of the stories of the Arabian Nights I loved hearing as a little boy.

Looking at these wonders, I thought how nice it would be to get a present for Zosia, something charming and feminine that she would treasure. Because she was now my adopted mother, I wanted to buy her something that would last forever. Several miles up the road, I came upon a silver shop and stopped, awed by the assortment of pretty things displayed in the window. A silver powder case stood out. After finding a place out of public view to transfer half of my money from one of my shoes to my pants pocket, I entered the shop. Not able to speak Persian, I said a few words in Polish and pointed toward the case. The man brought it out and laid it on the table, watching me curiously, not knowing why a skinny little boy speaking a foreign language would want to look at a lady's powder case.

I wanted that case for Zosia even though it was surely too expensive for my pocketbook. I knew, however, that in Persia no one ever paid the price first asked for merchandise. I dug into the pocket where I had put half my money and gave it to the man. He took out paper and pencil and wrote down a number, which was twice as much as all the money I had. I took off the shoe with the rest of my money, emptied it on the counter, and pushed all of the money I had to my name toward him. He still showed me the paper with the price. I did not know what to do, so I told him the truth, as my mother had taught me to do, not stopping to think that I was not speaking his language.

I said in Polish: "I do not have any more money, but I wish to buy this as a present for my sister."

The man looked at me strangely, wrapped the silver case, took my money, and smiled. He handed me the package. I thanked him in Polish, said good-bye, and started to walk out, thrilled to have something so nice to give to my sister.

"Czekaj," the man said.

I stopped and turned, thinking he had said something to me in Persian. It sounded very familiar, almost as if he had said "stop" in Polish. He approached me, reached into his pocket, and gave me back half of the money I had paid him for the case. I was puzzled but ever so grateful.

"Idz z Bogiem," he said to me. "Go with God."

"God will reward you, sir," I answered, hardly able to believe what had just happened.

I walked out, stunned with the man's kindness and the realization that there were still good people in the world. Soon afterward I realized that this man probably understood Polish but did not reveal that to me when I entered the store. The Persians possess an affinity for languages, and many merchants had learned to speak Polish rather well since the arrival there of so many Poles.

Once out of town and having found the road leading to the camp, I took my first-ever ride on a bicycle. It was wobbly and dangerous, but it didn't matter. The silver case was pressing against my body, and I was very happy to be able to do something nice for my sister for being my guardian. I understood that she, too, was an orphan like me and was lonely for our parents.

The road leading to the camp was made of cobblestones, and riding a bicycle over it was not a prudent way to travel, especially when riding one for the first time. As I approached the camp, a passing truck nearly hit me. Trying to swerve away, I flew off the bicycle, landing on my face.

I had chipped my front tooth and my lip was bleeding from a deep cut, yet there was nothing to do but get up, check for the case, and continue riding to the camp. When I arrived, I went to the area where refugees were living in tents and rode back and forth looking for Zosia, but she spotted me first through an open flap as I rode near her tent. She ran out to greet me. Her first words rang with disbelief, not so much because of the surprise of seeing me, but rather because of how I must have looked.

"Dear God! Whatever happened to you, Wiesiu? You're covered with blood! Your lip is cut and swollen. You are bruised and battered all over!"

"Nothing as bad as you may think, Zosiu. I just fell off a bicycle and slid over the cobblestones. That's all."

She did not notice my broken front tooth until after I spoke. There was no need to tell her that I was almost killed by a truck, nor did she ask me any more questions. Instead, she told me to go inside and wait for her to come back with water and tincture of iodine.

"No iodine! I do not need it." She ignored me and left without another word.

I remembered the pain caused by iodine on small scratches and cuts. The bigger the wound the worse it hurt, with a terrible, razor-sharp burning sensation. Zosia came back with a bucket of water, iodine, and cotton. Giving orders like an army sergeant, she told me to take my shirt off and sit still. Dipping a towel in the bucket, she gently and repeatedly tapped at my scratches and badly cut lip until all the dirt and dried blood were washed off. Then she cleaned my chest. Just as I was going to remind her to skip the iodine treatment, she picked up the bottle and a swab of cotton.

"If you sit still, I will do it fast and it won't hurt so much."

I didn't want to be called a sissy, and I clenched my teeth against the pain so that I would not bite my tongue. When Zosia was finished, she said, "It wasn't so bad after all, Wiesiu, was it?"

When I declined to answer, she asked why I had appeared so unexpectedly. My answer was short.

"I am not going back to the orphanage."

She was not surprised. She knew how the news about our father's murder had affected me.

"Wiesiulku, say no more," she said, sparing me the pain of going into detail. "We will notify the camp authorities of your transfer." She also said we'd arrange for a truck to return the bicycle. I felt relieved and grateful.

I thought that this moment was as good as any to show Zosia my appreciation for her understanding and kindness. I was nervous about making such a gesture, something I had never done before, and wondered how I could do so without sounding awkward or adding to the seriousness of the situation. To ease my discomfort, I sought to lighten the moment.

"My dear sister. Since you were so nice and gentle to me today, I have a present for you."

"Do not tell me. Do not tell me. I already know what it is," she responded with a dubious smile.

Clearly, she could not mean that. She could not have the vaguest idea of the package I carried or what was in it.

"Well, if you know, tell me what it is."

"Of course, it is a bicycle."

We both started laughing. When our laughter passed and I relaxed a little, I reached into my back pocket, pulled out the little gift-wrapped package, and held it out to her.

"Thank you, Zosienko, for taking such good care of me for all this time."

Skeptical at first, she unwrapped her present and gasped in admiration at the sight of it, wondering how I could have saved enough money to buy the case. I replied that I used the money our cousin Jean had given me. Then I told her what had happened along my journey, omitting, of course, the incident with the truck.

Holding the case with both hands, Zosia promised me that she would always cherish it.

Then she opened it and looked into its mirror with obvious delight. I could see a radiant gleam in her eyes and a tender smile on her face. She looked very much like our mother.

PART VI

People without a Country

The Temple of Jupiter, with sixty-nine-foot columns, amid the Roman ruins in Baalbek near Baabdad, Lebanon, 1946. Seeing these ruins reminded us of the devastation of our own country at the hands of modern invaders during World War II.

CHAPTER 27

AT THE CROSSROADS

In February 1945, Roosevelt, Churchill, and Stalin met again, this time at Yalta, and it became ever more clear that Poland would remain in the Soviet sphere after the war. A little more than a month later, Roosevelt was dead.

In May, the war ended in Europe. To us it was bittersweet news. We were happy that the war was finally over but sad because in July the Allies recognized the Communist regime in Poland, which had been handpicked by Stalin. It meant that we could not go back to a free Poland. By the end of August, Truman and Churchill, meeting again with Stalin, this time at Potsdam, had finished giving away our nation. Again we cried. As the months passed, more details came out. Because the Soviets took over Poland immediately after the war, the Polish army that had fought in Italy and North Africa was not allowed to return home fully armed. Instead, the British allowed the Polish Corps to demobilize in Britain.

Jurek wrote to us from Italy that he would stay on there for a while guarding German prisoners. Shortly afterward he followed the Polish troops to London and began working for the Polish Resettlement Corps, which was organized by the British to help resettle disbanded Polish soldiers.

In the fall, Zosia and I learned that the Polish people still in Persia would be leaving for Lebanon, then still a French territory. This move was prompted by the threat that the Soviets, even after the war was over, would occupy Persia and trap the remaining Polish refugees. The government of Lebanon agreed to accept us, and the British arranged our transportation.

Once again, we had to prepare to leave one foreign country for another. With Father and Mother dead, and Jurek by now in England, there were only two of us to prepare for the next step of our family's odyssey. We left in November. We were given passports and visas, and the camp authorities loaded us onto a train to begin the trip. The first leg was back through Ahvaz and on to Basra, Iraq. The train made its way through the spectacular Zagros Mountains, traveling through 147 tunnels and crossing and recrossing the winding, muddy Karun River. Pulled by a coal-fired locomotive, our train was frequently enveloped in sulfur fumes that made our eyes water and breathing difficult. We found ourselves in the good company of American soldiers. They drank beer, sang, and were in a festive mood. These defenders of freedom had a good reason to be happy. They were going home.

In Ahvaz, after a layover, we proceeded by rail to Khorramshahr, where we switched to buses for a short ride to Basra and there boarded a narrow-gauge train destined for the fabled city of Baghdad. Along the way we passed the Euphrates River, which flows from Turkey through Syria and Iraq to join the Tigris. As we neared Baghdad, I grew more excited at the prospect of seeing the setting for so many of my favorite childhood stories. I hoped to see some of the beautiful Arabian stallions and their riders with swords and daggers covered with precious stones. Nor could I wait to see the beautiful Arabian women and the belly dancers so exotically portrayed in the American movies I had watched at the base in Ahvaz.

We arrived in Baghdad and after a rest were taken for a tour of the city. Though my imagination was filled with tales of the Arabian Nights, the world we encountered was quite different. We drove through an old, dirty city devoid of vegetation with narrow streets and shabby houses. Then we visited the main bazaar, where many Arab men sat outside drinking coffee and playing games unfamiliar to us. Mostly they sat in front of establishments apparently designated strictly for men, where they had their evening social life and entertainment. Surely, I thought, that is where beautiful women danced, as in the American movies. To my surprise there were very few women in the bazaar. The ones we did see all wore black chadors and walked several steps behind the men they were with. To my disappointment, I could not see whether they were beautiful because their faces were covered.

The crowded bazaar was typical of those we had seen in Persia. It had extremely narrow streets crowded with shops and stalls overflowing with various kinds of merchandise. Some carried expensive cooking utensils, most of which were made of copper. Some carried a wide variety of imported items, hand-carved from ivory. Some carried a variety of swords and knives studded with what had to be inexpensive stones, yet these at least looked as real to me as those I imagined from the adventure stories. Other shops carried a wide assortment of gold bracelets and other jewelry, much of it imported from India. More than anything, this display of finery left the girls and women in our group breathless. There were shops with beautiful handcrafted rugs from the region and other places, so expensive that we could not imagine owning one. Others offered an array of exotic spices and a wide variety of mouth-watering fresh fruits and vegetables. Still others displayed freshly butchered lamb carcasses hanging on hooks, waiting to be cut to order.

After a three-day stay in Baghdad we entered the tiny and extremely uncomfortable train cars owned by the Baghdad Company and continued our journey to Beirut. We sat on narrow wooden benches and each morning were given a day's supply of food, mainly sandwiches and fruit.

Between Baghdad and Syria lies a desert varying in texture between sand and minimal vegetation. As we traveled through this desert, we passed many oases where Arabs lived. Though the oases had date palms and other vegetation, they were surrounded completely by great stretches of golden sand, and I wondered how people could survive there and what their sources for food and water were. How did they make a living? Soon enough I had at least part of the answer. The train stopped at several of the oases, and though we were not allowed to get off, at every stop young mothers with babies in their arms and young naked children, their skin burned by the scorching sun, ran to the train to beg for food and whatever else they could get. We shared with these people the food we received on the train.

After a tortuous journey through part of Turkey and Aleppo, Syria, Zosia and I arrived in Beirut exhausted. We and the other refugees were taken to previously assigned villages throughout Lebanon. My sister and I were taken with a busload of others to a town named Ghazir in the mountains northeast of Beirut. We were provided with temporary quarters and with identification and subsistence cards issued by the United Nations Relief and Rehabilitation Administration. My serial I.D. number was 2647. Eventually the total number of Polish refugees in Lebanon rose to about fifty-three hundred. The monetary allowance was sufficient for food, clothing, and shelter. After the administrative details were finished, Zosia and I enrolled in a school run by Polish refugee teachers.

Soon afterward, we rented a room in a house on the side of a hill, about a twenty-minute walk from the center of the town, where our school was located. About one hundred yards from the peak of the hill, above where we were living, stood a towering statue of Jesus beautifully painted in gold and blue. At the base of the statue, we could see below us, to the southwest, the ancient city of Beirut, as well as Jounie Bay and the clear blue waters of the Mediterranean reflecting the golden rays of the equatorial sun and the pale blue sky. By day, we could see the red roofs of the white houses that made up much of the city and the date and orange trees and the vineyards that surrounded them and spread far away into the hills. At night, we could see the lights of the city and most of the villages spread throughout the crescent of Lebanon.

Standing next to the statue of Jesus, we could feel the divine presence from the very beginning. With his outstretched arms he appeared to be watching over not only our town but the rest of Lebanon—even the rest of the world. It was such a powerful feeling that when someone asked us where we lived, we would say "under Christ," taking comfort in thinking that Jesus was watching over us.

Still, disturbing news continued to reach us that confirmed what we had heard earlier—that Poland would not be restored as a free nation. Our dreams of returning to a free Poland vanished completely when the details surfaced about the agreements reached at the Tehran and Yalta Conferences and later the Potsdam Conference. It became increasingly clear to me that no matter where one may go on this earth, no matter how beautiful and peaceful a place one may live in, a person always carries with him the joy and sadness that lie in his heart and soul. Despite living among the kind and peaceful people of Ghazir—and being surrounded by places of worship—my soul was again filled with confusion, not only about the human race but also about God. Each day as I left or returned to the house I looked up at the statue of Jesus looming above. My doubts about his goodness grew as my faith waned. Yet I found myself playing out a strange ritual. Climbing alone up the hill to sit beneath the statue, I would recite verses from a ballad my mother had taught me titled "Father's Return," written by Poland's most famous romantic poet, Adam Mickiewicz. It tells of a mother's begging her children to go to the pillar on the hill and there, before a miraculous picture, to pray for their father's safe return. In the ballad, it is the power of their prayers that saves the children's father. My visits to the statue were my attempt not only to save my father and bring him back by some miracle of prayer, or to feel closer to my mother, but also to rekindle my faith.

We lived in Ghazir for about nine months, until Zosia finished her college preparatory classes. She was then accepted into a subsidized program for refugee students at American University in Beirut. The course covered Polish language, humanities, and history. It was taught in Polish, like the other classes we had sporadically taken since leaving the Soviet Union. The authorities who set up the program hoped the students would return to Poland as teachers. Before deciding to take the classes, Zosia was careful to confirm that agreeing to the program did not make returning to Communist Poland compulsory.

As in Persia, the question we then had to face was what would happen to me. Zosia was required to live in the university dormitories, where no children were allowed. She was determined not to place me in an orphanage, remembering my unhappiness in the orphanage in Tehran. After a considerable search, she found a Polish school principal and his wife in the ancient village of Baabdad who agreed to look after me. The town had a Polish school for me to attend and was only about fourteen miles east of Beirut in the mountains. My monthly expenses were covered by my United Nations relief allotment. The arrangement was not ideal, but I much preferred it to any kind of orphanage or cadet school in Palestine.

Zosia managed to work out a deal with the principal and his wife, who lived on the school premises, to let me use one of the many empty rooms on the second floor. It was agreed that three times a day I would join them for meals and that the principal's wife would wash my clothes. For my part, I was expected to observe a reasonable curfew and account for my whereabouts. Other than that, I was responsible for myself. Although they proved to be a very nice couple, staying in this huge stone building, empty every night except for the two people on the floor below, was spooky. Moreover, I again felt isolated, which only heightened my sense of guilt and shame at being an orphan. I realized that there was nothing I could have done to save my mother, yet I could not rid myself of guilt for not being able to see her one last time. Nor could I shake the sense of myself as someone destined always to belong nowhere, to no one.

About a year and a half passed uneventfully in Lebanon. All the while I searched for news of my father, and I clung to the hope that the Communists in Poland would somehow be kicked out and our lands regained from the Soviets so that our family could return to Sarny.

One Saturday in the late spring or early summer of 1947, I was alone in my dimly lit second-floor room, doing my homework, when a gentle knock on the door broke the silence and a familiar voice called my name. My sister was paying me an unexpected visit, for when school was in session we were unable to see much of each other.

"Come in, Zosienko," I called out, my usual response when I had not seen her for a while. Zosia opened the door and we ran to each other and hugged. To my surprise, she cut off our usual routine of greetings rather abruptly and then announced the purpose of her visit. She told me that something unexpected had come up and that we had to make a decision that would affect us for the rest of our lives. She paused as if trying to organize her thoughts and told me to sit down. My heart was pounding. What could possibly be of such importance after all we had gone through in the past seven years? We had escaped imprisonment in the Soviet Union and the war was over. And though our parents were dead and we were without a home, surely the worst was behind us.

Zosia sat on the edge of my bed while I grabbed the only chair in my room and pulled it up opposite her. She told me that the UN subsidies we had been receiving were going to stop. As a result, we were left with only two options for relocating and starting a new life. One was to return to Poland. She said that for some time a delegation of Polish Communists, now in Beirut, had traveled throughout the world trying to convince Poles who had escaped from the Soviet Union to return home. I stood up in disbelief and anger at what was immediately clear to me to be the real reason why they now wanted us back. We were the living witnesses to the brutality of life in "the workers' paradise" and the evils of Communism. I remembered what the old Russian, Mr. Petrovich, had told me: "The Communists would rather kill you than let you go because they are afraid of other people finding out how we live." (We found out many years later that thousands were coming back from Soviet captivity as late as 1956.)

The other option, she said, was to move to England, where Jurek was still working in the Polish Resettlement Corps. All refugees with relatives in the Polish Army under British command were eligible to go there and would be provided with passage, a place to stay, and temporary assistance until they were able to provide for themselves. If we chose to immigrate later to another country, the British would help with that as well.

My unease was becoming more obvious as I paced the room. Zosia paused. Then, with a note of regret in her voice, she said that unless something changed soon, these were our only choices, and that although she did not like them, either, we had to pick one or the other before too long. I stopped and stared past my sister, my thoughts tumbling around in my head. There was so much to consider and so much at stake. What would happen if we made the wrong decision? What would happen if Zosia and I were to choose differently? Then there was Jurek to think about. What would he decide?

Seeing my hesitation, Zosia touched my arm and suggested that we wait before making a decision. But I insisted that we decide now, before she returned to Beirut. Besides, there were things that had been on my mind for a long time, and I wanted to get them off my chest. I told her that I was fed up with being a vagabond, with living in foreign places—even in beautiful Lebanon—with not knowing what the next day would bring and what would become of us. "At age fourteen I live in an almost empty stone building on the second floor all by myself, like a hermit," I said. "I am lonely, and I miss my mother. This is no way for anyone to live, not even an adult."

Tears formed in my sister's eyes, and I stopped talking. Zosia embraced me and said nothing for a long time. Then she told me that she felt the same way, that she was sorry for us both. But, she wondered, did this mean that I wanted to return to Poland, even if we could not go back to Sarny?

No, I replied, I just wanted her to know how I felt—and how painful a decision this was going to be. I pointed out that we lost our home and country when the Communists deported us, then we lost it all again when the Allies, with whom the Poles had fought for a free world, sold us out to the Soviets. The war had been over for two years, yet Polish refugees the world over simply sat waiting for a miracle to happen. "Now we are told we have two choices: go back to Poland and live under Soviet-controlled Communism or go to yet another foreign country and live with the people whose government had sold us out," I said with indignation rising in my voice. "What kind of a choice is that? There is no justice on this earth!"

Zosia listened intently, saying nothing. Thinking about the war always made me angry, and I had much more to say, but what would be the point? After all, she was my sister and had suffered as much as I had.

Regretting my outburst, I told Zosia that I did not want to go to Poland or to England. Zosia reminded me that we could not stay in Lebanon much longer. A decision had to be made.

I took a deep breath, then told her that I could never choose to live in another Communist country, not even Poland. I reminded her that our father died in the name of freedom, and our mother died leading us to freedom from our Soviet captors. We needed to stay free at all costs. At least England was a free country, and Jurek was there. If Zosia wanted to go to England, then we should both go and join him. Zosia's eyes became misty again. I was unable to read her response to all I had said but was relieved at having told the truth about how I felt. She told me again that she felt the same way I did—and at least from England it would be easier to join our relatives in America and make a new start.

The tension in the room was broken. We both felt relief at being in agreement about what we should do, and the details about our departure from Lebanon would be learned later. We descended the stairs and stepped out into the bright sunshine, but with the nagging realization that soon we would again be traveling to yet another foreign country. The home we had in Poland was lost; a new home was yet to be found.

Z osia and I were scheduled to board the British transport ship *Samaria* in late January 1948 at Port Said, Egypt, bound for Liverpool. The ship was to carry British military personnel stationed in the Middle East and Polish refugees. Before leaving, all travelers had to be tested for a variety of diseases. If a person was infected, he or she could not leave until cured. To accommodate the Poles leaving Lebanon for England, the British Army set up a testing compound in Beirut administered by British medics.

We had to wait a few days for the results of all the tests and, after being given a clean bill of health, were ready to be on our way. On departure day, we boarded buses to travel through Palestine, then still under British occupation. Because bands of Arabs and Jews were fighting, the drivers had to be vigilant. Indeed, we had to start the trip twice because our first attempt was turned back when it became clear that we would be going through an area where more fighting had just broken out. Once under way, we passed through Palestine and Jerusalem. The land was of clay, sand, and rock, scorched by the sun and a stark contrast to the lush beauty of Lebanon.

When we crossed into Egypt, we saw little but more sand and sun-scorched earth. Eventually we reached the Suez Canal, which teemed with British troops and Egyptians hard at work. Zosia and I remained there for three days in a transit camp near the town of Ismailiya, waiting for the transport ship to arrive in Port Said on the Mediterranean. When the *Samaria* did arrive, we were taken to the port, and we boarded the ship together with British soldiers returning home. Thus my sister and I embarked on yet another voyage by sea to another foreign country. Fortunately, we were accompanied by Iwona and her parents.

Zosia and I bid the Middle East good-bye with mixed emotions. We were leaving the continent where ancient Egyptians, Persians, Greeks, and Romans had built beautiful pyramids, towns, temples, monuments, viaducts, and bridges that remain for today's and future generations to marvel at. We were returning to twentieth-century Europe, a continent all but destroyed by war and left in chaos. The trip to England was uneventful except for a terrible storm near Malta, though the voyage took many days longer than had our earlier crossing of the Caspian Sea. We sailed the length of the Mediterranean, past the African coast, Gibraltar, Portugal, France, and the English channel, retracing the sailing lanes of thousands of trading and military ships through the centuries, including those of the invincible Spanish Armada.

During that journey I had plenty of time to think about where we were going and where we had been. I reflected on what we had lost and the harsh realities that life imposed on us, and I wondered whether there was a place on this earth with good and kind people, where there was justice, where there was peace, where there was love. I carried my home in my heart and found a way to escape there for comfort—in times of doubt, for wisdom; in times of fear, for courage; in times of loneliness, for love. And yet I began to recognize a longing to live fully in the present, to find a place I could call home, and to be free of the urge to live in the past.

CHAPTER 28

"WHERE THE SUN NEVER SETS"

As the *Samaria* approached England, I grew anxious about the kind of welcome we might receive. Although England had suffered considerable damage during the war, the British Empire was still a world power, so vast that it was often referred to as the place "where the sun never sets." It was composed of more than fifty colonies, dominions, dependencies, protectorates, mandates, and trust territories. The reach of the empire stretched from the British Isles around the globe, through Egypt and the Suez Canal, Palestine, Iraq, South Africa, Pakistan, India, Australia, New Zealand, Hong Kong, Singapore, Canada, and Newfoundland. It controlled resources necessary to meet every imaginable human need, and just as important, Britain's fleet was able to deliver the goods. I was convinced that the might of the British Empire was still such that the English would not long suffer from the effects of the war, at least in terms of meeting basic needs. I was equally convinced that England, with the help of the British Commonwealth of Nations, would be the first country in Europe to be rebuilt.

Zosia and I could see the lights on the shores of England. Soon we would step onto land as invited guests of the great empire, though it was an invitation I would accept with mixed emotions. The *Samaria* docked at Liverpool on a cold and foggy February evening in 1948. Having spent years in the hot climates of the Middle East, we did not welcome this change in the weather. After disembarking, we were taken to a transient refugee camp near Liverpool to await transfer to another camp. We were assigned to corrugated steel Quonset huts, which we later called half-barrels because of their semicircular shape. All I had on my skinny, cold, and trembling body was clothing that was adequate for the heat of the Middle East but certainly not for winter in England. And even though it was freezing outside, the hut Zosia and I were assigned to had practically no heat. We were each given an army cot and two blankets. Later, I learned that these Quonset huts were built primarily for Allied air force personnel during the war.

As we shivered from the cold throughout the night, we could not believe the lack of winter clothing and sleeping gear. Even used army clothes and blankets would have been welcome. The next day our ration consisted of a small scoop of potatoes, cabbage, figs, white bread, margarine, and tea. Although our first night on British soil was a cold and miserable experience, we tried to rationalize it as being only for a day or two.

After a few days, the British military shipped us to another temporary camp, but conditions there were just as bad. Again we were housed in Quonset huts with little or no heat. We still did not have suitable winter clothing or sleeping gear. There had to be warehouses full of blankets, winter clothes, and other cold-weather gear somewhere. For breakfast, we were given two slices of white bread with marmalade, margarine, and tea. For dinner and supper we had a scoop of mashed potatoes, a wedge of boiled cabbage, two slices of white bread, two dried figs, and tea. A few days on this diet left me, a growing teenager, progressively hungrier. Our reception was so contrary to what we expected that our disenchantment quickly turned from frustration into anger. As the mothers, wives, children, brothers, and sisters of Polish soldiers who had fought and died for England, we felt we should have received better treatment.

About three weeks after our arrival in England, we received a letter from Jurek saying that he would be coming for a visit. I had not seen him in five years, and the news made me feel both exuberant and apprehensive. The last time we had met had been in a foreign country after the death of our mother. Now we were about to meet in another foreign country, this time after having to admit against all hope that our father had been murdered.

On the day arranged for his visit, on hearing the anxiously awaited knock at the door, Zosia and I ran to open it and joyously embraced our brother before he could set down his suitcase and held him. Then we stepped back to look at one another while wiping the tears with the backs of our hands. Jurek was dressed in civilian clothes, unlike some of the Polish soldiers who came to meet their families. His expression was serious. Under his right cheekbone I could see a thick scar from shrapnel that was never taken out. He looked much older and more subdued than the soldier we had seen in Persia. From the moment I set eyes on him, I knew he was not the same man we had known before.

Jurek set the suitcase next to the table, straightened himself, and took a long look at my sister and me. He told Zosia what a beautiful woman she had become and gave her another long embrace and kisses. Then he put his arm around me and admitted that I had grown so much that had we passed each other on the street he probably would not have recognized me. We asked him dozens of questions, but Jurek was hesitant to answer. Instead, he opened the suitcase, took out two English wool sweaters, and laid them out on the table for us. We thanked him profusely. Then we apologized with embarrassment for not having been able to buy a gift for him.

Late that afternoon, Jurek took us to the closest English pub for fish and chips. The light was dim inside and we could smell the heavy odor of beer and fish. Four men were playing darts, and others were sitting by a heavy wooden bar drinking beer from mugs, talking and laughing loudly. Some sat at the tables, drinking and eating. The place was so noisy that we could hardly hear ourselves talk. Jurek decided to get three orders to go, and we went back to our Quonset hut.

After enjoying what was for Zosia and me the novelty of an English dinner, we sat around making small talk. It became progressively obvious that we were avoiding subjects weighing heavily on our minds and hearts. I was growing ever more uncomfortable. The man sitting with us, whom I loved but had not seen for the past five years—a third of my life—seemed in some ways like a stranger, and I hesitated to ask him about what I was most interested in learning: the fate of the Polish officers who were unaccounted for in the Soviet Union. Instead I asked him another question that had been of great interest to me for the past two and a half years. I wanted to know how he and the other Polish soldiers felt when they learned after the war that Churchill and Roosevelt had betrayed them and the cause they had been fighting for. Jurek had seemed withdrawn during the visit, but after hearing my question, blood rushed to his face and his eyes widened. He stood up and straightened his back while looking directly at me.

"Are you really sure you want to know how I feel?" he asked.

"Yes," I said, though I suddenly had the distinct feeling that I should not have asked that question. Still, I very much wanted to know.

Jurek agreed to tell me, "only because there is a lesson to be learned from it." He hesitated as if searching for words, then spoke passionately.

The Polish Army was betrayed, cheated, and insulted by the Western Allies. When the army was badly needed in Italy and in England, Western generals and politicians bestowed high praise on the Poles for their bravery and contribution to the war effort. But when the war was over and our army was no longer needed, what did we get in return?

All the Allied armies returned home, but the Polish Army was not allowed to go home for fear that this would offend the Soviets and hinder the Soviet takeover of Poland. In the history of warfare, had there ever been a time when a victorious army had not been allowed to return to its homeland? "Never," Jurek said, answering his own question. "The British government did not even have the decency to invite a representative unit of the Polish Army to march in its London victory parade—also for fear of offending the Soviets." Imagine having fought as a soldier, only to find out after the war that your own allies were more concerned about appeasing Stalin than honoring those who had fought and died to ensure a victory. How would you feel?

Zosia and I remained silent while Jurek spoke, although I could tell that she was becoming concerned about him as he grew more and more agitated. Jurek went on to tell us of disenfranchised Polish soldiers who had thought all along that they were fighting for their country's freedom. These same soldiers were the first to fly the Polish flag on the monastery of the supposedly invincible Monte Cassino. But they had all been deceived. When victory over the Germans was achieved, their own country's freedom was lost.

"At the end," Jurek said, "when our usefulness was over and we were left without a country, the British tried to redeem themselves by inviting us to England."

At this, Zosia broke in and asked Jurek to sit down. Surprised by the interruption, he hesitated for a few seconds and then sat down reluctantly. Zosia pointed out that England was the only country to offer refuge after the war. Shouldn't the English get some credit for this, despite what happened? Yes, Jurek conceded, and we should be grateful for their generosity. "On the other hand," he said, "we cannot ignore how this generosity balances on the scale of justice opposite their betrayal of us. How do they balance, I ask you?"

Once the Polish Army arrived in England, he continued, the soldiers were caught in the paradox of ostensibly living on friendly soil yet feeling that they lived among people who were not their true friends. Jurek reiterated his sense that the British had merely extended this gesture of hospitality as a way to ease their guilt. He looked at us and said, "Now both of you know how I feel about what happened."

Zosia leaned over and put her arms around him. My heart also ached for him. This was the first and only time we would talk about this subject. I wished that I had not asked him to do so.

With the coming of spring in 1948, we were transported to a permanent camp southeast of Liverpool called Five Oaks, where conditions improved, mostly in line with the more comfortable weather. Here we were sheltered in barracks, and Zosia and I had a unit to ourselves. Our daily diet was slightly improved.

One afternoon a few weeks after our arrival, I was studying alone—there was no school in the camp—while Zosia was visiting a girlfriend. A firm knock on the door surprised me. "It's open," I called out, curious as to who it might be. A slender young man clad in the dress uniform of a Polish Army officer stepped in. He wore a beret with the Polish eagle in front and a small red and white flag stitched on the side. His uniform was decorated with Polish, British, and Italian medals. The most outstanding one, which I recognized on sight, was the Virtuti Militari—the highest medal awarded by the Polish government for outstanding valor in battle. What could he possibly want with me?

My visitor asked whether my name was Wiesiu Adamczyk. I responded that it was, astonished that he knew my name. He asked how I was. My mind raced in an effort to place the visitor, but I was still drawing a blank. The best I could do was to answer that I was fine. Seeing my confusion, the officer continued.

"You do not remember me?"

"I am very sorry, sir, but I do not. I apologize." Where could I possibly have seen this officer and yet have no recollection of him? He came closer and extended his hand to shake mine. He told me that the last time we saw each other was about seven years earlier in Semiozersk. Then he was wearing Russian peasant clothing and looked disheveled. Maybe this was why I did not remember him. Then it struck me. I recalled his visiting our hut once in a while and then leaving with my brother to join the Polish Army in October 1941. It seemed ages ago.

"Are you Mr. Mietek?" I asked.

"Yes, I am Mietek Kaminski."

He gave me a hug. At that moment, the door opened and my sister stepped into the room. I noticed her first, because Mietek had his back to the door, and announced to her that we had a very special guest. Surprised as I was, she, too, was at a loss for words. Mietek turned to greet her, clicked his heels in the customary manner of Polish gentlemen, bowed slightly, and kissed her extended hand. Zosia beamed. Then after only a brief hesitation, she exclaimed, "Mietek!" They hugged each other. Then Zosia said, "Thank God you survived!"

I was mystified. My sister was immediately thanking God that Mietek had survived, yet I could hardly remember him. I wondered how well Zosia had known him in Semiozersk. And the hand kissing? Was it a play on my sister's vanity? The last time they had seen each other, Zosia had been hardly more than a skinny teenager. I glanced at my sister and realized, not for the first time, what an attractive woman she had become. As it turned out, that afternoon marked the blossoming of a romance.

As Mietek saw more and more of Zosia, I worried at first, not knowing what his intentions were. I could not help feeling protective of my sister. After all, we had been looking out for each other throughout our long journey together. I even resorted to obvious efforts to slow the course of nature. When Mietek visited, using every reasonable pretense, I would arrange to accompany them everywhere they went; when they wanted to stay home, I would be particularly busy studying. Despite my obstacles, he soon proposed.

Zosia and Mietek were married on September 4, 1948. Jurek came from London to give our sister away. Mietek's parents, who had also escaped from the Soviet Union, came for the ceremony. The only non–family member who attended the wedding was Zosia's best friend from Persia and Lebanon, Iwona Gronkowska. Though a wedding gown was well beyond our means, Zosia looked beautiful in a simple suit with a white hat. Mietek wore his full dress uniform decorated with all the medals he had received during the war. The wedding party went to a priest's office for a short service, and then the seven of us went out for a wedding dinner. We wished the newlyweds the very best and drank to their love, happiness, and health.

With Zosia married and Jurek working in an office in London, we had to address the question of where I could live and go to school. There was no school in our camp, but we learned that there was a high school for Polish boys at Beccles, a camp northeast of London. Classes were taught in Polish, though surprisingly English was not offered. Still, this was my only opportunity to continue my frequently interrupted education.

A few months after my arrival, the school at Beccles disbanded. Many of us were then sent to a camp in Bottisham, near Cambridge, which was another Polish school for boys that had been organized in December 1948. It had one chapel, an infirmary, and a common eating area, and it housed about six hundred boys. We learned from Polish teachers, from Polish books, and in the Polish language. We each wore flannel pants and blazers. Our curfew was 10:00 P.M.

Living conditions at Bottisham were about the same as at Beccles except that the boys with whom I shared a Quonset hut were better behaved. For my second winter on English soil, I lived with practically no heat. Although each hut was allotted one bucket of coal every two or three days, it was far too meager a ration to keep the steel hut warm. In the evening we would light our little stove in the middle of the hut and then gather around it trying to warm up. When the day's ration of coal was spent, we all went to our cots, covering up with the three worn blankets each person had been issued, vainly attempting to keep out the cold. If you were able to sleep, you could pretend that the heat had lasted all night. By now, all of us were experts at such make-believe. We joked about how in the Soviet Union we had used sleep as a way to escape the pangs of hunger. Now we went to sleep early and piled on the blankets in hopes of preserving the heat gained from the stove. It was ironic how in some ways little had changed. We were fed mostly herring, boiled eggs, jam, cabbage, dried figs, a scant amount of white bread, and occasionally milk; once a week we were given a thin slice of meat, and once in a great while we had fresh fruit.

To supplement our meager diet, I found a rather desperate but practical solution. In spring hundreds of pigeons nested in the oak trees of a nearby forest. A few of us made frequent evening trips to catch the young birds. We would climb the trees, kill the young pigeons, and cook them in a metal can scavenged from the kitchen's garbage heap. As revolting an act as this was, after listening to my stomach growl day after day, I became more concerned with my own health than that of the birds.

One day while I was lying on my bed studying, a young man about my age was brought into the hut by a camp administrator and assigned to a cot close to mine. He introduced himself to me as Christopher Flizak, although his Polish first name was Krzysztof. From this point on, I called him Chris. He also had been at Beccles, though we had not met there, and after that camp closed he had spent some time with his parents before coming to Bottisham. Before the war, he and his family had lived in a rustic area of eastern Poland, where his father served as a regular army officer. As with my family, they were prime candidates for deportation to the Soviet Union as "enemies of the people." Chris's odyssey from his home in Poland to England was very similar to mine. We became bosom buddies for life.

In the meantime, I began to experience incapacitating sinus attacks for the first time. I blamed this affliction on the change of climate from the heat of the Middle East to the cold and damp atmosphere of England

and on the conditions under which we lived. The attacks were so severe as to leave me unable to breathe through my nose or sleep at night. I first sought out the doctor who served the camp. When his prescribed treatments failed to work, he sent me to a specialist at a hospital in Cambridge. Because I went alone and was still unable to read or speak English, I could make no sense of the many forms they gave me to fill out. So I waited and waited, feeling worse and worse. After about three hours, a doctor examined me and then tried without success to show me using hand signs the nature of the procedure he intended to do. A nurse brought a washbasin of warm water and some medical equipment, one glance at which was enough to nearly scare me to death. She held a half-foot-long syringe attached on one end to a wooden handle. A two-foot-long piece of rubber tubing with an aspirating bulb was connected to the side of the needle. I still had no clear idea of what was intended and was filled with suspicion and fear. The doctor inserted the needle up through my nostril until it touched the sinus wall. He slowly raised his right hand next to the wooden handle and then suddenly slammed his hand against it. I felt a stabbing pain as the needle punctured my sinus wall. "God save me," I said under my breath. Then the nurse flushed the inside of the sinus cavity with warm water, which produced a strange and horrible sensation. I could hear and feel water swishing around inside my head. The doctor repeated the procedure on the other side. All the while I was cursing under my breath in Polish, Russian, and what little Arabic I knew.

When the doctor had finished, I felt better for about fifteen seconds. Then my head began to feel like an expanding balloon, and I still had the eerie sensation of water swishing around my brain. I had to leave right away, however, to catch the bus back to Bottisham. By the time I reached the bus stop, I again could not breathe through my nose. My head was pounding and I felt a hundred times worse than I did before the treatment.

About a week later, when I was feeling better, I took Chris aside and told him confidentially that we were going to take charge of and improve our situation. The things we needed most were food, heat, and female company. Chris agreed wholeheartedly. Of the three, finding girls was the easiest. We began to sneak out of the camp without permission to meet English girls in Cambridge. Once we had made contacts, we arranged dates for after-curfew hours, because it was easier to leave camp undetected in the darkness. Neither Chris nor I spoke English, but we soon discovered—as any soldier who has served in a foreign country can attest—that communication was possible using the common language of touching, feeling, and kissing. Not having a place to meet in private, we chose the only secluded spot—near the Cam River Bridge.

The problem of lack of heat was solved rather easily, once we put our minds to it. A short distance away from our Quonset hut was a fenced-in storage yard piled high with coal. There was no need to cut the locks or climb the tall wire mesh fence. Instead, we found an inconspicuous spot and cut a hole with a pair of wire cutters we had bought in Bottisham. From that day on, we had at least one bucket of coal a day.

The third problem, and the one that proved hardest to solve, was lack of food. There were two food supply bunkers serving the kitchen for the entire camp. During the war, they had served as bomb shelters and were covered with a heavy layer of dirt on which grass had grown. Each bunker had only one entrance, which was always securely locked. With a wink, I told Chris that he and I, coming from good Polish homes with solid religious backgrounds, were not the type to break locks.

"You are right, Wiesiu. That would be breaking and entering, and neither of us was raised to do such a thing."

We climbed on top of one of the bunkers to see what other means of entry might be available and promptly discovered two escape hatches. We tried one to see if it could be opened and found to our amazement that all we had to do was lift the cover. In the moonlight, we saw boxes of food stacked almost to the ceiling.

Chris and I returned to our hut to consider the problem of getting in and out of the bunker without being caught. We decided to enlist an accomplice, someone who was completely reliable and trustworthy. We chose a small boy also assigned to our Quonset hut. Because he had no family, we figured that he needed more help than most of the others and felt that he would be dependable. When we took him into our confidence, he readily agreed to join us and promised to keep our activities secret. The following night we proceeded on our first mission. Our new conspirator stood guard a block away ready to give a prearranged warning signal. I remained on top of the bunker to lower Chris inside and then to pull him out when the job was finished. It took Chris about seven minutes to learn what was stored in the bunker and where it was kept. We came away with bread, cheese, and dried figs, which we ate immediately.

After the success of our first venture, we went back regularly, though no more often than every ten days so as not to arouse suspicion. Our take was usually much the same, though occasionally we found apples and oranges as well. We became so adept at what we were doing that we could get in and out of the bunker in a couple of minutes, but we always took only as much food as we could finish at one time.

With extra food and heat, our plight certainly improved, but at the expense of our consciences. One day during our usual walk around the premises, the subject of our moral dilemma came up, as it did frequently in those days. I suggested that we exercise one of three options to resolve it. One was to let our consciences guide us. We could stop stealing food and coal and stay hungry and cold. Another option was to continue what we were doing and, on getting our first jobs, repay the British treasury the entire cost of food and coal we had taken. Chris listened attentively, but before I could explain the third option, he threw both hands in the air and with a slight smirk on his face commanded me to stop. He said he was willing to bet everything in his pockets that the next option would be nothing more than another one of my satirical jokes.

I replied that for one thing he could not bet anything because between the two of us we did not even have "a leaky pot to piss into." Even so, I was not joking. The third option would be a pure and simple financial transaction, like the ones banks have with one another and with their customers. "To best understand it," I said, "imagine you have a line of credit with the British treasury."

"I knew it," he interrupted again. "You are talking plain silliness. First you tell me that you and I do not have a pot to piss into and now you tell me we have a line of credit with the British treasury? This is nuts."

"Oh, yes we do, much more than you think," I answered.

"Wiesiu, you've had enough fun for one day, that's enough. Just drop the subject."

I let a moment go by, then asked him in a quiet voice whether I would ever lie to a friend. "No," he said. Then I described the third option.

Suppose someone steals all of your possessions and burns your house down. Overnight, you become penniless and homeless. In due time, you learn that it was your friend, the shopkeeper, who did these things to you. Still pretending to be your friend, he allows you to put up a tent in his backyard. Now, you know that this act of so-called kindness is motivated by reasons other than compassion, or he would not have stolen your possessions in the first place. It is wintertime, and you are hungry and cold. Desperate, you enter the man's store, take a loaf of bread, and walk out. For a second, put aside the legality of what you have just done. Did you steal the loaf of bread, or did you simply take back a tiny portion of what the man took from you? Would it matter if you told the shopkeeper that he could pay himself for the bread from the money he stole from you?

Chris's face grew serious as he reflected on what I said. Then, in an animated tone, he told me that my analogy was flawed.

"How?" I asked.

"It is not Churchill and Roosevelt who stole our possessions, but Stalin," Chris answered in earnest.

I countered that although it was Stalin who stole everything from us, it was Churchill and Roosevelt who sat with the thief at Tehran and Yalta, and it was they who signed the agreement allowing Stalin's theft. To the Polish people, it does not matter who did the actual stealing, does it? It is not we who should feel guilty, but rather those who gave away our home and country to the Soviet Union. "What was stolen from us is many times more valuable than the occasional loaf of bread or bucket of coal we take from the British," I said.

Chris put his arm around my shoulders and smiled, assuring me that now his conscience was clear. Still, he pointed out, many people believe that Roosevelt and Churchill made deals with Stalin not because they were evil but because they were under tremendous pressure to end the war at all costs. "By selling out half of Poland they were assured of having millions of Soviet troops to fight the Germans," he argued.

"But how did this justify betraying their ally?" I said. "Everyone has reasons for what they decide to do or not to do." But knowing the reasons does not mitigate the victims' suffering, I thought, and in any event I cared little about Churchill's and Roosevelt's reasons. "What I know is that two greatly admired defenders of freedom screwed the Polish people unjustly, and that you and I are two of the victims."

We continued walking the path around the school among tall oak trees but did not say a word. Some time later, Chris stopped and asked me how much I thought our line of credit with the British treasury was worth. I was not sure whether he was serious or joking. It did not matter. Without hesitation, I answered.

"Tell me, Chris, what is your home worth? What is your country worth?"

Both of us knew the answer because we had lost it all. No one knew better than we did.

We returned to our Quonset hut to study. At midnight, we went out for a snack of bread, cheese, and dried figs.

PART VII

Journey's End

The British ocean liner *Aquitania* leaving England for America on her last voyage with passengers, Southampton, England, November 15, 1949

CHAPTER 29

THE MAGNIFICENT
AQUITANIA

In October 1949 I received a letter from Aunt Maria in Chicago. I opened it eagerly and read the brief contents with a pounding heart. She wrote that the immigration visa applied for in my behalf was approved and that all arrangements for my going to America had been completed. The tickets for my ocean passage to Halifax, Nova Scotia, and for rail travel to Chicago were being forwarded to Zosia, along with telephone numbers and instructions. I was to leave on the British liner *Aquitania* from Southampton at 1:15 P.M. on November 15, 1949. Aunt Maria also enclosed a five-dollar bill for food on the train from Halifax to Chicago. She wished me a safe journey and told me that I would be arriving in time to celebrate a special American holiday, Thanksgiving.

I rejoiced that my dreams were about to come true. After years of wandering—lonely, scared, and bitter—I was finally going to a place I could embrace as a real home, a place where I was wanted. Three days before my ship was to depart, I left Bottisham by train for Brighton, where Mietek and Zosia had settled. I gave Chris what would be my new address in America and a telephone number in case of emergency and promised to ask Aunt Maria to help him come to America, too. He accompanied me to the railroad station in Cambridge. Bidding each other farewell was difficult. Before I boarded the train, we embraced and promised to meet again as soon as possible. As the train started pulling away, Chris's parting words to me were, "Do not forget, Wiesiu, when you get your first job, start saving money so that we can repay the British treasury."

As the train sped away, leaving the English countryside behind me, my thoughts turned to America and my family there. With the exception of Gerry and Jean Siepak, I had never met them. I wondered what this new beginning would be like. Sitting by the window, I watched the countryside hurtle by and was glad to be leaving England.

When the train reached Brighton, Zosia, Mietek, and little George, their three-month-old baby, were waiting for me. It was a typically dreary English November afternoon, and we went back to their apartment. Jurek joined us that evening from London, and we talked about our plans to meet soon in Chicago and begin new lives there. It was hard for me to believe this was really happening after so many years of our wandering in foreign lands, often separated from one another. Was it really possible that we would finally be together again in a place of our own choosing with our own lives to lead?

The next day, Jurek, wanting to do something special, took me on the train back to London. He had planned for me to see some more of the city before I left. We went to the dog races, my first exposure to a race-track. He explained how the totalizator board works and how the English bookmakers operate. I observed how they situated themselves strategi-cally around the track and continually updated the odds for the upcom-ing races on chalkboards. Jurek had a good day betting. We went out for dinner before returning to his flat with the intention of getting a good night's sleep but instead ended up talking into the morning.

The following day Jurek took me to see Buckingham Palace, West-minster Abbey, and the Tower of London, and I had my first ride on a sub-way. This time we saw more of the devastation caused by the Germans during the war. I began to have a clearer idea of how badly the British had suffered, and my attitude toward them softened as a result. Following our tour of London we took the train back to Brighton to join our family for a farewell dinner.

The next morning, November 15, we all took a train to Southamp-ton, where I would board the magnificent ocean liner *Aquitania*. When launched in Liverpool in 1913, she was the largest liner in the world and considered the most elegant and luxurious; one hundred thousand people went to see her launched. She was the longest-serving ship of the Cunard line; she had made only a couple of voyages before being pressed into service as an armed merchant carrier, troop ship, and hospital ship during World War I. During World War II she again served as an armed troop transport. For the past two years, the Canadian government had chartered her to carry immigrants between Southampton and Halifax.

I tearfully embraced Jurek, Zosia, Mietek, and the baby and kissed them for the last time in England. Then I walked up the gangplank clutching the small suitcase Zosia had given me as a bon voyage present. In it were my meager belongings, my passport, and the tickets for what I prayed would be the last stage of my odyssey. Once aboard I went di-rectly to the rail to wave good-bye.

Suddenly alone on the *Aquitania*, I felt like an old man, more worn out from traveling the world than ever before. I guess the ship was, too, because I was told that only one turbine was working. It was a curious coincidence that the biggest, most luxurious liner of her time was heading for her last destination, just as I hoped to be.

I was assigned to a bunk at the bottom of the ship with about two dozen men of different nationalities, only a few of whom spoke Polish. I was clearly the youngest in the room; most of my companions were between the ages of twenty-five and forty. Besides the clothes I was wearing, I had one shirt, one pair of pants, one jacket, some underwear, and an address book in my suitcase. I also had some British currency to spend on the ship and five U.S. dollars for the last leg of the trip. These were all my worldly possessions. But, though I spoke almost no English, I was finally going to America.

About four hours after departure, we ran into rough seas, which is common for the Atlantic in November. The motion of the ship made me sick. All around me were strange people speaking foreign languages. No Mother, no Zosia to hold me as I suffered. I was embarrassed to vomit in front of these strangers, but I had no choice. I decided to stay in bed until I began to feel better, and for the next four days had nothing to eat except for crackers and water that someone brought me. When I first tried to drag myself to the dining room, I made it to a spot only a few feet from the door before vomiting all over the corridor. I had no choice but to return to my cabin and live on whatever my cabin mates brought me.

As we came closer to the end of the trip, my condition improved enough that I could walk around and get some food and exercise. Then one midday we docked in Halifax, and the ship personnel announced that it would be a few hours before we could disembark. When the time came, I took my suitcase and headed for the washroom I had often used during the voyage to clean up—a spacious, beautifully designed washroom worthy of the finest hotel. This time, when I opened the door, I could not believe the sight. Human feces were spread all over the floor in piles about one foot apart. I recoiled in disgust and was immediately reminded of the train station on the first leg of our escape from the Soviet Union. Stunned, I stood in the doorway trying to figure out the meaning of this further lesson in human relations. This had been done on purpose, out of resentment or hatred. One person could not have done this alone; there had to have been a conspiracy on the parts of those on board who resented the British, as many of us did. This despicable act was an expression of revenge by those who had been stepped on and humiliated—those who felt themselves to be helpless pawns. Their vulgar demonstration left a clear message.

I found my way to an upper-deck washroom and minutes later went ashore and took my last look at the *Aquitania*. Her voyage and her life were over, but mine, though I felt as if I had already lived more than one lifetime, was just beginning. She would head back to her home port in England, where her furniture would be sold before she was scrapped.

CHAPTER 30

THANKSGIVING DAY

After disembarking, I went through customs. The Canadian officials, whom I thought of as British, were professional, courteous, and helpful. Because none of my family was to meet me in Nova Scotia, I had made arrangements with a Polish fellow who was riding the same train to Chicago to help me get to the train station. We found our way there and the train left late that evening, scheduled to arrive at Chicago's Union Station late in the evening of the next day. It turned out to be a milk train that seemed to stop every half-hour to pick up and deliver dairy products, mail, newspapers, and other goods. I was sure that it would never arrive on time.

By morning, I was very hungry, because I'd had little to eat while crossing the Atlantic. I went to the dining car and asked another Polish traveler who could speak English to order a good breakfast for me with all the trimmings. Even at that early hour, the waiter was dressed to perfection in a black tuxedo and a bow tie. He took my order and catered to me without reservation. The breakfast was magnificent, like nothing I had eaten in ten long years: excellent bacon and eggs, superb jam and plenty of it, fresh butter, rich coffee with real cream, and fresh fruit. When I finished eating, the smiling waiter bowed ever so slightly and presented me with a check for more than two dollars. "Jesus Christ!" I muttered under my breath. In 1949, two dollars was an exorbitant price for a breakfast. After paying the waiter, I had less than three dollars left and at least a day and an evening to travel. It was also possible that something could go wrong with the plans to be met by my relatives, in which case I didn't want to be entirely penniless. So for the duration of the trip I ran out during station stops to purchase bread and milk before running back to the train as fast as I could.

The train crossed the border between Canada and the United States at Port Huron, Michigan, the official point of entry. United States Customs and Immigration officers came aboard and began checking each passenger's papers. I was scared. What if something went wrong? What if they wanted to detain me to find out why a teenager was traveling alone? How would my family find me then? I tried to calm myself by recalling that at twelve years of age I had taken a bicycle through the unfamiliar city of Tehran and into the surrounding mountains looking for my sister, though unable to speak the language. I later did something similar in Lebanon, and nothing bad had happened to me either time. I was on American soil, not in the Soviet Union. And I repeated to myself my aunt's address in Chicago, which I had memorized. Just then an immigration officer approached me and asked for my passport, a request I understood because the English and Polish words for *passport* sound the same. He looked at it for only a few seconds and then smiled at me, said something in English that I did not understand, and walked away, not waiting for an answer. This was it? "Welcome to America!" I said to myself. After my previous experiences crossing borders, especially in the Soviet Union and Turkey, I was amazed that a person could enter a country so casually. I was also surprised at how efficient, calm, courteous, well-organized, and easygoing the Americans were in going about their business.

Traveling to Chicago from Port Huron, the train went much faster than it had in Canada, and the next thing I knew we had arrived in Chicago. Though I had dozed for much of the thirty-six-hour trip, I was still exhausted. And I knew I smelled terrible. The clothes I had on were the ones I had been wearing when I left England.

The train slowly came to a stop under a large canopy at Union Station. My heart pounded as I took my first step on American soil. A brief walk along the platform, amid people rushing this way and that, brought me to a huge, beautiful room the likes of which I had never seen before and could never have imagined being a railroad station. Confused, I thought I had walked through the wrong door and was in some other building, perhaps a basilica. But all around me were people carrying suitcases and consulting what must have been railroad tickets. So I had to be in the right place.

Collecting my thoughts, I began to relax a little. My aunt had earlier written that there would be nothing to worry about as long as I showed up at Union Station. What she had not known, of course, was that the train would be so late. After I had circled my way through the station for a good half-hour, it became clear that no one was there to meet me. I took out my little address book with my aunt's telephone number, but I did not know how to use a telephone. Worse, of course, was that I did not speak English.

I went up to a man walking alone through the station and pulled on his sleeve. I pointed to the telephone number and tried to explain in Polish that I would appreciate his dialing the number for me. At first he didn't understand and was obviously puzzled, but soon he realized my predicament and went with me to dial the telephone. Luckily, I had saved thirty cents of my five dollars. Within a few minutes I was speaking to my Aunt Maria, whom I had never met. Her first words were, "Welcome to America!" Then she told me that they had all gone to the station the day before to greet me. Since then they had been calling the station every hour to learn whether the train had arrived. She happily informed me that I had arrived on the perfect day after all—Thanksgiving. She said to look for a dozen people who would be there to greet me in about an hour.

Exuberant and eagerly anticipating the arrival of my family, I sat on a wooden bench nearby and observed the people. They were like no others I had seen in ten years: elegantly dressed, confident, rushing by with a sense of purpose and determination. I pondered my own destiny in this great country. Will my family accept me and love me? Who will I become? Will they be proud of me? Will I remember everything my parents taught me and live up to their expectations?

After nearly an hour had elapsed, I began to scan every entrance to the station. When I saw a group of people coming through the door at the other end of the immense waiting room, I knew immediately that they were my American family. I moved toward them in anxious anticipation. The first two people I instinctively recognized were my father's sisters, Maria and Michalina. We embraced and kissed. We all cried. I knew they did not cry simply because they were happy to meet me, though they were. They cried because seeing me alone reminded them of their murdered brother and of his wife who had died in Persia. And perhaps they saw in my face, my stance, a little of what we had all been through.

My aunts and I were meeting at last! "Could all this be only a dream?" I asked myself. But they were real and were right there in front of me, looking very much like their brother, my father. I could feel a bridge forming between us, connecting the past and the present. In one short step, I crossed that bridge. I cried from joy and sorrow.

We left the station with Steve, my cousin Gerry's husband, in their brand-new green Mercury sedan. I was totally enchanted with its beauty and amazed that a working person could own such a luxury. Gerry, whose visit to us in Poland in 1938 now seemed so long ago, sat in the front seat; Aunt Maria sat with me in the back. In a few minutes, we turned left onto Milwaukee Avenue, which, I was told, was one of the few diagonal streets in the city of Chicago. Steve explained that soon we would be passing through a Polish neighborhood commonly known as Little Warsaw.

As we drove, I began to notice glittering, multicolored lights in the windows and on top of the buildings. As a little boy in Poland, listening to Mother's tales of the Arabian Nights, I had pictured caves full of gold, silver, and jewels. This glitter was even more enchanting because it was real. I asked Steve, "What are these lights and why are there so many of them?" Somewhat surprised by my question, he told me that the lights were the neon signs of privately owned businesses advertising their products and services. There were many neon signs, he said, because the businesses want to stay competitive. He went on to explain how competition was the core of free enterprise and how it benefited all citizens by resulting in better products and services. I was captivated by this new concept, so different from the boastful propaganda but empty stores of the Soviet Union. That country was acknowledged by many to be as rich as or richer in resources as the United States. Yet the contrast was stunning. I thought about how the stores in the Soviet Union had no reason to advertise at all because most of the time there was nothing to sell. When there was something to sell, it was take it or leave it.

Why would two vast countries so rich in natural resources and fertile soil be so different? Why would one be a country of hope and opportunity and the other a country of fear, despair, and stagnation? I already knew the answer. It lies in the difference between the basic principles of capitalism and communism. But why would the Soviet people work against their own welfare? I did not know the answer then, nor do I know it now.

I also noticed as we drove that there were many metallic boxes sticking out of windows. Again puzzled, I asked Steve what they might be. "Air conditioners," he replied. "They keep the apartments cool in the summer."

I could hardly take it all in. After less than two hours on American soil, I already had encountered plenty to marvel at. The magnificent Union Station, public telephones, well-dressed people, well-kept buildings and private houses, Steve's new car, fit for a government dignitary, the heavy traffic of private automobiles, stores bulging with goods, air conditioners for personal comfort, the frequent traffic lights, and countless neon signs—all left me mesmerized. After only the briefest glimpse of America I could not wait to see the rest of it. We approached Armitage Avenue, where Steve made another left turn. Aunt Maria told me we would be home soon.

Home.

The sound of that word resonated deep within me. For most of my life, I had known of home only as a memory. My excitement and anticipation grew. We came to the intersection of Armitage and Kedzie Boulevard. Steve made another left turn and drove one block, pulling up in front of a well-kept three-story building. Over the main entrance were the large and freshly painted numerals "1906," the number I had carried in my heart since I had been a ten-year-old playing with scorpions in a Persian desert. I remembered it well from the letters I had written. All that lay between me and my new home were three flights of stairs with varnished woodwork and a carpet running down the middle. I climbed them eagerly. Aunt Maria opened the door, and I crossed the threshold to a three-bedroom apartment. As I glanced at the walls and the room, images of my home in Poland flashed before me.

My eyes rested first on a portrait of the Polish military leader Casimir Pulaski, who was killed in the Battle of Savannah while helping lead the fight against the British in the American Revolution. Next to his hung portraits of Jozef Pilsudski and Thaddeus Kosciusko. The pictures took me back to Father's study. A feeling of belonging overwhelmed me.

On another wall of the large, open room hung a tapestry of red poppies and golden wheat, a painting of a Polish peasant girl in a native costume, and a painting of an *ulan*, a cavalry man, with drawn saber on a magnificent galloping steed. All these reminded me of the Polish countryside. In a corner of the room hung a mountaineer's hat made from felt and meticulously embroidered with multicolored thread. Next to it were a *cipaga*, a mountaineer's cane with a metal head shaped like an axe, and decorative plates carved from wood by mountain people. All along the wall, wherever space allowed, were shelves full of costumed figurines representing the districts and traditions of my native land.

I looked around and knew this was truly a Polish household. Although they had come to America in search of a better life, these people still cared deeply about their native country, and they brought tradition and a little of their homeland with them when they crossed the ocean.

To one side of the room stood a solid oak dining table on a Persian carpet. It was covered with a heavy white linen tablecloth, hand-embroidered with red poppies and meticulously set for Thanksgiving dinner. Each place setting had a matching embroidered linen napkin. All of this, as well as the crystal wineglasses and goblets, came from Poland. Aunt Maria's finest china completed the splendor.

Soon after we entered and before I could fully appreciate the beauty of the room and the table, Aunt Maria discreetly asked me if I would like to take a bath. When a man stinks like a goat and knows it, he is not only ready for a bath, he is ready for a scrub brush. She had sat next to me in the car for more than half an hour, saying nothing about it. I answered that I could hardly wait to take a bath.

Aunt Maria took me to the bathroom, which separated the dining room from the kitchen. She already had started filling the tub with warm water. Clean underwear and socks had been laid out on a chair with a pair of Uncle Tony's pants and one of his shirts for me to wear. Also waiting for me were a new hairbrush and toothbrush, toothpaste, soap, and two towels. Before she left the bathroom, she checked the water temperature and told me to call her if I needed anything else. I took off my sticky, stinking clothes, tied them into a tight bundle, and laid them on the tiled floor. Then I carefully stepped into the bathtub, luxuriating in my first such experience in a decade.

Now I knew that my fortunes had really changed. This was my first bath in a tub since we were deported from our home in Poland. A brand new toothbrush, toothpaste, and soap! For many years, I had had none of these simple luxuries of life, which others think of as necessities. And two towels! Why does a man need two towels? After all, I was only taking a bath. Later, Aunt Maria explained that one was a bath towel and the other a face towel. For most of my wandering, there had been no towels but only old rags when we were lucky. After a decade of homelessness, I was reentering the world I had known as a young boy. I had almost stopped believing that it really existed, except in my memories.

I finished my bath, dried myself with the smaller of the towels, and dressed in Uncle Tony's clothes. Everything was much too large, but I rolled up the sleeves, tucked the shirt into the pants, and tightened the belt firmly. Then I stepped in front of the brightly lit, full-length mirror to comb my hair. In the mirror I saw the reflections of two people: a tired-looking teenager with the sad eyes and gloomy countenance of an old man, and next to him a little boy with bangs and a smile on his face. The teenager seemed to be a stranger, but I knew the boy and his voice very well.

I looked steadily into the mirror. In a few minutes, I would have to eat dinner at an elegant table in a nice home with nice people; not having done that for ten long years, I did not want to embarrass myself. I was afraid, so I asked the boy for advice.

Tell me: How does one talk, eat, and behave? Surely you must know.

There's nothing to it. I can tell you everything Mother taught me if you wish.

Everything?

Well, try to remember just a few important things: be especially nice and polite with the ladies; speak in quiet tones; speak only when you are spoken to; say "Thank you" for everything you are offered; say "May I please?" when you ask for something; eat slowly, as though you are not hungry; do not slurp your soup; do not put too much food in your mouth at one time; do not talk with food in your mouth; do not take more food than you can finish, but never refuse when the host or hostess offers you another small portion; do not leave the table until you are excused. And remember, at the end you must repeatedly compliment the hostess for an excellent dinner and thank her for all the trouble she has taken.

I will never remember all these things.

You must remember. These are the things Mother taught me and expected me to remember.

Just then I heard a knock at the door. Aunt Maria asked me if I needed anything else.

"I am finished, Aunt Maria," I answered quietly. When I looked again in the mirror, the little boy had disappeared, and the teenager—old and tired-looking beyond his years—was alone. My aunt opened the door and told me that I looked a hundred times better.

We went to the dining room, where everyone was waiting. Then we all sat down at the dinner table, my aunts and uncles and cousins, seventeen of us in all. My first day in America began with a truly appropriate celebration, Thanksgiving. I was awed to see a table laden with such an abundant variety of dishes. We had mashed potatoes, sweet potatoes, whole cranberries, cranberry sauce, Brussels sprouts, broccoli, cucumbers with sour cream, cauliflower with buttered bread crumbs, tomato salad, sausages, a golden brown turkey with stuffing, gravy, homemade bread and buns, and fresh butter. To finish the feast, there were wines and liqueurs, a pumpkin pie with whipped cream, many different pastries of the kind we had in Poland, and specially brewed coffee.

My uncle Tony sat next to me, and we wasted no time getting acquainted. As a young man he had come to America in search of a better life. His first job was making caskets, though he was already a qualified carpenter's apprentice. A short time later, he went to work in a furniture factory and there further developed his craft. Then he was hired by John M. Smyth, one of the finest furniture stores in the Midwest, located on the famous Michigan Avenue in Chicago. His job at the time of my arrival was to refinish damaged furniture for wealthy clients. During our conversation, he proudly pointed out many pieces of furniture in the house that he had made. He was a jovial man who enjoyed telling Polish jokes, and we were the best of friends from our first meeting. Every time I finished a plate of food, he loaded it up again, and I ate and ate and ate. I had never eaten so much in my life. After each additional helping, I had to loosen my belt.

My aunts, Maria and Michalina, hovered over me with tender loving care and affection. No one asked me questions about what had happened during the ten years of my odyssey, probably to spare me the pain of talking about it. Instead, we talked about all the members of the family—those at the table, those elsewhere in America, and those in Poland—including our cousin Jean, who was then working at a Veterans Administration hospital in Los Angeles.

We talked about America and its people. I learned about baseball, football, basketball, and hockey, Fourth of July fireworks, and hamburgers and hot dogs. I also learned how the Thanksgiving Day celebration originated with the Native Americans and the pilgrims and the significance of the turkey, corn, sweet potatoes, and pumpkin pie.

It was getting quite late by the time we finished our dinner. After much hugging, everybody went home. Uncle Tony retired for the night soon afterward, but not Aunt Maria. She still hovered over me like a mother over her newborn baby and asked if I was still hungry. I said no and thanked her profusely, but she still insisted on giving me some milk and honey with cake. I thanked her cordially and enjoyed some *babka*, one of the cakes of my childhood, which I had not eaten since before the war.

I had long been curious about the person who had searched so tirelessly for so many years for her brother's children, the nephews and niece she had never met. As we sat at the kitchen table, I built up my courage to ask her to tell me about herself.

Aunt Maria had left Poland in 1912 at age sixteen to search for a better life. Her brother Jan, my father, who was nineteen at the time, saw her off as she left for America, where she would join their older sister, Michalina, who had made the same journey four years earlier. He took her to Cracow, finished making the necessary travel arrangements, and put her on a train for Rotterdam, where she boarded a ship heading for Ellis Island.

In New York, after passing the physical examinations, she boarded a train for Chicago, where she moved in with Michalina and found a temporary job serving tables for the priests in their largely Polish parish. Soon thereafter she found her first permanent job as a seamstress. Within a year, she fell in love and married a young man who lived in her building. In due course, they had two daughters, Gerry and Jean, whom I had previously met.

Aunt Maria spoke of belonging to many charitable organizations. She organized blood drives during the war, helped send thousands of packages to lonely soldiers all over the world, and sent hundreds of packages at her own expense to poor relatives in western Poland, most of whom survived the war. She did all these things while working as a seamstress and taking care of her family. She also told me about her efforts to find us, beginning in 1940, and showed me documents she had sent to agencies all over the world, including the Polish Red Cross in London, the Polish government-in-exile in London, and even the Soviet government in Moscow. She never received a reply from the Soviets.

She turned the conversation to what she considered an urgent subject. Having learned how sporadic my schooling had been during the war, she told me about the public high schools in Chicago and about a very good private school, St. Bonaventure, located in Sturtevant, Wisconsin, and run by Franciscan fathers of Polish descent who would help me learn English. She offered to pay all the expenses and recommended that I go there but at the same time told me to take a few days to think about the pros and cons. On one hand, Saint Bonaventure would be the better choice for my education. On the other hand, if I attended a Chicago high school, I could stay with her and enjoy the comforts of a home and family. At that moment, I was glad that this difficult choice could wait.

Aunt Maria told me how happy she was that one of "the children" had finally arrived in America and that she could not wait to meet Jurek and Zosia. She referred to us as as if we were her own. She told me how sorry she was never to have met my mother but said, "Your father was a very good man." Then she asked if I wanted to go to sleep. Indeed I did; it was 1:30 in the morning. I thanked her for her kindness, for everything she had done and was doing for us, and for her love. I promised to repay her for everything. Her eyes misted as she replied that I owed her nothing. "Just wish me good health," she said, adding that it would make her very happy if Jurek and Zosia were to come to America. "You will make me even happier if you go to school, study hard, and grow up to be a good man like your father."

She showed me to my bedroom. She hugged and kissed me and told me to sleep as long as I liked, adding that breakfast would be ready when I woke up. She glanced back at me before quietly closing the door behind herself. My first day on American soil was ending. Again I thought how my fortunes had changed. I had my own room, my own bed, fresh sheets and pillowcases, a pair of pajamas, a quilt like the one I had back in Sarny, a soft carpet, and a pair of slippers on the floor. Most important of all, I had a kind and loving family just on the other side of my bedroom door. I was completely exhausted from the long journey, from the excitement of meeting my family, and from the thrill of being in America. Having quickly changed into my pajamas, I turned out the lights. The room was dark except for a tiny stream of moonlight shining through a break in the heavy curtain. Sleep came in an instant.

The next morning I heard whispers in the kitchen and then footsteps outside my bedroom door. I opened and closed my eyes several times to be sure this was not a dream. It was time to get up and begin my first full day in America.

CHAPTER 31

MAKING PEACE
WITH GOD

Ten days later, I walked the grounds of Saint Bonaventure High School for the first time, eager to start. My heart was filled with dreams and high expectations. Having lost four years of schooling, for the first time ever I would pursue my education with no other concerns or disruptions to distract me. This was the place where I was going to acquire knowledge, the one thing no one could ever take from me.

At day's end, when the administrative details were taken care of, Aunt Maria and Uncle Tony returned to Chicago. It was Sunday, and I had a few hours to myself. The atmosphere on campus was quiet and serene, giving me an opportunity to reflect and gather my thoughts. It was a perfect time to say a prayer and to give thanks.

I strolled to the main chapel. It was empty. For a few moments I stood in silence looking at the statues. I had not been in a church in more than three years. Many candles shone brightly, their light reflected in the multicolored mosaics and paintings of the saints. It was very tranquil. I felt as welcome in this chapel as I had been in our church in Poland when I was a little boy. Here, unlike so much of the world through which I had traveled, I found peace and an inexplicable closeness to God. In Lebanon, we had lived under the protective presence of the statue of Christ, which I thought at the time was an omen. On my first day on the grounds of Saint Bonaventure, I stood in a chapel surrounded by statues of Christ, the Blessed Virgin Mary, and many saints. I wondered whether this too was an omen.

I moved much closer to the altar, knelt, crossed myself solemnly, and meditated for a time. I prayed for my parents and for other members of my family who had perished, for all the Polish people who were left behind in the Soviet Union, and for those who had starved to death or been murdered there. These prayers took my mind to distant lands where I had not always prayed to God because I was so angry. Was I wrong to have been so bitter about our suffering? Should I make peace with God now? On reflection, I recalled Mother's advice to me as a child: "We should always give thanks to God for the blessings we receive despite those we did not get. And you can do so no matter where you are by saying a simple prayer."

I wanted to come to terms with God and reaffirm my faith, but it was very difficult. I tried to count my blessings, but doing so only brought back images and memories of all the terrible things that happened to my family and me. I pondered Mother's advice. Then, with my hands folded, I thanked God for our escape from the Soviet Union, for my family, who stood by me when I needed them most, and for the greatest gifts of all— life and freedom. At that moment I realized that throughout my ten-year odyssey, God had been looking out for me after all.

There remained someone else to thank—the skinny seven-year-old Polish boy I knew so well. Though his true home was in another time and place, he had traveled with me for ten lonely years through all the strange places to which fate had sent me. He was the boy who never gave up, who sustained in me hope, faith, and the will to survive. He was my true friend. I thanked him for everything he stood for and for being my conscience. Most of all, I thanked him for keeping alive the precious memories of home.

Though it was my day to offer thanksgiving, I had one favor to ask of God. I pleaded with him to help me find my father's grave before I died. Then I walked out of the chapel at peace with myself, hoping that I would be at peace with God as well.

PART VIII

The Passage of Time

The final resting place of 3,739 Polish officers shot in the back of the head by the NKVD in spring 1940, Piatichatki cemetery, Kharkov, Ukraine, 2002

FOR WHOM THE
BELLS TOLL

On Sunday, April 22, 1990, a large crowd gathered in front of an old Polish church in Chicago. Magnificent Saint Hyacinth Church stood basking in the sun, its three steeples stretching up to heaven, its huge wooden portals wide open. The church had filled to capacity long before the commemorative Mass was to begin, and now, even with every seat taken and people standing shoulder to shoulder in the aisles, it had an eerie silence. Those unable to squeeze their way inside stood outside expectantly. Former U.S. representative Roman Pucinski was in attendance, along with dignitaries of local Polish organizations. More than thirty-five hundred Poles and Polish Americans of all ages had come to pray for and honor the victims of the Katyn massacre exactly fifty years earlier at the beginning of World War II. Only a week earlier, the president of the Soviet Union, Mikhail Gorbachev, had announced to the world that it was the NKVD that had committed the mass murder of the Polish POWs. The long-kept secrets of the graves were beginning to surface.

Through the years, I had prayed for and honored my father in my heart, hoping that one day in my lifetime the truth about the massacre and his burial site would be made public. Soon we would learn the full story, but for now we focused on praying, honoring, and remembering. My brother and his wife, my sister, and I were among those paying homage to our father and the other victims.

The steeple bells rang out, and the Mass began. Thirty-five hundred worshippers sang "Rota," one of the most popular patriotic hymns of Poland. It was written in 1910 for the unveiling of the Cracow monument commemorating the victory in the 1410 Battle of Grunwald of Polish-Lithuanian forces over the Order of Teutonic Knights. I had sung it on the cattle train while being deported to the Soviet Union, on the desolate steppes of Kazakhstan, in the scorched desert of Persia, in the mountains of Lebanon, and in the freezing Quonset huts of England. Though their experiences were all different, the people singing this glorious hymn were much the same, bound together with a common thread of love for their native land and the love of freedom.

Father Zygmunt Waz, a young priest not yet born when the massacre took place, delivered the homily for the victims of the Katyn Forest massacre. His somber words penetrated the huge chambers of the church as the silent crowd listened. More singing and more hymns followed. As I stood lost in prayer and meditation, my thoughts carried me thousands of miles away to a distant place and time. The line between past and present blurred, and vivid images of my father's murder began to run through my mind, just as they had done for half a century.

Suddenly I see myself standing in the Katyn Forest, a gentle breeze rustling through the pines and softly shaking the budding branches of birch and oak. Then, breaking the peace of the forest, a Soviet bus pulls up, called by the Russians *Chorny Voron* (Black Raven), and I see emerging from the back of the bus Polish Army officers in their green uniforms and high leather boots, proudly displaying medals for merit and valor. Great coats are slung over their shoulders to shield them against the lingering chill of the fading winter. They are marched down a beaten path of needles and dry leaves deeper into the forest. The officers were brought here from the POW camp where they had been held. When they had left the camp a short time earlier, a Soviet military band had played to bid them farewell. They had been promised freedom—freedom to return to their homes and families and later to rejoin the Polish Army to fight the Germans.

In one group I see my forty-seven-year-old father. He is strong, yet serene, marching past the remnants of the winter snow still present on the shady side of the trees. A popping sound in the distance grows louder as the column moves closer. Father pauses, shocked, though not completely surprised, as he comes to a clearing. He looks around and steels himself for what he now knows is the truth. Behind him there are sounds of scuffling, resistance. Soviet guards grab the prisoners and bind their hands with ropes and wire precut for that purpose. The great coats are pulled over the heads of the more unruly, sawdust or felt gags stuffed into their mouths. The guards inflict deep bayonet wounds on some while forcing them to move forward. At the edge of a long trench, my father and his fellow officers are forced to kneel. They see below them the stacked bodies of those who have preceded them to "freedom." Father hears the footsteps approaching from his left, the sound of a gun being fired, and the thud of a body falling forward into the pit.

Step. Step. *Bang*. Thud.

Step. Step. *Bang*. Thud.

Step. Step . . .

Father thinks of Mother, my brother, my sister, and me and of our home in Sarny in the days before this nightmare began. Fear grips him, but he draws strength from his love for us as he feels the pressure of a gun barrel on his neck, just above the collar of his uniform.

I stand nearby, horrified, frozen with fear. My heart is bursting with pain and sorrow. I try to scream to heaven but cannot; my mouth is filled with sawdust. Then I struggle to move forward but discover that my hands are tied with wire like the prisoners'. A sickening feeling of utter helplessness overpowers me. I silently ask God for help, but there is no answer.

When the body of the last of the thousands to be murdered falls into the pit, the mass graves are covered with dirt and saplings are planted over them. With the passage of time, the trees grow tall, drawing strength from Poland's finest men, buried underneath their limbs.

After the last pistol shot, the Katyn Forest is silent, its buried secret remaining untold for decades. But for me there has never been silence. A half-century later I still hear the approaching footsteps of the executioners, then the gunshots, each louder than the preceding one.

As the Mass neared its end, I came out from under the spell. But painful memories of wartime still tumbled in my head. Old wounds reopened as though they had never healed. I could only withdraw to the solitude and comfort of prayer, as I have done many times before. I prayed for my grandmother, buried in Frysztak, Poland; for my grandfather, buried in Prague, a victim of World War I; for my mother, buried in Tehran, and my father, buried somewhere in the Soviet Union, both victims of World War II.

When the Mass ended, my family and I were among the first to leave the church. We waited on the stone steps listening and watching the people who followed. Many were old and crippled. Some were middle-aged mothers with babies in their arms; others were young children in Boy Scout and Girl Scout uniforms. As they walked by, I silently thanked the many strangers for honoring all the victims. This outpouring of patriotism among Poles and Polish Americans for their native land and compassion for the victims of the Katyn massacre inspired me to face my long-hidden feelings of pain, sorrow, and bitterness. These people gave me the strength I needed to begin writing the story of my ten-year odyssey and the events at Katyn that lie at my life's center. For that, I will be forever grateful.

CHAPTER 33

THE CIRCLE CLOSES

It was a beautiful day in early June 1998. The sun had risen into a cloudless blue sky, warming the earth and all living creatures. Just outside my window, an array of yellow, gold, red, pink, and purple flowers basked in the morning's glory, while the green leaves of gently swaying willow trees reflected the sun's golden rays like thousands of tiny mirrors. Only traces of the morning dew remained as small birds chased one another from tree limb to tree limb. A pair of white swans tenderly guided their brood across the still waters of the pond, swimming majestically and diving now and then through the mirrored surface.

Surrounded by nature's beauty and tranquility, I was at peace with myself. Only a day earlier, after eight long years and multiple interruptions, I had finished the first draft of this book. It was time to relax, to get away from reliving the past.

Then the phone rang. I answered, and within seconds everything had changed. As I listened, my heart raced faster and faster. I had waited for more than a half-century for such a call. How ironic that it should come at this moment. Professor Edward Kaminski, head of the Katyn Families Foundation of Chicago, was on the line. He informed me that the president of Poland, Alexander Kwasniewski, had extended an invitation for five individuals from our foundation to be the guests of the Polish government at a commemorative ceremony in Ukraine. The ceremony, which would take place in Kharkov, would honor the Polish POWs, almost all of whom were officers, murdered in April 1940 by the NKVD as part of the Katyn massacre. He asked me if I would like to represent the foundation and lay the memorial wreath at the ceremony. I was deeply moved and honored to accept, especially because I now knew that my father was one of the victims buried there.

My son George and I left Chicago on June 21—ironically, Father's Day and almost exactly fifty-eight years from the day my mother, brother, sister, and I were deported from Poland to the depths of the Soviet Union. George, born in America eighteen years after his grandfather's death, insisted on accompanying me on this long and painful journey. He too wished to pay homage to his grandfather and the other murdered officers. There was no greater gift my son could have given me that Father's Day. I had waited many years for the day when I would be able to honor my father, see his final resting place, and bring home a handful of soil from his grave to bury with dignity in the United States. The circle was beginning to close.

After George and I arrived in Cracow, we spent a few days with our cousins before departing on the five-day round-trip journey to Kharkov. On June 25, we checked in with the others making the trip at the headquarters of the Polish Army in Cracow, which would be our host and guardian. Fellow passengers included other deportees, Polish military officers, an armed contingent of the Polish Army from Cracow, the Guard of Honour of the Polish Armed Forces (PAF), and the band of the PAF. The train's commander, Colonel Stanislaw Roginski, cordially greeted us. He understood that most of us were deathly afraid to travel in the direction of the former Soviet Union. After repeatedly assuring us that it would be a "safe train," the colonel received a long round of applause. We were then taken to the station in Olkusz, near Cracow, where a military band was waiting to greet us.

After boarding the train, we met the others with whom we would be making the pilgrimage. Introductions began with handshakes, embraces, and kisses among the 220 people, all members of the Katyn Families Foundation, whether in Poland, England, or the United States. Most were children of the murdered officers, now between the ages of sixty and seventy-five. Many recalled their childhood in Poland and their wartime experiences, telling stories about their fathers with reverence and pride. Some in their sixties did not remember their fathers at all; others were born shortly after their fathers had left for the war. But because of the shared experience that had brought us together, we were quickly able to form a bond. Only two of our group were wives of officers; they were more than ninety years of age. There were three grandchildren—one from Poland, one from England, and one, my son, from the United States.

The first person to whom we introduced ourselves was Doctor Eva Gruner-Zarnoch, a member of the Polish team that exhumed the mass graves in Kharkov. She had spent four weeks at the site in 1995 and 1996, and her own father was buried at the site. During the excavation, the team found her father's signet ring and watch. Hearing her story sent chills through my body. She related that the NKVD routinely planted trees over mass graves in order to cover their crime. In time, as the city of Kharkov expanded toward the site, the officials decided to build a park over the graves. Then, almost forty years later, around 1980, as the ground settled owing to its unusual composition, children playing in the park began to discover the skeletal remains of human heads, hands, and feet emerging from the soil, along with various artifacts belonging to the Polish POWs. But rather than admit the crime, officials decided to bring drilling equipment to the gravesite and hide the evidence by crushing the remains. Then they covered the graves with more dirt.

Doctor Gruner described the cruelty of the executions. The prisoners were brought from Starobelsk a few hundred at a time and separated into smaller groups. Then they were transported by bus to the NKVD building in Kharkov where they were to die. Each prisoner, in assembly-line fashion, was taken to the basement, his identity was confirmed, and his hands were bound behind him. Then the prisoners were taken across the hallway, where they were told to sit on a bench next to the execution room, which presumably was soundproof. One at a time, prisoners were taken inside and executed with a single shot from a pistol, pressed to the back of the head and aimed precisely at the nerve center. According to German and Soviet research, this was the most efficient way of killing with one shot while producing minimal bleeding. The dead men's overcoats were placed over their heads to soak up the blood, then their bodies were dragged through the outside door, using a metal hook made for that purpose, into a waiting truck marked MILK AND CREAM. When darkness fell, the trucks were driven to Piatichatki, a suburb of Kharkov, and the bodies dumped into mass graves.

Our train was moving eastward and before long approached what is now the independent country of Ukraine. Prior to the war, much of this land was Polish, and my family had lived in the region. But after the Soviets took it in 1939, it was never returned. Throughout the cold war it remained Poland's border with the Soviet Union. As the train crossed the border, a frightening feeling overpowered me. My family and I had traveled to our enslavement on these very same tracks in a cattle car on the way to the Soviet Union. Repressed memories of our degradation and starvation began to flood my thoughts. My body stiffened and my palms became wet with perspiration. I did not want to go in the same direction ever again. But I had promised myself that if given the opportunity I would honor my father, even if it meant returning to the Inhuman Land.

Now and then the train made brief stops, usually no more than a few minutes at a time, allowing us to stretch and catch a breath of fresh air. During one such stop, George and I were interviewed by Olenka Frenkiel, a correspondent for the British Broadcasting Corporation. She was making a documentary of our pilgrimage. For her this assignment was most unusual: fifty-eight years earlier her own mother had traveled on the same tracks in a cattle car with other Polish people enslaved by the Soviets, heading to an unknown place somewhere deep in the Soviet Union. She too survived and eventually made her escape from Siberia. While Olenka was interviewing us on the platform, a priest dressed in a black robe approached. Without hesitation, he looked at the correspondent and asked, "May I tell you something?" She focused her camera on him and replied, "Please, do." The priest continued, "I want you to know that when I was seven years old and the war broke out, the Soviet soldiers shot and killed my mother in front of me. I started running. They shot at me and missed. They shot again and missed." He turned and walked away without saying another word.

I was stunned. His words filled me with compassion. Having lost my mother and father at about the same age, I understood the years of sorrow and pain he must have endured. But why did he reveal this painful personal drama so stoically, so matter-of-factly, in public and on camera? Was it for sympathy? I thought not. I had the sense that this man was trying to say something to the world about the terrible evils that exist and the need for all of us to guard against them. Having lived most of his life under Communism in Poland, he had had to remain silent.

After a grueling thirty-six hours, the train arrived in Kharkov. Dressed in black suits, George and I picked up two memorial wreaths that we had brought from Poland and stepped anxiously onto the platform. One wreath was from the Katyn Families Foundation in Chicago and the other was from the entire Adamczyk family, which is scattered all over the world.

After a brief interview with a Polish television reporter, we entered a large train station and were met with an astonishing sight. In the middle of the station stood the splendidly uniformed band of the PAF playing "The March of the First Brigade," which was written for Marshall Jozef Pilsudski. My father had served under his command when the Polish troops beat back the Bolsheviks in 1920. On both sides of the band and some distance away, local Ukrainians were cordoned off by policemen. Many stood there silently with their mouths wide open, disbelieving what was happening before their eyes. In one corner of the station still stood a larger-than-life statue of Lenin and on the other a statue of Marx. Never in my life would I have been able to imagine such a sight.

At the rest area I informed Colonel Roginski that a small number of us would like stop on the way back to Kharkov and visit the NKVD headquarters where the executions took place. Ukrainian authorities flatly denied the request.

After a brief rest, we reboarded the buses for a twenty-minute ride to the cemetery in Piatichatki. As we neared it, we could make out members of the secret police, half-hidden by trees and bushes, lining both sides of the road. The buses stopped outside a narrow steel gate guarded by local authorities. A steel fence surrounded the cemetery. Soon I would step down on the ground where my father and 3,738 other victims were buried so long ago.

It had taken eight years since Gorbachev's admission of the Soviet crime before an agreement was reached between the Poles and the Ukrainians as to how the cemetery in Piatichatki would be built and how the memorial ceremony would be structured. The main point of disagreement was the fact that the site contained mass graves of not only the Polish POWs but also thousands of Ukrainians and Russians murdered by the NKVD.

At last, on June 27, 1998, the time had come to pay homage to my father and his colleagues. I stepped down from the bus onto the grounds of the cemetery trembling. George and I made our way through the crowd close to the altar where the Mass would be celebrated. Between the dignitaries and the altar, a cement slab had been laid to hold an eternal flame and a large memorial stone, set with an inscribed plaque, which had been brought from Poland on our train.

The atmosphere was surreal. For years the Poles and the Ukrainians had been bitter enemies. In Kharkov some of the executioners of the POWs had been Ukrainians. Now in front of my very eyes the presidents of Poland and Ukraine stood side by side, Polish Catholic and Ukrainian Orthodox priests stood at the same altar, and the combined Polish-Ukrainian honor guard was a mere six feet in front of me. Never did I imagine that these two peoples would come together to mourn the victims of a massacre. Representatives from the United States, Great Britain, and Russia were conspicuously absent.

To begin the Mass, the sergeant major of the Guard of Honor of the PAF solemnly read the Prayer of the Faithful in a voice that reverberated through the forest. Throughout the afternoon, and for days upon returning home, I heard his voice quoting Ezekiel 37:3: "Will these bones come back again to life? Dear God, only you know." Following the Mass, the presidents of Poland and Ukraine and other dignitaries made speeches. Then the Charter of Foundation for the cornerstone was read magnificently by Colonel Wieslaw Grudzinski, the commanding officer of the Guard of Honor, and finally the two presidents laid the cornerstone while the band played Chopin's Funeral March.

At that point the woman standing next to me asked me to look up toward the only large opening in the canopy of oak trees. "Look," she said, "this is like a beautiful cupola of a cathedral and God himself is looking at the victims." I looked up, then looked at her and answered, "Yes, ma'am, today God is looking at all of humanity."

Next followed a salvo in honor of the dead by the entire complement of the Guard of Honor, composed of representatives of the air force, the navy, and the infantry. Three times the thunder of their rifles was heard in honor of Poland's finest men. We laid our wreaths near the cornerstone and then the procession of priests and dignitaries moved toward the mass graves, the largest of which contained 1,025 bodies. The graves were lit with hundreds of candles and decorated with as many white and red Polish flags.

The hardest part of the pilgrimage faced me. In which mass grave was my father buried? I realized that the others shared my quandary. One of them desperately hugged an oak tree, thinking that her father might be lying under its roots. She looked very old, yet she cried like a little child missing her daddy. My heart went out to her. At that moment I decided that there was no need to torture myself any longer. I went around to all the mass graves and said a short prayer at each one, just to be sure that I would not miss the one where my father was buried. Then I went to the largest one, knelt down, and began to recite the Lord's Prayer, but the words did not come easily. I was numb, speechless, lost, and confused. Instead, I whispered, "Father, I love you" and scooped up some soil and some oak leaves that had fallen on the grave.

As I knelt, my son quietly approached and told me he had something for me. He stretched out his hand and gave me an empty cartridge from a bullet. Foolishly, I asked him if he had found it in the forest.

"No, Dad," he replied. "It is from the salvo of the honor guard."

I clutched it tightly in my hand and looked at him as tears welled in my eyes. "Did you also find one for yourself in memory of your grandfather?" I asked after a moment.

"No, Dad, this is your day. This cartridge is for you in memory of your father."

A number of Polish officers who had traveled with us were visiting the graves and mingling among the pilgrims. I overheard some of them saying that at a different time and in a different place it could have been they to whom these pilgrims were paying homage. Some said that it felt as if they were walking over their own graves. Suddenly my fellow pilgrims and I were young again, children of the victims of Katyn, whom I now saw embodied in the young officers who had accompanied us. It had been fifty-nine years since I had seen my father. Yet for a few moments I was no longer the husky American with a graying beard but a six-and-a-half-year-old Polish boy being kissed good-bye by my father as he left for the war. I could see him leaning over my bed to pick me up and hug me. I could clearly hear his last words to me.

The strange interlude faded away. I looked around me. Somewhere, in one of these mass graves, my father's remains would lie for eternity, but never would he be forgotten. I was ready to leave, comforted by the knowledge that my grandchildren and theirs would always remember him as well.

We moved toward the cemetery gate, taking one last look at the candlelit graves, the fluttering Polish flags, and the many paper signs stuck in the ground, each bearing the name of one of the victims. As we were leaving, I could still read one of the wind-blown signs: KAPITAN JAN ADAMCZYK. I turned to George, remarking that the truth had finally risen from the graves for all the world to know. "Neither the planting of the trees over them nor the grinding of their bones could hide this horrible crime that we and the world should never forget," I said. He put his arms around me and remained silent. Before leaving the cemetery I said a prayer for my father's soul, grateful that I had finally had an opportunity to visit his grave. The burden I had carried for so much of my life had been lifted at last.

The buses took us back to the train station in Kharkov. Before leaving I witnessed an unusual farewell. Olenka Frankiel was interviewing a local Ukrainian journalist on the platform in front of our train. She asked him whether he knew who was buried at the cemetery where the ceremony was held. In broken English he replied with obvious hesitation.

"Officer Poland."

"Who killed them?"

"Hitler," replied the journalist, nodding his head as if to give approval to his own answer.

"Hitler?" Olenka repeated in a voice marked with surprise and disbelief.

"Yes, yes, Hitler. I think Hitler," replied the man sheepishly.

As we boarded the train, the man stood on the platform waving at us and smiling. The train started moving, and the man walked along still waving and smiling. I could not help but wonder whether it was because he was happy to see us leave or because he would be asked no more questions.

Not far from the Polish border a surprise announcement was made that the train would shortly make a half-hour stop for a special occasion. We were told that the Ukrainian military had organized a special ceremony for us at the request of Leonid Kuczma, their president. It was to be the sharing of bread and salt between a group of Ukrainian officers and ourselves, an old Ukrainian and Polish tradition and now an offering of peace and friendship.

When the train stopped, people poured onto the platform and headed in the direction of the ceremony. My son, eager to witness this historic occasion, rushed out as well, followed by the two travelers who shared our compartment. For a few minutes I sat on the train, alone with my thoughts. Then, deciding to join the others, I stepped onto the platform and found myself almost directly in front of the entrance to the main building of the station. Over it was a word written in Cyrillic. A fellow traveler translated it for me as "Luck."

I stood frozen in place, my heart pounding. This was our hometown before the war. *This was Poland.* My father had walked on this very platform hundreds of times. The last time I had been here was in mid-December 1938, when my entire family came to bid farewell to Gerry Siepak. Though almost sixty years had passed, I could still recall the occasion clearly. I remembered how Father tightly held my hand as I tried to get a closer look at the approaching train on which my cousin was to depart. Of all the places in a five-day journey where our train could have stopped for the ceremony, it stopped here! Was it possible that I was being led toward making peace within my soul by forgiving the Soviet perpetrators of the crime? Was this the time and place to do it, in my old hometown?

I turned my gaze toward the end of the platform where the ceremony was taking place. The Ukrainians and the Poles were sharing bread and salt. Some Ukrainians, perhaps the fathers or uncles of those now celebrating peace and friendship, had been members of the NKVD who had massacred the Polish POWs. But it had not been many hours since both peoples had stood side by side in the Piatichatki cemetery to honor the victims and prayed to God at the same altar. I began to walk toward the thinning crowd. Officers of both nations held loaves of rye bread and salt. I walked up to the Ukrainian officer and broke off a small piece of bread, and he did likewise. We dipped it in salt and ate it. At that moment the crowd began to sing "Sto lat, Sto lat," a Polish birthday song that wishes for the celebrant to live at least a hundred years. In this case it was sung with the hope that the two nations would live in peace at least that long.

On the train the evening before we returned to Cracow, George and I met with some of the Polish officers for a farewell celebration. We thanked them for the kindness and consideration they had extended to us throughout our pilgrimage. They presented us with a copy of *Grob Nieznanego Zolnierza* (Tomb of the Unknown Soldier). The following day we were again greeted by the music of the military band as we disembarked in Olkusz. The good-byes took much longer than had the hellos. It seemed no one wanted to break the bond that united us and had strengthened us on this pilgrimage.

The following morning we left Cracow for Warsaw, where we boarded a Polish jetliner for our return to the United States. That evening, even before unpacking the suitcases, I rushed to the retirement home where my aunt Maria, then 102 years of age, was living. When I entered her room, her first words were, "You're back. Thank God you're back."

Her fear prior to my departure was that the Soviet police would imprison me again and send me back to Siberia for hard labor. As she sat in her wheelchair, I kissed her and handed her some pictures from the memorial service. One showed a cross that was dedicated to Katyn. Despite her poor eyesight, Aunt Maria was determined to read for herself the inscription on the cross. After a while, she whispered softly, "Pomoz Przebaczyc 1940" ("Help to Forgive 1940"). She meditated for a long time while holding another picture, that of the Blessed Virgin Mary caressing a skull pierced by a bullet.

After several minutes passed, I removed the pictures from her hands. Then I hesitated, not knowing how she would react to what I was about to do. "Grandma," I said, using the name by which we called her now, "I have something very special for you. This is from your brother's grave." I handed her the plastic bag with soil and leaves from one of the mass graves. With hands twisted by rheumatism and arthritis, she accepted my gift and held it tightly to her breast. For a long time, she said nothing. Then she cried.

I looked at her with amazement and admiration. All her years of hard work—sending thousands of packages to Polish soldiers in Italy during the war and to poor relatives in Poland, opening her home to Polish immigrants, serving on committees for the Polish National Alliance—derived from the love of her brother, my father, whom she had not seen since 1912, eighty-six years earlier. Now, at last, she was able to hold him close to her heart.

I took the bag from her hands and placed it in a drawer, thinking it might be best for her not to get overly emotional. She said nothing at first, but a few minutes later, with tears rolling down her wrinkled face, she pleaded, "Wiesiu, may I hold him just a little longer?"

I fulfilled her wish.

After a while, she looked at me and apologized for being so old and forgetful, for not being able to tell me more about my father. Then, without breaking her sad, intense gaze, she said, "Wiesiu, I cannot remember anything now, how your father looked, except for his face.

"He had such a beautiful face."

CIRCUMSTANCES SURROUNDING THE KATYN TRAGEDY

A great myth developed that only the fascist enemy was capable of genocide, of mass crime. If the crimes of the Soviet Union were to be put into
the same category as those of the Nazis, the whole moral story of why we
fought the Second World War would have been ruined. We now know that
during the war, Stalin actually killed more of his own people than Hitler
killed during the Holocaust.
—Norman Davies

Today most people think of World War II as a struggle of the Allies
against the evils of Nazi Germany. It is important to keep in mind, however, that for the first two years of the war the Soviets were allied with the
Germans. It was not the Germans alone who attacked Poland to begin
the war; together both nations planned and orchestrated a program of
genocide against the Polish people in which about five million Polish citizens lost their lives. It was only after the Germans had a change of heart
and attacked the Soviets that the latter joined the Western Allies in a
common effort to defeat the Nazis.

When the war ended and the time came to try the European war criminals for their actions, the Western Allies faced a dilemma. If they truly
were intent on seeking justice, then they should have charged the Soviets with the acts they committed in Poland prior to joining the Allied effort. They knew that the Soviets had waged a war of aggression against
Poland in September 1939, had deported Polish citizens to the USSR,
and had slaughtered between thirty thousand and fifty thousand Polish
"political prisoners" from June to August 1941. In the end, not wanting
to be embarrassed by their alliance with the Soviet war criminals, the
United States and Great Britain in particular turned a blind eye to the
acts of the Soviet Union.

Some of the wartime acts of Stalin and the Soviet Communists were
perpetrated against millions of their own people, including executions,

imprisonment, and starvation. But much of that same brutality was also directed against those whom the Soviets had conquered and tried to convert to Communism. During World War II, the Polish people generally and Poland's intellectual leadership in particular became prime targets.

In April and May 1940, on orders of Stalin, about fifteen thousand Polish POWs (more than half of whom were officers) who had been held on Soviet soil were executed one by one by a pistol shot to the back of the head. Their bodies were dumped in common pits located in the Katyn Forest, Miednoye, and Kharkov. Although this massacre occurred in three different locations, it is often collectively referred to as the Katyn massacre or, simply, Katyn (to be distinguished from the massacre that occurred specifically at the Katyn Forest, which I will call the Katyn Forest massacre).

WHY DID THE MASSACRE HAPPEN?

Most historians agree that the Soviets ordered the massacre for two reasons. First, they believed that if they were to take over Poland, the country's intellectual leadership had to be eliminated, and army officers constituted a large segment of this group. Second, the Russian Communists deeply hated the Polish officers for their defeat of the Bolsheviks in the War of 1920, which effectively ended the Soviets' plans to spread Communism to all of Europe and the rest of the world. The Communists' revenge found its expression in the Katyn massacre and also in the killing of thousands of other Polish military men and civilians who were deported to the Soviet Union.

There was, however, another motivation for the Katyn massacre, the roots of which can be found in Marxist philosophy itself. Even before the events leading up to the Russian Revolution transpired, the early Russian Communists were committed to the Marxist conviction that "the workers of the world" were brutally oppressed by the upper classes. Undeniably, in many cases they were. But under Lenin and Stalin, this philosophical assertion was quickly turned into a political principle that claimed that all persons in the upper classes were oppressors. Anyone in a position of power or authority or who owned property became a target for vengeance. Eventually even the local baker and shoemaker, who were eking out a living, were suspect in the eyes of the Communists; whoever did not toil for the state was perceived to be an "oppressor" and an "enemy of the people." Intoxicated by this principle, the Russian Communists attempted to eradicate their "class enemies" in the hopes of creating a paradise for the downtrodden workers.

Poland, with its Western culture and superior airs, was viewed as a bourgeois state, and as such it posed a threat to Communism that had to be destroyed. The actual planning by the Soviets for the obliteration of Poland as a nation, and the elimination of the leaders that would help make this possible, had been completed long before the outbreak of World War II. The Communists were simply waiting for an opportune moment. When the army officers were taken prisoner at the start of the war, the Soviets found themselves holding the crown jewels of Polish intellectual leadership.

HOW THE SOVIETS SET THE TRAP

In August 1939, Nazi Germany and the Soviet Union publicly signed a treaty of nonaggression commonly known as the Ribbentrop-Molotov Pact. At the same time they reached a secret agreement to divide Poland between themselves along the Narew and the Bug Rivers. Everything to the east would come under Soviet control and everything to the west under German control. The two new allies gave themselves unlimited license to deport Poles to slave labor camps and to murder them indiscriminately without cause and without trial. Their goal was to wipe Poland off the map.

On September 1, 1939, German troops attacked Poland. Most of the Polish Army was rushed to the western frontier to defend the border against the German invasion. Then, on September 17, the Red Army crossed Poland's eastern border in violation of the Soviet-Polish non-aggression treaty. The advance of Red Army troops came as a shock to the Poles, who were confused as to exactly what the Soviets' intentions were and unsure how to respond. The Soviets said they were on their way to help the Polish Army fight the Germans. Many Polish Army units that were stationed along the eastern border believed this to be true. Still wanting to respect its nonaggression treaty with the Soviet Union and hoping for help in repelling the Germans, the Polish government issued orders not to offer organized resistance to the Red Army. In any event, the Polish leaders knew they could not successfully fight two powerful armies on two different fronts.

The Soviets were successful in keeping their true intentions a secret in order to prevent the Polish Army from engaging them before their forces were in place. As soon as they were strategically positioned, the terror began. When the Soviets' intentions became clear, sporadic fighting broke out between the Polish Army and the Red Army, but it was too late. The small units of the Polish Army, greatly outnumbered by the

Soviets, were quickly overwhelmed and ordered to lay down their arms or risk being shot. In actuality, surrender only delayed execution for many, in particular the Polish officer corps.

By the end of September, about two hundred thousand Poles were taken prisoner by the Soviets. Officers were immediately separated from their units and sent to prisoner-of-war camps in Kozelsk, Ostashkov, and Starobelsk, all located on Soviet soil. Other targeted individuals were arrested later by the NKVD and were also sent to these camps. They included political leaders, professors, teachers, engineers, doctors, lawyers, journalists, musicians, priests, sportsmen, policemen, and border guards. By October 1939, the Soviets had interned about 45 percent of the Polish military and civilian elite.

THE SOVIET MASTER PLAN FOR GENOCIDE

Unlike most prisoner-of-war camps in the Soviet Union, which were guarded by ordinary Russian soldiers, the camps at Kozelsk, Ostashkov, and Starobelsk were guarded by specially selected NKVD agents. On orders from Moscow, their goal was to identify prisoners who might be sympathetic to Communism. The plan was to use those men in the formation of a puppet Polish government controlled by the Communists in the postwar era. High-ranking NKVD officials were brought in to lead the interrogations. Repeated interviews lasted day and night. The interrogators relentlessly probed the Polish officers about every detail of their lives, in particular their thoughts about Communism and about the world order projected by Marx. Significantly, each officer was asked whether he had fought in the War of 1920. After six months of intensive questioning, the NKVD and the Soviet leaders in Moscow concluded that the vast majority of these men not only would be useless in the new Communist order but would likely pose major obstacles to the planned worldwide expansion of Communism after the war.

On March 5, 1940, the Soviet leaders in the Kremlin—Stalin, Voroshilov, Molotov, and Mikoyan—signed a top-secret memorandum, proposed by NKVD chief Lavrenti Beria, outlining a plan to execute 25,421 Polish prisoners of war held on their soil. All interrogations in the three camps stopped abruptly. The prisoners who had been deemed sympathetic to the Communist cause—448 in all—were transported to a new camp at Pavlishchev-Bor, a reorientation and indoctrination facility. On April 3, the camps at Kozelsk, Ostashkov, and Starobelsk began to empty. Six weeks later, the prisoners who had occupied them were executed and buried in three secret locations.

THE DISCOVERY OF THE
KATYN FOREST MASSACRE

On June 22, 1941, little more than a year after the executions, the German Army attacked the Soviet Union. Caught by surprise, the Soviets suffered a devastating defeat and in response made a complete about-face and joined the Western Allies in the fight against Hitler. For the time being, however, owing to the success of their attack, the Germans occupied much of the Soviet territory, including the Katyn Forest area. It was there in the spring of 1943 that they discovered the site of the mass murder of Polish officers and announced their find to the world. Three commissions of forensic experts were formed to exhume the bodies of the victims and establish their identities and the dates and causes of death. One commission was composed of German officials, another of international forensic experts and pathologists from twelve neutral countries including Switzerland, and a third of medical experts from the Polish Red Cross. The Germans also brought to the gravesite as observers two British and two American officers who were German prisoners of war (the Americans later testified before the U.S. congressional committee investigating the Katyn Forest massacre).

On April 30, 1943, the forensic experts began to investigate the massacre. Without explicitly assigning guilt, they concluded that the Polish officers were murdered in the spring of 1940. In view of this finding, no explicit assignment of guilt was necessary: the German Army had been nowhere near the Katyn Forest at the time. And in any event, Germany at that point was still allied with the Soviet Union. Even the Soviets, publicly indignant at the clear implication of their guilt, never denied that fact.

With the assistance of the Polish Red Cross and local workers, the German commission oversaw the digging up of the burial pits in the Katyn Forest and over a two-month period examined 4,142 bodies, tagged them, and returned them to the graves. Most of the bodies carried some sort of identification papers. The thousands of articles recovered included Polish and Russian currency, small personal objects, letters to be mailed to relatives in Poland, diaries, and Russian newspapers, none dated later than the middle of May 1940. All the bodies identified in the Katyn Forest were those of men who had been imprisoned in Kozelsk. It is significant that the order in which the bodies were found was the exact order in which the prisoners, in groups of 50 to 360 men, had been marched out of the camp in Kozelsk by the NKVD guards. It was further determined that, to hide the crime, saplings had been planted over the graves in the spring of 1940.

The location of the sites where eleven thousand other Polish POWs interned in the camps of Ostashkov and Starobelsk were buried was not revealed until 1990.

THE LIES AND THE BEGINNING OF THE COVER-UP

In the fall of 1941 the Soviet government granted an "amnesty" to Polish prisoners of war and to civilians who had been deported to the Soviet Union. At the same time an agreement was signed that allowed for an immediate formation of a Polish army on Soviet soil. But only the old and the sick or the very young arrived to enlist. The best and the brightest Polish officers, who had been held in the three camps, were missing. All inquiries into the status of the men by the American, British, and Polish governments led to evasiveness or silence; the Soviets refused to discuss the matter. Poles alone made more than two hundred such inquiries. The Soviet answer was always the same: they did not know what happened to the Poles. When Stalin himself was questioned, he replied that they escaped. When asked where, he replied, "To Manchuria."

After the discovery of the Katyn Forest massacre, however, when the Soviets were questioned again about what happened to fifteen thousand Polish POWs, they "remembered" for the first time that they had fallen into German hands and were murdered by them. When this was clearly shown to be impossible by the investigators, the Soviets accused the Western Allies of "imperialist conspiracy." When the Polish government-in-exile in London, without pointing the finger of guilt at anyone, asked that the International Red Cross be allowed to participate in an investigation, the Soviets refused to cooperate and became belligerent.

The Western Allies, in particular Roosevelt and Churchill, had embraced Stalin as a comrade-in-arms and now faced a major moral and military dilemma. They could demand that the International Red Cross be allowed to investigate the massacre and risk the loss of Soviet military support, or they could accept the Soviet explanation and remain silent about what they knew to be the truth. They chose the latter course. Churchill went so far as to promise the Soviet ambassador in London that neither the International Red Cross nor any other organization would ever be allowed to investigate the Katyn Forest or any other place under German occupation.

Very shortly after the discovery of the massacre, the Western Allies knew who was responsible and had more than sufficient evidence to indict the Soviets at the anticipated war crimes trials. Sir Owen O'Malley, ambassador to the Polish government-in-exile, wrote a secret memorandum on the subject of British collaboration with the Soviets in the cover-up of the Katyn massacre. It was distributed to senior members of the British cabinet and Foreign Office and was circulated throughout the upper echelons of the U.S. government. Roosevelt received a copy. According to the historian Louis Coatney, "The memorandum pointed out that collaborating with the Soviets in the coverup of their atrocity would destroy the Allies' claim to moral ascendancy in their crusade against Nazi Germany and could compromise the moral credibility and the legitimacy of the expected postwar war crimes trials." The governments of the United States and Great Britain did not heed O'Malley's advice but instead maintained for years a conspiracy of silence.

The Soviets, meanwhile, overtly engaged in a variety of cover-ups. One of the most significant was their own Katyn massacre investigation, conducted in the fall of 1943 by the Burdenko Commission, after the Germans were pushed out of the area. The commission's members were handpicked by Stalin and the Soviet secret police; its title was "Special Commission for Ascertaining and Investigating the Circumstances of the Shooting of Polish Officer Prisoners by the German-Fascist Invaders in the Katyn Forest." As the title makes clear, the Soviets seemed to have known before the investigation began who it was that murdered the Polish officers. The commission issued a report of its investigation on January 24, 1944, stating that the Germans murdered the officers after July–August 1941. This report became the official version of what happened.

What the public did not know for decades after the 1943 discovery of the massacre was that the Soviets made an extreme and most bizarre effort to conceal their crime. It was the Luftwaffe that captured on film some of the Soviets' activities. The German reconnaissance planes took photos of the Katyn Forest from July 9, 1941, to June 10, 1944, covering the time period before the Germans arrived in the area, after they were driven out, and following the Burdenko Commission's own investigation of the massacre.

At the end of World War II, thousands of German reconnaissance photographs were captured by the Americans, including those of the Katyn Forest. They were indexed and classified in Medmenham, England, by a team of expert American and British photo interpreters in a project codenamed Dick Tracy. The preliminary catalogue was published in 1945, prior to the Nuremberg war crimes trials. At that point the Western

Allies had in their possession ineluctable evidence that the Soviets not only committed the Katyn massacre but also how and when they excavated the graves, removed the corpses, and bulldozed the area in a futile attempt to hide their misdeeds.

THE NUREMBERG WAR CRIMES TRIALS

While the Soviets were busy covering up their crime, the American and British governments did everything they could to conceal documents pointing to the Soviets' guilt. After the war was over and before the International Military Tribunal was convened at Nuremberg in 1945, the Western Allies had ample time to investigate and turn over to the tribunal all the evidence in their possession concerning the Katyn Forest massacre. Doing so, however, would have meant admitting not only their mistakes in dealing with Stalin and the Soviet Communists during the war but also their involvement in the cover-up. If they revealed the truth about Katyn, then they would have to reveal the rest of what they knew about the war crimes committed by the Soviets. This would have been impossible for them to do without provoking domestic and international outrage.

The problem then facing the Western Allies was twofold. The first and most significant was how to set up the prosecution and trial of the major European war criminals (not only the Germans) at Nuremberg so as to avoid charging one of their own allies with genocide. The second was how to make it appear that they did not know who committed the massacre. The Western Allies had catered to Stalin's every whim during the war, and they certainly were not going to offend him now. History may never reveal exactly what happened behind closed doors and why. What is known is that, to the exclusion of other allies, only the Big Four (the Americans, the British, the French, and the Soviets) met in London between June 26 and August 8, 1945, to decide how the trials would be handled. They decided to distribute the responsibility for overseeing the indictment and prosecution of the major European war criminals in the following way: the United States would handle the overall conspiracy to incite and wage a war of aggression; the British would handle the violation of specific treaties and crimes on the high seas; and the other two major allies would deal with war crimes divided between them on a geographic basis, the French handling crimes that occurred in Western Europe and the Soviets those in Eastern Europe, which included Poland and the Soviet Union. This agreement meant that only the representatives of the Soviet Union could prosecute the mass murder of Polish officers in the Katyn Forest, even though the Soviets, as yet, had neither been investigated for nor cleared of having committed the crime.

Not only were the political, moral, and legal implications of this arrangement disturbing, but they created a new dilemma for the Western Allies. Although the evidence pointed clearly to the Soviets, it was they who were allowed to prosecute the war crimes committed in the area of the Katyn Forest. On one hand, if they failed to indict the Germans for the massacre, then, under the agreement reached by the Big Four, no one else would be responsible for or capable of doing so, and the Western Allies could not technically be held accountable for failing to prosecute a major act of genocide. They would be absolved from charging the Soviets. On the other hand, if the Soviets charged the Germans with committing the Katyn Forest massacre, how could the Western Allies withhold conclusive evidence of Soviet guilt and get away with it? Under Western law, those involved in the cover-up, albeit after the fact, could be found guilty of complicity in the genocide and later be charged in criminal court.

Despite the possibly grave consequences, the Western Allies decided not to charge the Soviets with any war crimes—not even for conspiring with the Germans to incite and wage a war of aggression against Poland in September 1939—and pretended that they did not know that the Germans would be charged with the massacre. When the case came up for trial before the International Military Tribunal in July 1946, the Soviets, who had vigorously blamed the Germans all along, indeed charged them with the crime; the Western Allies withheld evidence to the contrary, while volumes of incriminating evidence offered by the Poles were disallowed.

The strongest evidence the Soviets submitted against the Germans came from three Soviet "eyewitnesses," but the German defense team promptly discredited their testimony. The Soviet prosecutor also produced the findings of the Burdenko Commission. This evidence also was easily overturned. No other witnesses were allowed to testify.

Notwithstanding the enormity of the crime, the American presiding judge quickly dismissed the charges for lack of evidence, and the Katyn Forest massacre was dropped from the agenda. The final verdicts were read on September 30, 1946. Katyn was not mentioned, and even the charge concerning the massacre was omitted without explanation. It is interesting to compare this with the way other charges were handled by the tribunal. When, for example, the case of fifty members of the Royal

Air Force who had been shot by the Germans came up for trial, it was fully investigated and prosecuted to a successful conclusion.

Four years after the Nuremberg trials, while writing his wartime memoirs, Churchill found himself in a dilemma of his own making. He could not afford to omit any mention of the Katyn massacre. But neither could he afford to tell the truth about what he, Roosevelt, and the Western Allies knew about the massacre and when they knew it. One of the most eloquent speakers of the twentieth century, and an admired defender of freedom and human rights, solved his dilemma by stating, "It was decided by the victorious Governments concerned, that the issue should be avoided, and the crime of Katyn was never probed in detail."

CONGRESSIONAL INVESTIGATION OF THE KATYN FOREST MASSACRE

In 1951 the U.S. Congress decided to form a select committee to investigate the Katyn Forest massacre. The purpose of the investigation was to establish which nation was guilty of the murders and whether any American officials were responsible for suppressing the related facts. The hearings were held in Washington, Chicago, Frankfurt, Berlin, Naples, and, despite resistance from the British Foreign Office, London. Invitations to attend were extended to the Soviet government, the Polish Communist government in Warsaw, the Polish government-in-exile in London, and the Federal Republic of Germany. The latter two accepted, but the Soviets and the Polish government in Warsaw (on instructions from Moscow) declined. Churchill also received an invitation but did not attend.

Eighty-one witnesses testified, 100 depositions were taken from people who could not attend, 183 exhibits were studied, and 200 other witnesses offered to appear with testimony that primarily was of a corroborating nature. The select committee published a report finding that the massacre was committed by the NKVD and recommended that the Soviets be tried before the International World Court of Justice.

The committee uncovered substantial evidence that the State Department, Army Intelligence (G-2), the Office of War Information, and the Federal Communications Commission, among other government agencies, deliberately withheld information about the massacre from the public. The committee also established that Roosevelt and the State Department ignored numerous documents from various diplomats—among them Anthony Joseph Drexel Biddle Jr., the U.S. ambassador to the Polish government-in-exile in London; Admiral William H. Standley, the U.S. ambassador to Moscow; and John G. Winant, the American emissary to London—who reported information strongly pointing to Soviet guilt.

It also found that in 1944, former ambassador George Earle, who served as a special emissary to the Balkans for President Roosevelt and who was a family friend, informed the president that the Soviets were responsible for the massacre. The president, however, ordered him to maintain silence. When Earle advised Roosevelt that he might go public with the information, the president issued an order to send him to American Samoa for the duration of the war.

Another example of the U.S. cover-up brought to light by the House report was the disappearance of a statement made by Colonel John H. Van Vliet Jr., one of the two American POWs held by the Germans who were brought to the Katyn gravesite as witnesses. In May 1945, Van Vliet arrived in Washington, D.C., from Europe and met with Major General Clayton Bissell, the army assistant chief of staff in charge of army intelligence, to describe what he saw during the exhumation. Van Vliet emphatically and unequivocally stated his conviction that the Polish officers were murdered by the Soviets. Bissell, on whose orders Van Vliet's report was taken down, promptly classified it as top secret and ordered the colonel to maintain absolute secrecy concerning this report. Curiously, no copies of it were made; after a thorough investigation and the interrogation of Bissell, the select committee concluded that the original document had been either intentionally removed from army intelligence files or destroyed.

More astonishing to the committee was the secret testimony of three high-ranking army intelligence officers under General Bissell's command. These officials asserted that a pool of "pro-Soviet employees and some military in Army Intelligence" acted as apologists for the Soviets and exerted "tremendous efforts . . . to suppress anti-Soviet reports." In its conclusion, the committee report observed ruefully that "in those fateful days nearing the end of the Second World War there unfortunately existed in high governmental and military circles a strange psychosis that military necessity required the sacrifice of loyal allies and our own principles in order to keep Soviet Russia from making a separate peace with the Nazis. For reasons less clear to this committee, this psychosis continued even after the conclusion of the war."

There were at least two reasons for the Western governments' continued "psychosis," which resulted in their ongoing silence on the subject of Katyn. For the West to have officially accused the Soviets of the

Katyn massacre would have been tantamount to waving a saber in the face of a new enemy. Doing so would have exposed the same governments and individuals who were involved in the cover-up to serious legal and political consequences, both domestic and international, not to mention possible military confrontation with the Soviets.

WHEN THE SILENCE WAS BROKEN

Yet as the decades passed, the political atmosphere in the Eastern bloc countries started to change. In 1981, the Solidarity movement began to press the Communist government in Poland to reveal the secrets of Katyn. In 1988, fifty-nine Polish intellectuals made an appeal to Russian intellectuals to meet in order to break the silence on Katyn, among other historical "white spots." In 1989 Polish Communist authorities for the first time allowed information to be published about Katyn, admitting that all the evidence of the massacre pointed toward the Soviets. Slowly, the walls of secrecy surrounding the Katyn massacre began to crumble.

Finally, on April 13, 1990, Mikhail Gorbachev, during a meeting in Moscow with General Wojciech Jaruzelski, president of Poland, made the stunning admission that the NKVD was responsible for the massacre of nearly fifteen thousand Polish POWs. Gorbachev also disclosed that they were buried in mass graves in the Katyn Forest, in Miednoye, and in Kharkov. At the same time, Gorbachev carefully avoided any mention that the Soviet government and the Communist Party were responsible. He also did not reveal what happened to thousands of others who have never been found. Nor did he offer a copy of Stalin's execution order of March 5, 1940, which would have shown that 25,700 Polish POWs were sentenced to be shot. It was later learned that this order had actually been in Gorbachev's possession for some time. On the following day Tass, the official Soviet news agency, reported Gorbachev's admission. On October 14, 1992, a representative of President Boris Yeltsin delivered a copy of the execution order (see gallery) and forty-one other pertinent documents concerning the massacre of Polish POWs to President Lech Walesa of Poland.

In 1996, in response to demands by Polish émigrés, the Foreign and Commonwealth Office (FCO) issued its final report on the question of British involvement in the cover-up of the Katyn massacre. The commission of FCO historians, convened by John Major, simply denied the cover-up. In July 2002, *BBC History* magazine printed an article based on newly declassified documents titled "Britain Helped Cover Up Katyn Massacre." In April 2003, the FCO historians published *Katyn: British*

Reactions to the Katyn Massacre, 1943–2003. Denis MacShane, Minister for Europe, said in his foreword:

> Successive British governments had no illusions about the likelihood of Soviet responsibility for the massacre. But in the absence of conclusive evidence, they, like other Western governments, remained reluctant to accuse the Soviet authorities of the crime. Though they condemned the massacre in the strongest terms, the refusal publicly to charge the USSR with responsibility for Katyn angered many, in this country and beyond, who wished to see justice done. It is in recognition of those feelings that this report is published today.

The FCO report does not state that there was a cover-up or that the crime was hushed up for pragmatic reasons. Nevertheless, one can infer from the report that the FCO historians knew that the British government strongly suspected the Soviets of the crime but chose to suppress the truth. The assertion that the British did not have conclusive evidence with which to accuse the Soviets is simply untrue. It has been firmly established that both the Americans and the British had more than sufficient evidence to indict the Soviets at Nuremberg; this would have allowed the court to decide whether the evidence was adequate to convict.

CONCLUSION

One can understand that during the war there may have been compelling reasons for the West not to broadcast the evidence about the Katyn massacre pointing to Soviet guilt. But once the war was over, what basis was there for maintaining the silence, other than political, moral, and legal expediency? During the six decades since the Katyn massacre, no one has been prosecuted for the crime and no one has been prosecuted for its cover-up. At the very least, the victims of Katyn and their descendants deserve a full admission of the truth by all parties who have denied them justice.

LETTERS TO AMERICA

While going through family archives, I came across two of the many letters my cousin Jean wrote from Persia to her family in America. (She died of cancer in 1963 at age forty-three while working at the Veterans Administration hospital in Los Angeles.) The first letter, dated December 13, 1943, was written to our cousins Helen, Barney, and Gene Pazera in Gary, Indiana.

Dear Helen, Barney, and Gene:

Just returned to our post after being on "Detached Service" up north. The trip was great as we made the round trip by Army Transport plane. Persia certainly looks beautiful from the air, especially while flying over the mountains. We flew as high as 17,800 ft. and the windows were just coated with ice. We had to wear our boots and heavy overcoats because it was so cold.

I am very happy to write you how fortunate we were in arriving just in time to see our President Franklin D. Roosevelt, Winston Churchill, Josef Stalin and others representing allied countries. Helen, it was an episode of my life I will never want to forget. So many presidents gathered in one particular country at the same time. My only regret is that the intense restrictions that we had to live under made it impossible for me to see the children more often. However, Ambassador Dreyfus has his lovely wife here, and I have made arrangements with her to see that the children get the money coming to them from the States and see to it that they will be properly clothed for the Christmas holiday. All the food such as candy, cookies, etc. that I have been receiving from home are generously shared with the Polish refugee children who are here.

Helen, I do hope you do not mind my writing this. The Holy Wafer you sent me for Christmas was shared with some of the Polish refugee mothers whose sons are fighting in various countries. Am proud to tell you that even though it may be just a scarce amount, that wafer has been broken up in tiny pieces and sent by these mothers to their boys in Africa, England, Egypt, Palestine, and many other countries.

If you could only see the tears in these eyes and expressions of joy on these faces, Helen, I am sure your heart would beat with pride. They just sighed and said, "Oplatek z Ameryki" ("Holy Wafer from America"). I am certainly happy you sent it, and do hope you realize how much it means to believe in faith and have confidence in our "good Lord" at a horrible time like this.

Though these people have only a crude camel stable to protect them, when we announced that we had some Holy Wafer from America for them, even the little old crippled grandparents got enough strength to come a little closer to me and just begged to at least touch the Holy Wafer with their lips.

Helen, I do not think it's necessary for me to tell you that I stood there with tears in my eyes thinking, "God have mercy on us." Please, Helen, if you have any more left, send it to me and you will make a lot of homeless, depressed, and heartbroken people happy even if it is for only a few moments.

It makes me feel so bad that we are unable to do more for Zosia and Wiesiu. I, too, hope that the folks back home realize how difficult circumstances are for me. I have tried everything in my power to get the children back home.

May I end this letter saying that we will work until we can assure the folks back home happiness, contentment, and security.

My sincere love to all,

Jean

The second letter was written to Jean's mother, father, and sister in Chicago. It is hard to read its date but it appears to have been written January 12, 1945.

Dearest Mother, Dad, and Gerry:

Just received your letter with attached snapshots of Mother and Dad. After showing them proudly around the camp, am happy and thrilled to say that Mom and Dad now have hundreds of admirers.

Haven't seen the children all that much because they are going to school. Friday is Wesley's birthday party, so I will have them both over the weekend. Wiesiu is going to be all dolled up in his new suit and so is Zosia in her blue wool skirt and pale blue cardigan sweater with a white Peter Pan collar. For Christmas, I gave her money to get a permanent, so I will set her hair and pin a nice little blue bow in her hair. Wiesiu is having a lovely birthday cake made and everyone is looking forward to the party.

So sorry I cannot tell you just when they are leaving. Apparently, something is happening and transports are being held up. This sure is getting to be hard on me. Every time I have a few minutes, off I go to visit the children with hands full. Zosia got a beautiful Persian bracelet from "her" Major, a patient of mine who adores her. Wiesiu, who got books of foreign stamps, also begs me for permission to adopt him. Honestly, they really got to be the mascots of the U.S. Army in Persia. Wiesiu has already gained five and a half pounds and is getting to be such a big boy. He's always saying something in American. Sometimes he says the craziest things that Irene and I have to hold our sides from laughing.

This business of gum cracking is going to stop pronto. Aunt Jean put her foot down and took all the gum away from Wiesiu until he can promise he can chew quietly. Zosia is having fits because he learned how to chew gum. All the mothers at camp are having trouble cutting gum out of their youngsters' hair. (Oh, dear what a mess.) From now on, Mr. Wrigley better furnish some gum remover or he will have an entire nation of mothers causing a spontaneous blitz.

Gerry, trouble continues and I am doing all in my power to get these children home. Conditions here are perfect hell! They live in camel stables with no heating installed and no running water. They sleep on boards ten inches from the ground.

10 A.M.	Breakfast	Tea, Cheese and white bread
4 P.M.	Dinner	Soup, Cheese and white bread
7 P.M.	Supper	Tea

Gerry, that's what they get to eat. Please tell Council Ryba it's about time to get down to business and look into the matter. Things are getting worse and nothing is being done. Mortality rate is terrifically high. Please tell them for the sake of God—WAKE UP AND HELP THEM. Little babies crying and dying because they are starved and cold.

Oh, Gerry, if I could only write what I have seen, heard, and experienced. Remember, everything that I have written you is also what our little cousins are suffering from.

Honestly, I am so sorry I am writing in such anger. But Gerry, please impress on everyone back home that Holy Hell is going on over here and something must be done about it.

The weather is lousy. We are having our rainy season now and practically break our necks trying to get to the mess hall from our barracks in all the slippery mud. What a hell of a place to be stuck. Boy, it sure gets cold now. The days are warm and if it isn't raining, we can get by with only a little sweater. At night, we sleep under four blankets and wish we had at least six more.

Guess the War looks pretty good. We are all hoping to be home this year. Keep your fingers crossed and be good. Maybe I will surprise you. Wish the children could come along.

Will write again tomorrow.

Loads of love,

Will be seeing you soon

Jean, Zosia, and Wiesiu

24 *and the Soviet double-cross worked*   In reality it was a double double-cross, but the Poles did not know this at the time. On August 23, 1939, a week before the war started, the Nazis and the Soviets had signed the Ribbentrop-Molotov Pact and also agreed in secret to divide Poland between themselves with the intention of wiping out the country forever. The West did not know about this secret agreement until shortly before the war ended in 1945. The Soviet government denied its existence until 1989.

25 *was equivalent to the Gestapo*   In Russian, "NKVD" stands for Narodny Kommissariat Vnutrennikh Del, or People's Commission for Internal Affairs. Its main function was to carry out the Soviet government's suppression of its own citizens and of those who had been conquered.

32 *to be deported by the NKVD*   Four major deportations from Soviet-occupied Poland to the Soviet Union took place. They occurred in February, April, and June–July 1940 and in June 1941. Most of those deported were women and children.

    The number of people deported is a subject of controversy. For nearly fifty years, the prevailing estimates of Polish citizens "transported" to the Soviet Union ranged from 1.5 million to 2 million people, according to Polish historians. This total comprised four groups: deportees taken in 1940–41, POWs taken in September 1939, individuals arrested by the Soviets (usually on trumped-up charges) and sent to prison, and individuals forced to join either the Red Army or work battalions. It was estimated that the largest group were the deportees, numbering from 980,000 to 1,080,000 people (note that this range does not include persons deported in 1939 or in 1944–47).

    After the fall of Communism the newly opened Soviet archives revealed that the total number of individuals deported between 1940 and 1941 differed dramatically from Polish estimates, causing major disagreements among researchers and historians. As of 2002, the count, according to the Soviet archives, stood at 320,000 individuals, or about one-third of the original Polish estimate.

    With such a disparity between the original Polish estimates and the Soviet archives, I decided to travel to Poland in May 2003 to seek the opinion of two professors. I first interviewed Professor Wojciech Materski, director of research and studies at the Institute of Political Studies, an organization within the Polish Academy of Sciences. He believes that the Soviet archives are in principle correct and states that today most Polish researchers and historians studying the matter agree. He added that if some factors that are unverifiable at this time were to be considered, the total number of deportees could be between 320,000 and 350,000.

He explained that the Polish estimates were based primarily on visual observations of transports leaving Poland and heading east toward the Soviet Union. The count was calculated by taking the total number of cars in a transport and then multiplying it by some average number of people in a car, although some cars had as few as thirty people and others as many as seventy or eighty. It is likely that some transports going through a number of towns may have been counted more than once by different observers. After the Soviet "amnesty" in 1941, individuals coming from various gulags, work camps, prisons, and settlements provided their own personal observations as to the number of Polish people in their area.

When I asked Professor Materski about the credibility of Soviet archives given the Soviets' history of spreading false information, he responded that whatever disinformation the Soviets made public was a completely different matter from internal NKVD records, which were never meant to be seen by anyone other than designated NKVD individuals. The most persuasive argument in favor of the records' accuracy, he said, lies in the extreme fear that the NKVD recordkeepers had for their own lives. Any discrepancies found in such records could have easily caused the recordkeepers to be sentenced to prison, sent to Siberia for hard labor, or shot.

Next I asked Professor Materski whether the Soviet archives opened to historians and researchers after the fall of Communism in the nineties were complete. This question was a complicated one, he said, and the answer could not be a simple yes or no. Rather, it could be answered only by "describing the process of documentation in its entirety."

Once the security of the archives was threatened by the German attack on the Soviet Union, with the exception of the Smolensk region, the Soviet government began to remove the most important and most sensitive parts of the archives from their western territories to Moscow. It is not known how many of these documents came back to Belarus and Ukraine after the war and how many were left behind in Moscow. For the most part, the documents that were returned to Belarus are not accessible, but those returned to Ukraine are. Also, the NKVD office procedures for the Soviet republics required that the most important single-copy documents be sent immediately to Moscow. During the war there were two archives to which these documents could have been sent: the NKVD archives and the NKGB archives. After the war, those two archives were temporarily combined but subsequently were divided again into the KGB archives and the MSW archives. Up to the present, the KGB archives (currently called the Central Archives of the Federal Security Service) are inaccessible, as are the deportation documents sent to those archives. The documents not sent to the KGB archives were separated and sent to other central archives. The deportation documents that are currently available can be found in the Archive of the President of the Russian Federation, the State Archive of the Russian Federation, and the Russian State Military Archive.

I also interviewed Andrzej Korzon, a retired docent at the History Institute of the Polish Academy of Sciences and a professor at the Masovian Higher School of Humanities and Pedagogics in Lowicz, Poland. He was more skeptical of the Soviet figures, noting that they needed to be examined more closely—for example, to determine whether Ukrainians, Belorussians, Jews, and other minorities who were Polish citizens were counted as such by the Soviets. He estimates the number of Polish citizens deported in the years 1940–41 to the Soviet Union during four major deportations to be at least 400,000 and possibly up to 450,000. These numbers take into account three classes of individuals: "amnestied" deported Polish citizens who returned to Poland after the war (263,000), Polish citizens who left the Soviet Union in 1942 after the amnesty with the Polish Army (115,000), and deportees who died in the Soviet Union (estimated to be about 10 percent of the verified 320,000 deported individuals, or 32,000).

For further information on the subject, the reader should consult Stanislaw Ciesielski, Wojciech Materski, and Andrzej Paczkowski, *Represje sowieckie wobec Polakow i obywateli polskich*, 2d ed. (Warsaw: Osrodek Karta, 2002); and Katherine Jolluck, *Exile and Identity: Polish Women in the Soviet Union during World War II* (Pittsburgh: University of Pittsburgh Press, 2002).

49 *you can see your own ears* We learned much later that Poles throughout the Soviet Union were given the same answer, word for word, and concluded that it had to be of long-standing origin and was probably said to other deportees from other nations as well. The Bolsheviks had not invented deportation as a means of political punishment. Their predecessors, the Russian czars, had done the same for more than a hundred years. The only difference between them was in the method used. The Soviets used cattle cars to transport their prisoners by rail, but the czars had been crueler still, forcing prisoners to march thousands of miles to Siberia, even in winter. Few survived the journey, and fewer returned.

88 *a Polish army would be formed on Soviet soil* A few weeks before Jurek's interrogation the Soviet Union, the British government, and the Polish government-in-exile in London had agreed to form a Polish army in the Soviet Union. Still, attempts to recruit Poles into the Red Army continued. Often the NKVD used more coercive tactics, telling potential inductees that they would be charged with treason if they refused to sign up. Fearing for their lives, many did. The main reason for their recruitment of Poles was that Moscow desperately wanted able-bodied Poles scattered throughout their own army's ranks rather than concentrated within their own country as a viable and fundamentally hostile army. This became evident to the newly formed Polish Army command when the new arrivals from POW camps,

prisons, and work camps turned out to be for the most part the old and the sick. Many were hardly more than living skeletons and died shortly after their arrival in the Polish Army camps.

92   *and exposure to the weather*   Why did they do it? No one had promised them immediate salvation, not the Poles and certainly not the Soviets. Why would a mother with small children risk her own and her children's lives traveling thousands of miles simply to be near the Polish Army, still on Soviet soil, and much closer to the war zone? The army was likely to move away and leave them in a worse predicament than the one they had left. For decades I have sought an answer to this question, asking literally hundreds of Polish escapees from throughout the Soviet Union why they joined this leaderless exodus. Why did they not wait until the war was over or at least until the Germans could be pushed back?

Their answers have always been the same. They were driven by a desperate hope for freedom, willing to achieve it at all costs and against all odds, believing that somehow the Polish Army would lead them out of the Soviet Union and to that freedom, just as Moses led the Jews to the Promised Land from their bondage in Egypt.

105   *as he breaks down in tears*   From its inception after the Russian Revolution, the Soviet secret police force was used as a means of suppressing the citizenry by means of fear, intimidation, acts of brutality, and murder. The Soviet government, faithful to the Communist mentality, believed that by regularly changing the name of this body—CHEKA, GPU, OGPU, NKVD, MGB, MVD, KGB—its reality could be masked. Regardless of the name, Soviet citizens lived in terror of the secret police. None of the publicly accessible Soviet archives deal with this subject, but unofficial estimates mention between 250,000 and 350,000 border guards, 1.5 million NKVD agents, and millions of informants, paid and unpaid, at any one time.

To make the people forget their misery and degradation, the government provided them with plenty of vodka: for the masses, it was a general anesthetic; for the soldiers, a morale booster before battle; for the executioners, a reward for each day's work. (For many of the dedicated Communist servants in the execution corps, when vodka could no longer assuage their guilt, bullets could: they shot themselves. Many others were spared such a tragic decision by being executed by order of the government.) Once hooked, the disgruntled addicts, whenever there was a shortage of vodka, would supplement their habit by drinking shaving lotion, wood alcohol, and even antifreeze.

In 1990, at the request of the Soviet government, the KGB reported that between 1935 and 1950, at least nineteen million citizens in the USSR were arrested. Seven million others were forcibly starved to death in Ukraine because they did not want to accept collectivization. Nikita Khrushchev admitted in his memoirs that cannibalism took place in the Soviet Union during this period of mass starvation.

No one will ever know the exact number of people executed and starved to death in the Soviet Union between the time of the Russian Revolution and the collapse of Communism. Soviet archives at this point do not reveal the total numbers. Unofficial estimates have ranged from twenty million to as high as eighty million. The wide range is explained in part by the fact that some estimates do not include certain groups of people who were murdered or those who died from hard labor, exhaustion, starvation, or disease (such persons were considered by the Soviets to have died of natural causes).

107 *in view of the constant hunger and starvation*   Another example of this propaganda is related by the Polish general Zygmunt Bohusz-Szyszko in his book *Czerwony Sfinks* (Red Sphinx). The general had flown from London to the Soviet Union on military business during the time we were there. While waiting on a Douglas plane that was to take him to Moscow, he approached a young Soviet pilot and asked him whether the plane was American or Soviet-built. The pilot replied boastfully that the plane was designed by the famous Soviet engineer Douglas and was manufactured in the Soviet Union from Soviet-made materials.

131 *the Soviet-controlled transports would be abruptly discontinued*   The second evacuation, which we were most fortunate to be part of, was the last. Army trucks making their way through the mountains transported about twenty-six hundred late arrivals, who missed the last ship for Persia at the end of August. About one hundred sixteen thousand civilians and soldiers left during the spring and summer. Of the remainder, thousands were forced to accept Soviet citizenship, others were forced to join the Red Army, and still others were forced into the newly formed Polish Army under strict Soviet control.

131 *for a chance to reach freedom*   Our friend Krystyna Ziemlo later told us that her mother, three sisters, and she traveled from northern Siberia for three months to reach Krasnovodsk for their chance to escape. She and two sisters made it out, but her mother and three-year-old sister died trying.

149 *taking us to face a new world on our own*   Months later, Zosia and I arranged to have Mother's gravesite marked with a stone carved with her name and the dates of her birth and death. There was no formal ceremony when it was set in place. We placed flowers on her grave and went back time and again while we remained in Tehran. Some time later, and without telling me about it, Zosia had someone take a picture of us kneeling by Mother's grave. I saw it for the first time fifty years later. She never told me she had it, as if to protect me.

151 *I clung to her for comfort, lost for words*   Family archives revealed that our meeting with Lieutenant Jean was described in the Polish newspaper *Zgoda*, published in Chicago, on September 7 and 13, 1943. Jean submitted the articles from Persia. She wrote about the joy and sadness of meeting her orphaned cousins under such deplorable conditions and described meeting

with other Polish refugees, the conditions of our camp, and her impressions of Persia (see also the letters in the appendix).

167 *America's contribution to the combined war effort* After the war was over, Brigadier General Donald P. Booth stated in a letter to all U.S. Army soldiers under his command that by December 1944 nearly five million tons of vital materiel had been transported to the Red Army through the Persian Gulf.

Not all war equipment went by truck via the desert to the Soviet Union. The Americans had a huge air base in Abadan, near the port of Khorram-shahr and about thirty miles northeast of the Kuwait border. The base included an airfield, a control tower, an air transport command depot, a depot for assembled planes awaiting test flights, and an assembly point for U.S. planes to be flown to the Soviet Air Force.

170 *and simply killed itself* Years later, I came across the following legend. A scorpion who was deathly afraid of water asked a turtle to give him a ride on his back across a lake.

The turtle refused, saying to him, "I am afraid that you will sting me and I will drown."

"Do not be afraid," the scorpion replied, "because if I sting you, then both of us will go under."

Reassured, the turtle permitted the scorpion onto his back and started across. When they were halfway to the other side, the scorpion did indeed sting the turtle on the neck. As the turtle began to sink, he said, "But you promised that you wouldn't."

The doomed scorpion replied, "But it is my nature."

192 *would be learned later* As it turned out, of fifty-three hundred Poles in Lebanon in 1947, thirty-five hundred chose as we did and went to England. Six hundred people who were old or ill returned to Poland. The rest went to other countries and a small group stayed in Lebanon.

197 *the supposedly invincible Monte Cassino* The battle of Monte Cassino, the most significant of the Italian campaign during World War II, took place in three phases between January and May 1944. The victory not only opened for the Allies the only north-south road to Rome, but it also crushed the Germans' most heavily fortified defensive line in Italy.

During the three major offenses, units from America, Britain, Canada, France, India (including Nepalese Gurkhas, considered the world's best soldiers for mountain combat), and New Zealand, as well as some "free Italian" units, failed to take the hill and its Benedictine monastery while suffering very heavy losses. In the end it was the Second Polish Corps under General Wladyslaw Anders that succeeded in taking Monte Cassino. Most of the corps had been forcibly deported from Poland to the Soviet Union in 1940–41.

199 *their love, happiness, and health*   I saw Iwona again eleven years later in Chicago. Shortly after Zosia's wedding, she met a Polish officer, Janusz Rzeczkowski, and soon afterward they were married. Like Mietek, he had fought in Italy, but he followed a different route to get there. At the beginning of the war he fought the Germans in Poland as part of the underground army. Then, when the Russians swept westward through Poland, they arrested him and thousands of other underground fighters. He escaped to Czechoslovakia and joined the Polish Army in Italy.

207 *so that we can repay the British treasury*   Chris and I met again in Chicago in 1953 and have kept in touch ever since. Our careers have mirrored each other's: he received a doctorate in psychology, and I received a bachelor's degree in science and a minor in philosophy. Both of us received commissions in the U.S. Army, operated our own businesses, and lectured on various subjects. Chris was recognized for his professional achievements in *Who's Who in Polish America,* and I was recognized for my achievements in tournament bridge in the Leading Bridge Personalities section of the *Official Encyclopedia of Bridge.*

208 *I went directly to the rail to wave good-bye*   I wondered when we would meet again. As it happened, Zosia, Mietek, little George, and his one-year-old sister, Barbara, arrived in America in 1951, when the United States opened the gates to stranded Polish refugees. Mietek worked as a building estimator for the Chicago Housing Authority and Zosia worked as an accounting supervisor. Their third child, Yvonne, was born in the United States. My brother arrived a year later. He married Cesia Szkudlarek, who had also escaped the Soviet Union, and they both became successful in real estate.

219 *a good man like your father*   Not only did I promise to do my best, but I have felt honor-bound to keep that promise all my life. As far as wishing her good health is concerned, I did it every time I saw her until she died in April 2002, one month before her 106th birthday. During each visit our conversation centered on relatives and conditions in Poland, helping those in need, and the traditions of our native land that we still followed in America.

245 *the expected postwar war crimes trials*   Louis R. Coatney, "The Katyn Massacre: An Assessment of Its Significance as a Public and Historical Issue in the United States and Great Britain, 1940–1993" (master's thesis, Western Illinois University, 1993), p. 16.

245 *Invaders in the Katyn Forest*   See J. K. Zawodny, *Death in the Forest: The Story of the Katyn Forest Massacre* (Notre Dame: University of Notre Dame Press, 1962), p. 49.

246 *to hide their misdeeds*   Copies and selected originals were kept by the CIA and British intelligence until the late 1970s. Then the Americans and the British distributed some of their holdings to, respectively, the National Ar-

chives in the United States and the Public Record Office, the Joint Reconnaissance Intelligence Center, and the University of Keele in England.

In 1981, Robert G. Poirier, one of the CIA's most experienced photo interpreters, wrote an internal memorandum titled "The Katyn Enigma: New Evidence in a 40-Year Riddle," which was immediately stamped CONFIDENTIAL by his superiors. Filed at the National Archives, this report was never intended to be seen by the outside world. In 1990 it was mistakenly shown to Waclaw Godziemba-Maliszewski, a scholar of modern photo interpretation techniques who has devoted years of his life to the study of the Katyn photos. In researching the Katyn cover-up, I have relied on Waclaw Godziemba-Maliszewski, "Katyn: An Interpretation of Aerial Photographs Considered with Facts and Documents" (in English and Polish), in *Fotointerpretacja w Geografii: Problemy Telegeoinformacji* (Warsaw: Polskie Towarzystwo Geograficzne, 1996), and on Frank Fox, *God's Eye: Aerial Photography and the Katyn Forest Massacre* (Westchester, Pa.: Westchester University Press, 1999).

246 *which included Poland and the Soviet Union*   See Zawodny, *Death in the Forest*, p. 64; House Report, pp. 10–11.

248 *was never probed in detail*   Winston S. Churchill, *The Hinge of Fate: The Second World War* (Boston: Houghton Mifflin, 1950), p. 761.

248 *suppressing the related facts*   See House Report No. 2505, *The Katyn Forest Massacre: Final Report of the Select Committee to Conduct an Investigation and Study of the Facts, Evidence, and Circumstances of the Katyn Forest Massacre*, 82d Cong., 2d Sess. (Washington, D.C.: Government Printing Office, 1952).

248 *before the International World Court of Justice*   Ibid., p. 2.

248 *from the public*   Ibid., p. 4.

249 *pointing to Soviet guilt*   Ibid., p. 6.

249 *for the duration of the war*   See Zawodny, *Death in the Forest*, pp. 182–83; House Report, pp. 6–7.

249 *or destroyed*   House Report, pp. 8–9.

249 *to suppress anti-Soviet reports*   Ibid.

249 *the conclusion of the war*   Ibid., p. 11.

251 *this report is published today*   Denis MacShane, foreword to *Katyn: British Reactions to the Katyn Massacre, 1943–2003* (London: Foreign and Commonwealth Office, 2003).